BIBLE TRUTH
FOR SCHOOL SUBJECTS

Volume I

Social Studies

Revised

HISTORY
GEOGRAPHY
ECONOMICS
GOVERNMENT
LEADERSHIP & ADMINISTRATION
SOCIAL RELATIONSHIPS
THE FAMILY
THE CHURCH
SOCIAL PROBLEMS

Ruth C. Haycock, Ed.D.

 **Association of Christian Schools International**
P. O. Box 4097, Whittier, CA   90607

All Scripture quotations are from the King James Version of the Bible.

Table of Contents

Foreword

One of the most significant things God is doing in the Body of Christ today is the rapid development of Bible-centered Christian schools. In order for Christian schools to maintain their Biblical integrity, they must have access to Bible-based curriculum materials. The *Bible Truth for School Subjects* series, written by Dr. Ruth C. Haycock and published by the Association of Christian Schools International, is the kind of valuable curriculum material that will keep the Christian school movement on course spiritually.

I praise God for Ruth Haycock. She has devoted a lifetime of Bible study to this important project. This is volume one in a four-volume series. The four volumes are: *Social Studies, Language Arts/English, Science/Math* and *Fine Arts and Health.* Each of these is an essential tool in the all-important task of integrating Scripture into the academic curriculum of the Christian school.

This volume, *Social Studies,* has been revised and esthetically upgraded since it was originally published in 1979. Hundreds of copies have already been sold and I know it will continue to be a blessing for many years to come.

While this valuable series was designed for use by teachers and administrators to facilitate Biblical integration in the classroom, it is also useful as a topical index of Scriptures for chapel talks and sermons.

I commend this volume to you. It will enrich your life as a teacher, educator and servant of God.

Dr. Paul A. Kienel, Executive Director
Association of Christian Schools International

Preface

This book is designed as a handbook for teachers at every level. Its goal is to bring together Biblical concepts related to the various social studies, providing assistance to the busy teacher who must prepare several lesson plans every day, yet wants to include what God says that is relevant to the topic for the day.

The lists of concepts, together with the Biblical basis for them, are the results of inductive Bible study stimulated initially by a reading of Frank Gaebelein's classic, *The Pattern of God's Truth.* In 1965 several other experiences contributed to a concern for determining a Biblical view of school subjects: attendance at my first Christian school conference in Houston, a Wheaton College intersession under John Blanchard, dorm association with students who were thrilled with Mark Fakkema's presentation of a Christian view of academics, several secular graduate courses showing the contrast, and finally the challenge of teaching a course on the Christian school in Baptist Bible Seminary.

During the intervening years, God added stimulus to pursue this project. My students were struggling to develop a Christian perspective in academic subjects. Service on the faculty of the National Institutes at Grace College required digging as preparation for workshops. Teacher's conventions gave opportunity for interaction with mature teachers, eager to teach a Biblical viewpoint, but with scanty Bible background and little time for study. Out of all this comes the four volume series of which this is the first.

This second edition of Volume 1, *Social Studies,* is both an enlargement and a revision of the 1979 edition. It includes new concepts, added Bible background, two new chapters on social institutions, dealing with the family and the church. Secular writers may question the priority of these institutions, but no Bible-believing Christian can do so. The resource section has been enlarged and updated.

A book of this nature does not come into being without the efforts of many people. The content is the responsibility of the writer; typesetting, proofreading, paste-up and camera work is the work of Mary Thompson and Doris Manuel of Piedmont Bible College. Their labors have come after hours and far into the night. Their willingness to disrupt their schedules to meet deadlines makes this book possible; many thanks are due them. The work of ACSI personnel in actual publication and distribution is equally essential and much appreciated.

The compilation of principles and supporting Scripture passages included here is incomplete, and some statements may even be debatable. God has much to say in the social sciences, and for a writer to wait until he has found every Biblical concept and expressed it without fault is to wait too long to be of help to Christian schools. In eternity schools will not be needed!

If this publication can be used by the Lord to stimulate you to study your subjects in the Word of God as well as in other sources, and to develop curriculum guides and lesson plans which honor His thoughts, its mission will be accomplished.

Ruth C. Haycock
Winston-Salem, NC   27103
April, 1983

Introduction

It has often been said, *The Christian pupil attending a secular school is being sheltered from the truth; consequently he is conforming to the world rather than to the image of Christ.* In a general way those of us involved in Christian schools are quick to agree, recognizing that without the written Word of God and the living Word, Jesus Christ, a child is being cheated. He is not getting the things in life which are most crucial to his becoming what God intends.

Even in a Christian school however, it is very possible that a child may also be sheltered from truth, especially in his academic studies. He may be involved in Bible class and chapel, be subject to Christian standards and discipline, be active in Christian service, and still be getting primarily a secular academic education. What he is taught, and how he is taught, may be so similar to what is done in the neighboring non-Christian school that a visitor would not detect a difference.

As Christian schools have multiplied, many Bible-believing teachers have moved from public to Christian schools. They have rejoiced in the freedom to mention the Lord and all that is most precious to them. They have been happy for higher standards of discipline and achievement. In many cases though, they have brought to their new schools the old viewpoint of their subjects. It is what they know best. They learned it in the public schools themselves. They built upon that foundation in college. They learned how to teach it and then for some years used the secular humanistic textbooks and teacher's manuals which were provided.

New teachers too have often had all their training either in secular institutions or in Christian colleges where their academic and education professors were the products of humanistic colleges and graduate schools. Too frequently the feeling is, *After all, social studies is social studies, isn't it, regardless of where you teach it, so why expect a different social studies in a Christian school?*

If we actually believe that the Bible is authoritative in every area in which it speaks, in history and science as well as in salvation and prayer, we are obligated to find out what it says about every topic we teach. If we fail to present what God says but teach other aspects of a subject, we shelter pupils from the truth and give them only part of the story.

What we do teach may be purely humanistic and opposed to the truth found in the Bible, or it may be true as far as it goes, but incomplete. In either case pupil thinking is being shaped according to the world's pattern. God asks instead for transformed lives, not conformed to the world, but based on renewed minds able to prove *what is that good and acceptable and perfect will of God.*

If Christian schools are to be Christian in the academic areas and to present a Biblical life and world view, teachers must become increasingly familiar with what the Word says in each area; they need to search for ways to involve pupils in learning, ways which enable them to understand and accept that Biblical viewpoint which is part of God's perfect will. In addition, Christian teachers must assist one another in producing textbooks and other materials based on Biblical principles.

It is not enough that we moralize in Bible classes to teach socially acceptable or even Christian conduct. Neither is it adequate that we use incidents from history, or observations from science, to illustrate spiritual truth. Though history and science furnish many possible object lessons, their use in this fashion is not a true integration of truth from Scripture and truth from other sources. It is not equivalent to searching out what God actually teaches about money, or capital punishment, or the treatment of animals, and then teaching it as part of the academic study of that topic.

Again, neither does the use of sentences from the Bible in a grammar lesson, or Scriptural words in a spelling lesson, necessarily mean that a Biblical view is taught. The frequent quotation of Bible verses in workbooks or textbooks, or the use of Biblical themes for art work, does not guarantee that the subject itself is being taught Biblically. While education in a Christian school should surely include a study of Bible sentences and words, and the use of Biblical quotations and themes, the integration of truth is more and deeper.

Basic to the whole concept of teaching God's truth in every area, and of helping pupils to see all truth as from God, are two prerequisites for the Christian school. **First**, the Bible must be thoroughly taught at each grade level as the inerrant Word of God, whether it deals with trusting Christ or the qualifications for leadership, with prayer or history. **Second**, Christian aspects of a subject must be included as part of that academic discipline, not relegated to Bible class alone.

For example, as the literary classics are studied, Christian writings must be included; as the Middle East is considered historically or geographically, Palestine and Israel must be given a rightful place. To fail here is to say to young people that Bible and the academic subjects are separate -- that only in Bible class do we consider what God says. With such a message conveyed to them, students will graduate with what some have called intellectual schizophrenia, and defeat the whole purpose of the Christian school.

Much attention is given in the Bible in relationships among people -- what is commonly called social studies, or the social sciences. True, the most basic of all teaching deals with the relationship between God and man, but second to that is human interaction. Christ spoke first of loving God with wholeheartedness, but next of loving one's neighbor as oneself.

Not only is the importance of these studies underscored in Scripture, but they are also areas of attack in our society today. Secular humanism centers in man and promotes man, society, and the state as the gods that really matter. Hence the double need in a Christian school for attention in the social sciences to the teachings of the Word of God.

In each of the chapters a list of Biblical concepts is presented first. Then follows Scripture passages which may be used in the classroom as a basis for study and investigation.

1

History

BIBLICAL CONCEPTS

I. **Our attitude toward history**

   1. God has directed that written records be kept.
   2. God wants us to know history.
   3. God expects us to learn from history.
   4. God has a plan He is carrying to completion; history records the progress of that plan.
   5. God's dealings in history show us what He is like.
   6. God holds believers responsible for fitting into His plan and being His instruments.

II. **God's relationship to the events of history**

   1. God is sovereign; no man or nation can overrule Him.
   2. God is never taken by surprise; things that happen fit into His plan.
   3. God plans the history of nations; He has purpose in what He plans.
   4. God controls the rise and fall of rulers.
   5. God leads rulers when they look to Him for guidance.
   6. God uses even heathen nations to accomplish His purposes.
   7. God deals with individuals, as well as with nations.

8. God sometimes withholds judgment that is due, most often to bring honor to His name.
9. God, in time of general judgment, often spares those who trust Him.
10. God has frequently revealed to His servants future events not known to others.

III. Nations and their relationship to God [in addition to previously stated concepts]

1. God is interested in all nations.
2. All nations are responsible to God.
3. The history of nations is dependent on their responses to God and to His people.
4. No nation is secure if it departs from God, or exalts itself above God.
5. The fact that God uses a nation to judge another does not relieve that nation from its own responsibility to God.
6. God has a special place and future for Israel.
7. God has promised that the descendants of Ishmael [Arabs] will be a great nation.
8. Satan's opposition to God has affected the history of nations.
9. All nations will ultimately worship God.

THE CYCLE OF A NATION

1. **BONDAGE** -- captivity, slavery
2. **SPIRITUAL FAITH** -- turning to God
3. **ACTS OF GREAT COURAGE** -- doing what is right despite difficulty, danger, pain
4. **LIBERTY AND ABUNDANCE** -- freedom and great blessing
5. **SELFISHNESS** -- regard for one's own interest (at others' expense)
6. **COMPLACENCY** -- quiet satisfaction
7. **APATHY** -- indifference, lack of emotion
8. **DEPENDENCY** -- control or influence by another
9. **BONDAGE** -- captivity, slavery

--Source unknown; quoted in Temple Times, September 28, 1980

BIBLICAL BACKGROUND

I. Our attitude toward history

1. God has directed that written records be kept.

Exodus 17:14

The account of victory over Amalek: *14 And the Lord said unto Moses, Write this for a memorial in a book, and rehearse it in the ears of Joshua . . . .*

Exodus 34:27, 28

At God's giving of the commands a second time: *27 And the Lord said unto Moses, Write thou these words: for after the tenor of these words I have made a covenant with thee and with Israel. 28 And he was there with the Lord forty days and forty nights; . . . And he wrote upon the tables the words of the covenant, the ten commandments.* Not only did God record the words, but He directed Moses also to write.

Deuteronomy 17:18-20

God's command to Israel's future king: *18 And it shall be, when he sitteth upon the throne of his kingdom, that he shall write him a copy of this law in a book out of that which is before the priests the Levites.* God's reasoning is given in verses 19, 20. The king himself must own and study daily the record of God's dealings, even if to do so he must copy by hand.

Deuteronomy 31:19, 21, 22

The Lord speaking to Moses: *19 Now therefore write ye this song for you, and teach it the children of Israel:* *put it in their mouths, that this song may be a witness for me against the children of Israel.*

Jeremiah 30:2

God speaking to Jeremiah: *2 Thus speaketh the Lord God of Israel, saying, Write thee all the words that I have spoken unto thee in a book.* See also 36:2, 27, 28; Ezekiel 43:11.

Daniel 12:4, 8, 9

God told Daniel to seal up the record, the prophecies He had given, until the end time. Daniel did not understand all that he had been told, but he was to record it for the future.

Luke 1:1-4

Though no specific command is recorded here, Luke explains the importance of his writing his Gospel account.

Revelation 1:11, 19; also 2:1, 8, 12, 18; 3:1, 7, 14; 19:9; 21:5

Christ to the Apostle John: *11 . . . What thou seest, write in a book, and send it unto the seven churches which are in Asia . . . . 19 Write the things which thou hast seen, and the things which are, and the things which shall be hereafter.*

2. God wants us to know history.

A large portion of the inspired Word is an historical record. Consider the Pentateuch, the twelve books of history in the Old Testament, the many historical accounts in the prophetic books, the Gospel accounts of the life and ministry of our Lord, the Acts account of the history of the early church, Paul's historical and autobiographical sketches interspersed in the Epistles, and the Apostle John's report of his experience in the early chapters of the Revelation. With this much that is of historical significance, we cannot doubt God's interest in our knowing history.

Deuteronomy 1:1 through 4:2

Here is a somewhat detailed account of the wilderness wanderings recorded and rehearsed for the new generation about to enter the Promised Land. God considered it important that this new group know what had happened previously.

Joshua 24:1-13

Here too, just before his death, Joshua was instructed by God to rehearse again their history and their need for seeking the Lord and serving Him alone.

Psalm 78

The history of Israel is recorded in song, with a prelude that expresses concern for the knowledge of history by the coming generations. *4 We will not hide them* [i.e., what our fathers told us] *from their children, shewing to the generation to come the praises of the Lord, and his strength, and his wonderful works that he hath done. 5 For he established a testimony . . . and appointed a law . . . . which he commanded our fathers, that they should make them known to their children: 6 That the generation to come might know them, even the children which should be born; who should arise and declare them to their children.*

See also Psalm 136.

3. God expects us to learn from a knowledge of history.

Deuteronomy 4:32-34

32 For ask now of the days that are past, which were before thee, since the day that God created man upon the earth, and ask from the one side of heaven unto the other, whether there hath been any such thing as this great thing is, or hath been heard like it? 33 Did ever people hear the voice of God speaking . . . as thou hast heard, and live? 34 Or hath God assayed to . . . take him a nation from the midst of another nation . . . according to all that the Lord your God did for you in Egypt . . . ?

Deuteronomy 7:17-19

When Israel would fear the nations in the land, she was encouraged to look back at what God had already done. Also Judges 10:11-13.

2 Chronicles 20:6-13.

King Jehoshaphat's knowledge of God's earlier dealings with Israel became the basis of his faith in God for deliverance from Moab and Ammon now. (Numbers 20, perhaps 450 years earlier.)

Ezekiel 5:13

Thus shall mine anger be accomplished . . . and they shall know that I the Lord have spoken it in my zeal, when I have accomplished my fury in them. Also Ezekiel 25; 35:2-4.

Daniel 5:18-23

Daniel reminded Belshazzar how God had judged Nebuchadnezzar's pride, saying, *And thou his son, O Belshazzar, hast not humbled thine heart, though thou knewest all this; But hast lifted up thyself against the Lord of heaven . . .* (v. 22, 23).

Daniel 9:2, 3, 11-14

Daniel, over in Babylon, studied the writings of Jeremiah, as God had revealed to him a seventy-year period in which Jerusalem would be desolate. He acted upon the information recorded earlier.

In 11-14, he recognized the calamities that came to Israel as fulfillment of the writings of Moses a thousand years earlier (Deut. 28:15-68).

1 Corinthians 10:11

Now all these things happened unto them for ensamples: and they are written for our admonition, upon whom the ends of the world are come.

See also Exodus 1:8, 13 and Judges 2:8-12 for examples of the lack of knowledge of history and the tragic results of that lack. In Esther 6 is an exciting account of a king learning from history, just in the nick of time.

"History is but the unrolled scroll of prophecy."
--James A. Garfield, U.S. President, 1831-1881.

4. God has a plan He is carrying to completion; history records the progress of that plan.

Isaiah 45:18

He created the earth to be inhabited.

Genesis 1:26

He created man to have dominion under God.

Genesis 3:15

He promised a Savior and King. Also Isa. 9:6,7; Micah 5:2.

Genesis 12:2

He promised the nation Israel -- a great nation through whom all nations would be blessed. Also 22:17,18; 26:24; 28:3,4; 35:9-12.

Jeremiah 32:37-44

He promised Israel's restoration after scattering to the nations.

Matthew 5:17,18

The words of Christ: *17 Think not that I am come to destroy the law, or the prophets: I am not come to destroy, but to fulfill. 18 For verily I say unto you, Till heaven and earth pass, one jot or one tittle shall in no wise pass from the law, till all be fulfilled.*

Luke 24:27

On the road to Emmaus: *27 And beginning at Moses and all the prophets, he expounded unto them in all the scriptures the things concerning himself.*

1 Corinthians 15:23-28

He plans to rule over all.

Ephesians 1:10

Everything is to culminate in Christ. God's ultimate purpose is that everything should glorify Him. See also the following Scriptures.

Ephesians 1:12

That we should be to the praise of his glory . . . .

Ephesians 2:7

That in the ages to come he might show the exceeding riches of his grace in his kindness toward us . . . .

Ephesians 3:10

That now unto the principalities and powers in heavenly places might be known by the church the manifold wisdom of God.

Psalms 150:6

Let everything that hath breath praise the Lord.

5. God's dealings in history show what He is like (His attributes).

For example:

Genesis 6:8,13,14,21; 7:1; 8:1

God showed His grace to Noah in the midst of a wicked generation whom He was about to destroy.

Psalm 107

1 O give thanks unto the Lord, for He is good: for his mercy endureth forever. 15 Oh that men would praise the Lord for his goodness, and for his wonderful works to the children of men! 43 Whoso is wise, and will observe these things, even they shall understand the lovingkindness of the Lord. The whole psalm rehearses God's actions down through history, as an illustration of His goodness and lovingkindness.

Psalm 136

Here God's wisdom, as well as his mercy is demonstrated by His work in the creation of the universe and the provisions He made for Israel down through her history.

Jeremiah 44:20-23

God spoke to the Jews in Egypt through Jeremiah about their burning of incense to the queen of heaven. God shows His omniscience and also His holiness as He deals with this sin in Israel's history.

John 3:16

For God so loved the world that He gave . . . . His love is manifest by this the greatest event in history.

1 Timothy 1:13,14

Paul the Apostle, in giving his testimony, exclaims over God's mercy and grace, as manifested in His dealings with him, one who was a blasphemer and persecutor.

"What are all histories but God manifesting himself, shaking down and trampling under foot whatsoever he hath not planted."

--Oliver Cromwell, 1599-1658.

6. God holds believers responsible for fitting into His plan and being His instruments.

Romans 6:13

Neither yield ye your members as instruments of un-righteousness unto sin: but yield yourselves unto God, as those that are alive from the dead, and your members as instruments of righteousness unto God.

Romans 12:1,2

1 . . . Present your bodies a living sacrifice . . . which is your reasonable service. 2 And be ye transformed . . . that ye may prove what is that good, and acceptable, and perfect, will of God.

Ephesians 2:10

For we are his workmanship created in Christ Jesus unto good works, which God hath before ordained that we should walk in them.

II. God's relationship to the events of history

1. God is sovereign; no man or nation can overrule Him.

Judges 7:1-8

God reduced Gideon's army, saying, *The people that are with thee are too many . . . lest Israel vaunt themselves against me, saying, Mine own hand hath saved me* (v. 2).

Ezra 6:22

When the Passover was kept once again after the return from captivity in Babylon and Assyria: *22 . . . For the Lord had made them joyful, and turned the heart of the king of Assyria unto them, to strengthen their hands in the work of the house of God, the God of Israel.*

Job 12:23

He increaseth the nations, and destroyeth them; he enlargeth the nations, and straighteneth them again.

Psalm 22:28

For the kingdom is the Lord's; and he is the governor among the nations.

Proverbs 21:1

The king's heart is in the hand of the Lord, as the rivers of water; he turneth it whithersoever he will.

Isaiah 23:7, 8

7 Is this your joyous city [i.e., Tyre; see v. 5] whose antiquity is of ancient days? . . . 8 Who hath taken this counsel against Tyre . . . ? 9 The Lord of hosts hath purposed it, to stain the pride of all glory . . . .

Isaiah 40:13-17

14 With whom took he counsel, and who instructed him . . . ? 15 Behold, the nations are as a drop of a bucket and are counted as the small dust of the balance; behold he taketh up the isles as a very little thing . . . 17 All nations before him are as nothing . . . less than nothing, and vanity. Also 46:9,10.

Jeremiah 46:1-26 (especially v. 19,20,24-26)

God promises destruction to Egypt -- takeover by Babylon.

See also the following, where God promises destruction to a series of nations: 47:1-7, Philistia; 48:2,7,8,11-13, 42, Moab; 49:15, Edom; 49:35-38, Elam; 50:9, Babylon.

Ezekiel 25:5

God speaking against the Ammonites: *5 And I will make Rabbah a stable for camels, and the Ammonites a couchingplace for flocks: and ye shall know that I am the Lord.*

God's actions against nations are designed so that all nations will recognize Him as Lord. For example: Ezekiel 25:7,11,14,17; 26:6; 28:22-24; 29:6,9,16; 30:8,19,25,26; 33:29; 35:9-13; 36:34-36; 39:21-29.

Ezekiel 29:3,9

God specifically promised destruction to Egypt because she considered the Nile River her own and of her own making, refusing to recognize God's hand.

Ezekiel 38,39

In the future, when the nations from the north and east band together to plunder and destroy Israel, God will destroy them by earthquake (38:19,20), by internal fighting (38:21), by disease (v. 22) and by violent storms. In doing so, He will make His power known to the nations: *23 Thus will I magnify myself, and sanctify myself; and I will be known in the eyes of many nations, and they shall know that I am the Lord.* Also 39:7.

Obadiah 3,4,8

God speaking to Edom: *3 The pride of thine heart hath deceived thee, thou that dwellest in the cleft of the rock, whose habitation is high; that saith in his heart, Who shall bring me down to the ground? 4 Though thou exalt thyself as the eagle, and though thou set thy nest among the stars, thence will I bring thee down, saith the Lord. 8 Shall I not in that day, saith the Lord, even destroy the wise men out of Edom, and understanding out of the mount of Esau?*

Malachi 1:4

Whereas Edom saith, We are impoverished, but we will return and build the desolate places; thus saith the Lord of hosts, They shall build, but I will throw down . . . The people against whom the Lord hath indignation for ever.

Matthew 28:18

And Jesus came and spake unto them, saying, All power is given unto me in heaven and in earth.

Acts 5:39

Gamaliel's reminder: *39 But if it be of God, ye cannot overthrow it; lest haply ye be found even to fight against God.*

2. God is never taken by surprise; things that happen fit into His plan.

Genesis 45:4-11

Joseph speaking: *7 God sent me before you to preserve you a posterity in the earth . . . ; 8 So now it was not you that sent me thither, but God . . . .* Also 50:19-21.

Exodus 3:19-21

God told Moses: *I am sure that the king of Egypt will not let you go, no, not by a mighty hand. And I will stretch out my hand and smite Egypt with all my wonders . . . and after that he will let you go (19, 20).*

Exodus 4:21-23

The Lord said unto Moses, When thou goest to return into Egypt, see that thou do all those wonders before Pharaoh . . . but I will harden his heart that he shall not let the people go (v. 21).

Also 9:35; 10:1, 2, 20, 27; 14:4, 8, 17.

3. God plans the history of nations; He has purpose in what He does.

Deuteronomy 7:7, 8

God didn't choose Israel because she was the largest nation, but because of His love and His covenant.

Deuteronomy 8:3

He let Israel hunger and then fed her so she would know the importance of living by the Word of God.

Daniel 7

Daniel's vision interpreted; four great nations are described in sequence. Also 8:3-12, 20-25.

Daniel 9:22-27

The seventy weeks described; the future of nations.

Zephaniah 3:8

God will judge the nations: *8 . . . My determination is to gather the nations, that I may assemble the kingdoms, to pour upon them mine indignation, even all my fierce anger: for all the earth shall be devoured with the fire of my jealousy.*

Zephaniah 3:14-20

God promises restoration to Israel: *20 . . . A name and a praise among all people of the earth . . . .*

Zechariah 14

All nations to be gathered to battle against Jerusalem (v. 2); the Lord to appear and set up His kingdom (v. 3, 9); all nations to worship the King (v. 16).

Also the many national prophecies in the Major and Minor Prophets.

4. God controls the rise and fall of rulers.

General statements:

Proverbs 8:15, 16

15 By me kings reign, and princes decree justice. 16 By me princes rule, and nobles, even all the judges of the earth.

Proverbs 20:29

Mercy and truth preserve the king: and his throne is upholden by mercy.

Daniel 2:20, 21

20 Daniel answered and said, Blessed be the name of God for ever and ever: for wisdom and might are his: 21 And he changeth the times and the seasons: he removeth kings and setteth up kings . . . .

Daniel 2:44, 45

Daniel interpreting Nebuchadnezzar's dream: *44 And in the days of these kings shall the God of heaven set up a kingdom, which shall never be destroyed: and the kingdom shall not be left to other people, but it shall break in pieces and consume all these kingdoms, and it shall stand for ever. 45 ... The great God hath made known to the king what shall come to pass hereafter ....*

Daniel 4:17

... The most High ruleth in the kingdom of men, and giveth it to whomsoever he will, and setteth up over it the basest of men.

Hosea 13:11

God speaking to Israel: *11 I gave thee a king in mine anger, and took him away in my wrath.*

Romans 13:1

Let every soul be subject unto the higher powers. For there is no power but of God: the powers that be are ordained of God.

Examples (not all of Israel):

1 Samuel 9:16,17 - Saul

17 And when Samuel saw Saul, the Lord said unto him, Behold the man whom I spake to thee of! this same shall reign over my people.

1 Samuel 16:12 - David

... The Lord said, Arise, anoint him: for this is he.

1 Kings 14:7,8 - Jeroboam

7 ... Forasmuch as I exalted thee from among the people, and made thee prince over my people Israel, 8 And rent the kingdom away from the house of David, and gave it thee ....

1 Kings 14:14 - Jeroboam's successor

Moreover the Lord shall raise him up a king over Israel, who shall cut off the house of Jeroboam that day .... Also 15:29.

1 Kings 16:2,3 - Baasha

God speaking to Baasha: *2 Forasmuch as I exalted*

thee out of the dust, and made thee prince over my people Israel ... 3 Behold I will take away the posterity of Baasha ....

1 Chronicles 22:9,10 - Solomon

God speaking to David: *9 Behold, a son shall be born to thee, who shall be a man of rest ... 10 He shall build an house for my name; and he shall be my son, and I will be his father; and I will establish the throne of his kingdom over Israel for ever.* Also 2 Chronicles 2:11, 12, where a foreign king, the king of Tyre, recognized God's appointment of Solomon.

Isaiah 44:28 and 45:1-4 - Cyrus, king of Persia

28 ... Cyrus, he is my shepherd, and shall perform all my pleasure: even saying to Jerusalem, Thou shalt be built; and to the temple, Thy foundation shall be laid. 1 Thus saith the Lord to his anointed, to Cyrus ....

Ezekiel 30:22-25 - Pharaoh of Egypt, and the king of Babylon

God states His determination to bring Pharaoh to nought and to strengthen the king of Babylon over Egypt.

Daniel 2:37,38 - Nebuchadnezzar, king of Babylon

Daniel interpreting the king's dream: *37 Thou, O king, art a king of kings: for the God of heaven hath given thee a kingdom, power, and strength, and glory 38 And wheresoever the children of men dwell ... [He] hath made thee ruler over them all. Thou art this head of gold.* Also 5:18-21, where Daniel reminds Belshazzar of this fact.

Daniel 5:26-31 - Belshazzar, king of Babylon

The handwriting on the wall, and the subsequent downfall, as a judgment from God.

5. God leads rulers when they look to Him for guidance.

For example:

1 Samuel 23:2

Therefore David enquired of the Lord, saying, shall I go and smite these Philistines? And the Lord said unto David, Go, and smite the Philistines, and save Keilah.

Also v. 4, 10-12; 30:6,8; 2 Sam. 2:1; 5:10,12,19,23, etc.

1 Kings 5:2-4

God directed that David should not build the temple but that his son Solomon should do so.

1 Kings 12:22-24

God directed Rehoboam not to fight Israel.

6. God uses even heathen nations for His purposes.

For example:

Judges 2:14, 15

And the anger of the Lord was hot against Israel, and he delivered them into the hands of spoilers that spoiled them, and he sold them into the hands of their enemeies round about . . . . Also 3:7, 8, 12, etc.

2 Kings 17:6-18

Assyria took Israel captive because of Israel's sins against God.

Ezra 5:3-17; 6:1-14, 22

Enemies in the land stopped the building of the temple by the returned Jews. A letter was sent to King Darius the Mede by these enemies, asking that a search be made in the records to find out if Cyrus of Persia had actually authorized this building. Chapter 6 records what they found, and not only resulted in their permission to continue the building, but in the requirement that supplies be provided for the building, and for sacrifices. *22 . . . For the Lord had made them joyful, and turned the heart of the king of Assyria unto them, to strengthen their hands in the work of the house of God, the God of Israel.*

Ezra 7:6-26

Artaxerxes, king of Babylon, authorized Ezra's expedition to Jerusalem. His decree on Ezra's behalf is recorded in verses 11-26, listing all the provisions the king was making.

Nehemiah 2:4-9

Artaxerxes also commissioned Nehemiah to rebuild Jerusalem. He sent letters to governors who were to provide for needs on the way, and a letter to the forestry department to provide lumber for the palace and the wall.

Isaiah 44:28; 45:1-4

God promised to use Cyrus, king of Persia, to subdue nations before Him.

Jeremiah 5:15-17

God speaking to Israel: *Lo, I will bring a nation upon you from far, O house of Israel, saith the Lord . . . a mighty nation . . . an ancient nation, a nation whose language thou knowest not . . . .*

Jeremiah 25:8-11

God promised to use Nebuchadnezzar and all the families of the north to destroy Israel and take them captive for seventy years. Also 32:28-30; Hab. 1:6ff.

Jeremiah 36:1-3

God justified to Israel the desolations brought by heathen nations under His guidance.

Jeremiah 46:24-26

God promised to use Babylon to judge Egypt. Also Ezekiel 29:19, 20.

7. God deals with individuals as well as with nations.

Many examples from the patriarchs; also Moses, Joshua, Elijah, Elisha, Paul, persons in the Gospels and Acts.

John 1:12

But as many as received him, to them gave he power to become the sons of God, even to them that believe on his name.

John 21:21-23

Peter's concern over what would happen to John; Jesus' assurance that He does not deal with all in the same way.

Ephesians 1:4-6

Chosen, predestinated, adopted, accepted in the Beloved -- such terms refer to individuals.

8. God sometimes withholds judgment that is due, most often to bring honor to His name.

Exodus 32:9-14

After the golden calf worship, (especially v. 12, 13) lest the Egyptians think He brought them out to kill them.

Numbers 14:11-21

After the people complained against Moses and Aaron,

when the spies brought back their report of giants in the land -- lest the Egyptians hear of the judgment and spread the word to other nations (esp. v. 12-14, 20).

Isaiah 48:9

God speaking to Israel: *9 For my name sake will I*

defer [or delay] *mine anger, and for my praise will I refrain for thee, that I cut thee not off.*

Ezekiel 20:7-22

God rehearses several instances of withholding judg-ment. One example: *14 But I wrought for my name's sake, that it should not be polluted before the heathen, in whose sight I brought them out.*

9. God in time of a general judgment often, though not always, spares those who trust Him.

For example:

Genesis 6:5-8; 8:1; 9:1

God remembered Noah.

Genesis 19:17-24

God spared Lot and those of his family who believed.

Numbers 14:23, 24, 35-38

God rewarded the faith of Joshua and Caleb, when all others were destroyed.

Malachi 4:1-3

Yet future: *1 . . . And the day that cometh shall burn them up* [i.e., the proud and wicked], *saith the Lord of hosts . . . . 2 But unto you that fear my name shall the Sun of righteousness arise with healing in his wings . . . .*

Hebrews 11:31

God made special provision for Rahab.

Hebrews 11:36-40

Many believers were not delivered from persecution and death for their faith. Also 2 Peter 2:5-9.

10. God has frequently revealed to His servants future events not known to others.

The principle stated:

Amos 3:7

Surely the Lord God will do nothing, but he revealeth his secret unto his servants the prophets.

Examples:

Genesis 18:17, 18

God told Abraham about the coming destruction of Sodom.

Genesis 41:25, 38, 39

God showed Joseph the planned seven years of feast and famine for Egypt and the surrounding area.

1 Samuel 3:11-14; 2:27-36

God told Samuel of the coming judgment upon Eli.

Daniel 9:21-27

God showed Daniel much truth concerning the end times.

Matthew 24:15-26; Mark 13:14-23

God tells us that a sure sign of the beginning of the Tribulation period will be the Anti-Christ's assuming the place of rulership in the temple in Jerusalem.

Matthew 24:29-51; Mark 13:24-37

God promises that the time of Tribulation will end with the coming of Christ with great power and glory, with accompanying violent changes in the heavens.

Mark 13:4-13

God gives believers many details of events coming before the Lord comes: increasing wars, earthquakes, famines, false Christs, persecution of believers even by their families, the international preaching of the Gospel.

1 Thessalonians 4:16, 17

God revealed through the Apostle Paul that *16 . . . The Lord himself shall descend from heaven with a shout, with the voice of the archangel, and with the trump of God: and the dead in Christ shall rise first: 17 Then we which are alive and remain shall be caught up together with them in the clouds, to meet the Lord in the air: and so shall we ever be with the Lord.*

"You took the good things for granted; now you must earn them again. For every right that you cherish, you have a duty which you must fulfill. For every hope that you entertain, you have a task that you must perform. For every good that you wish to preserve, you will have to sacrifice your comfort and your ease. There is nothing for nothing any longer."

--George Washington

III. Nations and their relationship to God (in addition to previously stated concepts)

1. God is interested in all nations, and in persons from those nations.

Genesis 12:3

God speaking to Abram: *3 . . . In thee shall all families of the earth be blessed.*

Psalm 96:1-10

1 . . . Sing unto the Lord, all the earth. 3 Declare his glory among the heathen, his wonders among all people. 7 Give unto the Lord, O ye kindreds of the people, give unto the Lord glory and strength. 10 Say among the heathen that the Lord reigneth . . . . 13 . . . [The Lord] cometh for he cometh to judge the earth: he shall judge the world with righteousness, and the people with his truth.

Jonah 1:1,2; 3:1-10; 4:11

God sent Jonah His prophet to Nineveh, a wicked heathen city of 120,000 people so ignorant that they did not know right from left. See also Nahum 1-3; here are three chapters of prophecy concerning Nineveh.

Matthew 12:41,42

Jesus commends Nineveh for responding to Jonah's preaching; he also commends the Queen of Sheba for her efforts to hear the wisdom of Solomon.

Matthew 28:19,20

19 Go ye therefore, and teach all nations, baptizing . . . 20 Teaching them to observe all things whatsoever I have commanded you.

Mark 16:15

. . . Go ye into all the world, and preach the gospel to every creature.

Luke 2:10

Angels speaking to the shepherds: *10 . . . I bring you good tidings of great joy, which shall be to all people.*

John 1:6,7

6 There was a man sent from God, whose name was John. 7 The same came for a witness, to bear witness of the Light, that all men through him might believe.

John 3:16

For God so loved the world that he gave his only begotten Son, that whosoever believeth in him should not perish, but have everlasting life.

Acts 17:30,31

Paul speaking in Athens: *30 And the times of this ignorance God winked at; but now commandeth all men every where to repent: 31 Because he hath appointed a day, in the which he will judge the world in righteousness by that man whom he hath ordained . . . .*

Romans 16:26

Speaking of the Gospel: *26 But now is made manifest, . . . according to the commandment of the everlasting God, made known to all nations for the obedience of faith.*

1 Timothy 2:1-6

1 I exhort . . . prayers . . . be made for all men; 3 For this is good and acceptable in the sight of God our Saviour; 4 Who will have all men to be saved, and to come unto the knowledge of the truth. 6 Who gave himself a ransom for all . . . .

1 John 2:2

And he is the propitiation for our sins: and not for our's only, but for the sins of the whole world.

2. All nations are responsible to God.

See also several related concept statements in this section which indicate responsibility.

Isaiah 13:19-22; also 14:22-27

God judges nations that oppose Him. *19 And Babylon, the glory of kingdoms, the beauty of the Chaldees' excellency, shall be as when God overthrew Sodom and Gomorrah. 20 It shall never be inhabited . . . .*

Also Isaiah 15,16, Moab; 17:1,2, Syria and its capital Damascus; chapter 18, Ethiopia; chapter 19, Egypt.

Ezekiel 7:27

God speaking here to Israel: *27 . . . I will do unto them after their way, and according to their deserts will I judge them; and they shall know that I am the Lord.*

Ezekiel 14:12-20

If a nation [in this case Israel] sins against God, and God judges that nation, even Noah, Daniel and Job together cannot stop that judgment.

Daniel 2:37-45; 4:34-37; 5:22-31

God expects all nations to recognize Him, not just Jews and Christians. He revealed His plan for the sequence of kingdoms to Nebuchadnezzar, a Babylonian; He brought Nebuchadnezzar to submission after seven years of judgment; He destroyed Belshazzar for exalting himself against God and desecrating the vessels of Israel's temple.

Amos 1, 2

God pronounces judgment on specific nations for very specific sins:

1:3-5. Syria, for use of iron instruments of warfare against Gilead.

1:6-8. Philistia, for deporting an entire population, giving it to Edom.

1:9,10. Lebanon, also for delivering an entire population to Edom, as well as for failing to heed a previous covenant made under Solomon (1 Kings 5:1; 9:11-14).

1:11,12. Edom, for pursuing Israel with a sword, and refusing to let them go through their land (Num. 20:14-18).

1:13-15. Ammon, for extreme cruelty to pregnant women in time of battle.

2:1-3. Moab, for cremating the bones of the king of Edom.

2:4,5. Judah, for rejecting the law of the Lord; for refusing to obey Him; for idolatry.

2:6-16. Israel, for selling people for money and things, for harlotry, for keeping garments given as pledges overnight (Ex. 22:26), for ignoring Nazarite vows, for stifling God's prophets.

Obadiah 15

The Golden Rule for nations: *15 . . . As thou hast done, it shall be done unto thee: thy reward shall return upon thine own head.*

Matthew 25:32

The judgment of the nations, described by Christ.

3. The history of nations is dependent on their response to God and to His people.

For example:

Genesis 6:5-8, 13

Noah and the people of his day received different treatment, based on their attitude toward God.

Deuteronomy 23:3-8; 25:17-19

The actions of Moab, Ammon and Amalek, when Israel was on the way to the Promised Land, had long range effects on their history, and on God's attitude toward them.

Deuteronomy 27:14-26 and chapter 28

God lists for Israel the conditions of His blessing and judgment, based on specific actions on their part.

1 Samuel 7:3

Samuel related Israel's deliverance from the Philistines to obedience to the Lord.

1 Kings 9:4-9; also 1 Kings 11:14, 23, 30-39

The Lord promised Solomon the establishment of his kingdom, dependent on his walking in obedience to the Lord. Later came judgment for Solomon and the nation. God stirred up adversaries.

Proverbs 14:34

Righteousness exalteth a nation; but sin is a reproach to any people.

Jeremiah 46-51

A series of prophecies of judgment upon Egypt, Philistia, Moab, Ammon, Edom, Syria (Damascus), Kedar (Arabia), Elam, Babylon, Chaldea, Israel. Also Ezekiel 29:1-13; Zephaniah 2:4-11.

Ezekiel 28:1, 2, 6, 8

Judgment pronounced upon Tyre for her pride and arrogance.

Joel 3:1-8, 12, 19

God promises judgment in the end time upon the nations who have mistreated Israel and desecrated God's temple.

Jonah 3:5-10

Nineveh's repentance and deliverance from destruction. Later judgment in Zephaniah 2:13-15.

Zechariah 1:14, 15; 2:8, 9.

Although God promised He would use other nations to carry out His judgment against Israel, they were not to go beyond the limits He set. He also promises judgment to nations that plunder Israel.

Matthew 25:32-46

In the Olivet discourse, Christ describes the coming judgment of nations on the basis of their treatment of the Jews who have preached the Gospel of the kingdom during the Tribulation. See Scofield note.

4. No nation is secure if it departs from God, or exalts itself above God.

Isaiah 47

Here is a description of a proud nation, Babylon, determined that she is above any attack of judgment. Note some of the characterizations: *lady of the kingdoms* (v. 5); *I shall be a lady for ever* (v. 7); *given to pleasures, dwells carelessly, that sayest in thine heart, I am, and none else beside me; I shall not sit as a widow, neither shall I know the loss of children* (v. 8); *thou hast trusted in thy wickedness: thou hast said, None seeth me. Thy wisdom and thy knowledge, it hath perverted thee; and thou hast said in thine heart, I am, and none else beside me* (v. 11). Then note the judgment described.

Jeremiah 48:7,29,30,42

The description of Moab is one of trust in her own works and pleasure, loftiness, arrogancy, pride, haughtiness. *42 And Moab shall be destroyed from being a people, because he hath magnified himself against the Lord.*

Jeremiah 49:4-6

Ammon's trust was in flowing valleys, treasures, her own sense of security.

Jeremiah 49:15,16

Edom prided herself in the rocky terrain which was her security.

Jeremiah 50:35-40; 51:13,36,37

Chaldea and Babylon trusted in horses, chariots, a multi-ethnic people, treasures, idols, and a good water supply.

Ezekiel 29:3,9

God promises judgment to Egypt for refusal to recognize God's hand and rather claiming the Nile River to be her own and of her own making.

Hosea 8:14

For Israel hath forgotten his Maker, and buildeth temples . . . ; but I will send a fire upon his cities and it shall devour the palaces thereof.

Hosea 13:16

Samaria shall become desolate; for she hath rebelled against her God . . . .

Obadiah 3, 4

Spoken of Edom: *The pride of thine heart hath deceived thee, thou . . . that saith in his heart, Who shall bring me down to the ground? Though thou exalt thyself as the eagle and though thou set thy nest among the stars, thence will I bring thee down, saith the Lord. Also Mal. 1:4.*

5. The fact that God uses a nation to judge another does not relieve that nation from its own responsibility to God.

Isaiah 10:12-15

God promised to punish Assyria for her pride, after using her to judge Israel.

Isaiah 30:31

For through the voice of the Lord shall the Assyrian be beaten down, which smote with a rod.

Jeremiah 25:11,12

After promising seventy years of captivity to Babylon, God says: *12 When seventy years are accomplished,*

I will punish the king of Babylon, and that nation . . . for their iniquity, and the land of the Chaldeans . . . .

Zechariah 1:12-15

God has earlier expressed His displeasure with Israel (v. 2,4); now He shows His displeasure with the nations who oppressed her: *15 I am very sore displeased with the heathen that are at ease: for I was but a little displeased, and they helped forward the affliction.*

"America is great because she is good: if America ceases to be good, America will cease to be great."

Alexis de Tocqueville, 1805-1859.

6. God has a special place and future for Israel.

Exodus 31:13,16,17

The keeping of the Sabbath was to be a sign of Israel's special relationship to God.

Psalm 135:4

For the Lord hath chosen Jacob unto himself, and Israel for his peculiar treasure. Also Deut. 7:6-8; 26:16-19; 27:9,10; Isa. 41:8-14.

Isaiah 55:5

God promises that Israel shall become a center to which the nations shall come. Also 60:3-16; Micah 4:1,2.

Jeremiah 23:3-6

God promises to gather Israel from all nations, to make them fruitful, to give them a King -- the Lord Himself. Also Isa. 43:3, 5-7; Amos 9:14,15; Mal. 3:1-6.

Jeremiah 30:1-11

God promises restoration to the land, the time of Jacob's trouble, then freedom again to serve the Lord in the Kingdom. Also 18-22 and chapters 31-33; Dan. 9.

Jeremiah 46:27,28

God promises to treat Israel differently from other nations. He will make a full end of them, but not of Israel. Also 50:19-34; Ezek. 16:60-63; 36:21-38; Lev. 26:44, 45; Isa. 41:10-14; 49:25,26.

Hebrews 8:7-13

God promises a new covenant with Israel.

See also many other passages of Scripture, including the following: Ezekiel 20:39-44; 25:2-17; 26:2,3; 28:24-26; 36:8-11; Joel 2:18-27; 3:18-21; Amos 3:1,2; Micah 4:13; 5:2-5; 7:15-20; Haggai 2:7-9; Zechariah 1:16,17; 2:8,11; 3:9,10; 8:2-8, 13, 20-23 (cf. Genesis 12); 10:5-10; 12:8-10; 13:1-3; 14:1-21; Malachi 3:2-6.

PROJECT: Look up all of the verses referred to in this section, making a note of what specific promise or prediction is made in each concerning Israel. Then categorize them and prepare a summary describing God's special treatment of Israel and the verses which relate to each part.

7. God has promised that the descendants of Ishmael (Arabs) will be a great nation.

Genesis 16:10-12

10 And the angel of the Lord said unto her [Hagar], I will multiply thy seed exceedingly, that it shall not be numbered for multitude. 11 And the angel of the Lord said unto her, Behold, thou art with child, and shalt bear a son, and shalt call his name Ishmael; because the Lord hath heard thy affliction. 12 And he will be a wild man; his hand will be against every man, and every man's hand against him; and he shall dwell in the presence of all his brethren.

Genesis 17:20

God to Abraham: *And as for Ishmael, I have heard*

thee; Behold, I have blessed him, and will make him fruitful, and will multiply him exceedingly; twelve princes shall he beget, and I will make him a great nation.

Genesis 21:13,18

God to Abraham: *Of the son of the bond-woman will I make a nation, because he is thy seed.*

God to Hagar: *Arise, lift up the lad, and hold him in thine hand; for I will make him a great nation.*

8. Satan's opposition to God has affected history.

Genesis 3:14-24

The results of Satan's temptation and man's sin include a curse upon the serpent and a change of his lifestyle; sorrow, pain in childbirth, submission of woman to man; a cursed ground that brings forth only with work, hard work; death and removal from the garden.

Job 1:7,12

Satan attacks those who trust God, within the limits set by God. Also 2:6, 7.

Isaiah 14:12-17

When finally Satan is cast into Hell, his past influence will be noted -- he made the earth tremble, the kingdoms shake, the world a wilderness, the cities desolate, and held men as secure prisoners (v. 15-17).

John 8:44

Satan is a murderer and a liar and has people who follow him as his children.

Ephesians 6:12

For we wrestle not against flesh and blood, but against principalities, against powers, against the rulers of the darkness of this world, against spiritual wickedness in high places.

9. All nations will ultimately worship God.

Psalm 22:27, 28

27 All the ends of the world shall remember and turn unto the Lord: and all the kindreds of the nations shall worship before thee. 28 For the kingdom is the Lord's: and he is the governor among the nations. Also 72:11; Isa. 45:23-25; 66:23; Dan. 7:13, 14.

Philippians 2:9-11

9 Wherefore God also hath highly exalted him and given him a name which is above every name: 10 That at the name of Jesus every knee should bow, of things in heaven, and things in earth, and things under the earth; 11 And that every tongue should confess that Jesus Christ is Lord to the glory of God the Father.

Revelation 15:4

Who shall not fear thee, O Lord, and glorify thy name? For thou only art holy: for all nations shall come and worship before thee; for thy judgments are made manifest.

TURNING POINT IN HISTORY APPROACHING

"In addition to the grave political situation in the world today, we are witnessing the emergence of a wholly new situation, a crisis of unknown nature, one completely different, one entirely non-political. We're approaching a major turning point in world history, in the history of civilization. It can be seen in various areas by various specialists. I could compare it only with the turning point from the Middle Ages to the Modern Era, a whole shift of civilizations. It is a turning point at which settled concepts suddenly become hazy, lose their precise contours, at which our familiar and commonly used words lose their meaning, become empty shells, at which methods which have been reliable for many centuries no longer work. It's the sort of turning point at which the hierarchy of values to which we are dedicated all our lives, which we use to judge what is valuable and what is not, and which causes our lives and hearts to beat, is starting to waver and may perhaps collapse.

"And these two crises: the political crisis of today's world and the oncoming spiritual crisis, are occurring at the same time. It is our generation that will have to confront them."

--Alexander Solzhenitsyn, in speech at AFL-CIO meeting, July, 1975, as quoted in Christian Studies Center Worldview, October, 1980.

2

Geography

BIBLICAL CONCEPTS

1. God is responsible for the contour of the earth.
2. God controls His creation -- i.e., what we commonly call NATURE.
3. Natural resources belong to God.
4. We are stewards of the land and responsible to care for it.
5. Land is polluted as a result of man's sin.
6. God's desire for man was that he should populate the earth, not congregate in one place and make a name for himself.
7. God originated nations and languages to keep men scattered.
8. God distributed land to tribes and nations, and is concerned about boundaries.
9. God is concerned about all kinds of people, wherever they live and whatever their status.
10. All nations are related.

Note: Additional Biblical teaching related specifically to plants and animals is found in Volume 3 of this series, entitled Science and Mathematics.

BIBLICAL BACKGROUND

---

1. ### God is responsible for the contour of the earth.

Nehemiah 9:6

Thou . . . art Lord alone; thou hast made heaven . . . the earth, and all things that are therein, the sea, and all that is therein, and thou preserveth them all . . . .

Job 26:10

He hath compassed the waters with bounds, until the day and night come to an end.

Job 28:9-11

9 He putteth forth his hand upon the rock: he over-turneth the mountains by the roots. 10 He cutteth out rivers among the rocks; and his eye seeth every precious thing. 11 He bindeth the floods from over-flowing . . . . Also Psalm 46:8.

Isaiah 40:22

It is he that sitteth upon the circle of the earth, and the inhabitants thereof are as grasshoppers; that stretcheth out the heavens as a curtain, and spreadeth them out as a tent to dwell in. Also 42:5.

2. ### God controls His creation -- i.e., what is commonly called NATURE.

Leviticus 26:4-6

4 Then I will give you rain in due season, and the land shall yield . . . the trees of the field shall yield their fruit. 5 And your threshing shall reach unto the vintage, and the vintage shall reach unto the sowing time.... 6 . . . I will rid evil beasts out of the land. . . .

Leviticus 26:21, 22

21 And if ye walk contrary . . . I will bring seven times more plagues upon you . . . . 22 I will also send wild beasts among you, which shall rob you of your children, and destroy your cattle, and make you few in number. . . .

Psalm 107:23-31

25. . . For He commandeth and raiseth the stormy wind . . . He maketh the storm a calm.... Also 33-38.

"The world is God's epistle to mankind -- his thoughts are flashing upon us from every direction."

Plato, 427-347 B.C.

3. Natural resources belong to God.

Exodus 19:5

> *... All the earth is mine.*

Leviticus 26:32-35

> *26 And I will bring the land into desolation ... 33 ... your land shall be desolate, and your cities waste. 24 Then shall the land enjoy her sabbaths ... even then shall the land rest ... 35 As long as it lieth desolate, it shall rest ....*

1 Chronicles 29:14,16

> *David praying: 14 ... For all things come of thee, and of thine own have we given thee ... 16 O Lord our God, all this store that we have prepared ... cometh of thine hand and is all thine own.*

Haggai 2:8

> *The silver is mine and the gold is mine, saith the Lord of hosts.*

Psalm 24:1

> *The earth is the Lord's and the fulness thereof; the world, and they that dwell therein.*

Psalm 89:11

> *The heavens are thine and the earth also is thine: as for the world and the fulness thereof, thou hast founded them. Also v. 12; 95:5; Ezek. 36:29-36.*

Ezekiel 29:3,9,10

> God rebukes Pharaoh and Egypt for speaking of the Nile as their own. *9 The land of Egypt shall be desolate and waste; and they shall know that I am the Lord; because he hath said, The river is mine, and I have made it.*

4. We are stewards of the land and responsible to care for it.

Genesis 2:15

> *The Lord took the man, and put him in the garden of Eden to dress it and to keep it.*

Exodus 23:11

> The land was to rest every seventh year as a reminder of man's stewardship. Also Lev. 25:4.

Psalm 8:6

> *Thou makest him* [man] *to have dominion over the works of thy hands.*

5. Land is polluted as a result of man's sin.

Genesis 3:17,18

> *17 And unto Adam He said, ... cursed is the ground for thy sake ... 18 Thorns also and thistles shall it bring forth to thee ....* Also Lev. 18:24,25; Num. 35:33,34.

Psalm 106:37,38

> *37 Yea, they* [our fathers] *sacrificed their sons and their daughters unto devils. 38 And shed innocent blood ... whom they sacrificed unto the idols of Canaan: and the land was polluted with blood.*

Isaiah 24:5,6

> *5 The earth also is defiled ... because they have transgressed the laws ... 6 Therefore hath the curse devoured the earth ....*

Jeremiah 2:7

> *And I brought you* [Israel] *into a plentiful country to eat the fruit thereof and the goodness thereof; but when ye entered, ye defiled my land and made mine heritage an abomination.* Also 16:18; Micah 2:10.

6. God's desire for man was that he should populate the earth, not congregate in one place and make a name for himself.

Genesis 1:28

> *God said unto them, Be fruitful and multiply, and replenish the earth, and subdue it: and have domin-ion ... over every living thing.*

Genesis 9:1

> *And God blessed Noah and his sons and said unto them,*

Be fruitful and multiply, and replenish the earth.

Genesis 11:1-9

God judged the building of the tower of Babel and the motivation behind it. *So the Lord scattered them from thence upon the face of all the earth.*

7. God originated nations and languages to keep man scattered.

Genesis 10

Here is a detailed description of the distribution of the nations, the sons and grandsons of Noah after the Flood. Note these statements: *5 By these were the isles of the Gentiles divided in their lands; every one after his tongue, after their families, in their nations. 20 These are the sons of Ham, after their families, after their tongues, in their countries, and in their nations.* Also v. 31,32.

Genesis 11:1-9

1 And the whole earth was of one language, and of one speech. 4 And they said, Go to, let us build us a city and a tower . . . and let us make us a name, lest we be scattered abroad upon the face of the whole earth. 6 And the Lord said, Behold, the people is one, and they have all one language; and this they begin to do: and now nothing will be restrained from them, which they have imagined to do. 7 Go to, let us go down, and there confound their language, that they may not understand one another's speech. 8 So the Lord scattered them abroad . . . .

8. God distributed land to tribes and nations, and is concerned about boundaries.

Numbers 34:1-28

The division of Canaan among the tribes of Israel.

Deuteronomy 2:5 through 3:2

God speaks over and over of giving certain land to a particular people.

Joshuah 1:2-5

God said to Joshua: *2 . . . Go . . . unto the land which I do give . . . 3 Every place that the sole of your foot shall tread upon, that have I given you . . .* [boundaries are listed] *5 There shall not any man be able to stand before thee . . . .* Also Joshua 15:22.

Jeremiah 27:6-8

God has shown concern even for lands being judged by the conquering of other nations. For example: *6 Now have I given all these lands into the hand of Nebuchadnezzar the king of Babylon . . . . 8 And it shall come to pass, that the nation and kingdom which will not serve the same Nebuchadnezzar . . . that nation will I punish, saith the Lord, with the sword, and with the famine, and with the pestilence, until I have consumed them by his hand.*

Acts 17:26

And God made of one blood all nations of men for to dwell on all the face of the earth, and hath determined the times before appointed, and the bounds of their habitation.

9. God is concerned about all kinds of people, wherever they live and whatever their status.

Acts 10:34,35

34 . . . God is no respecter of persons: 35 But in every nation he that feareth him and worketh righteousness, is accepted with him.

Romans 10:12,13

12 For there is no difference between the Jew and the Greek: for the same Lord over all is rich unto all that call upon him. 13 For whosoever shall call upon the name of the Lord shall be saved.

James 2:1-9

Believers are warned against deferring to the rich on the basis that God chooses the poor (v. 5); to treat people unfairly because of their status is sin (v. 9).

Some examples of God's concern:

John 3
   Nicodemus, a ruler, a Pharisee

John 4
   A woman, Samaritan and immoral

John 5
   A helpless man

Matthew 28:19
   All nations. Also Acts 1:8

Acts 2:5-11
   Devout Jews from every nation

10. All nations are related.

Genesis 10:32
   All are descendants of Noah and of Adam.

Acts 17:26
   God *hath made of one blood all nations of men for to*

dwell on all the face of the earth.

1 Corinthians 15:39
   All flesh is not the same flesh; but there is _one_ *kind of flesh of men, another flesh of beasts . . . .*

"The word <u>geography</u> is derived from two Greek words, meaning <u>to write about the land</u> or <u>to describe the land</u>. The discipline of geography thus must be related to God, since He is the Creator of the land, the world (Gen. 1:1; John 1:1; Heb. 1:10; etc.). The creation is His handiwork, and points to Him. The teacher must continually remind his students of this fact. Someone has summed it in these words: 'God left His fingerprints all over creation.'"
   --Byron Snapp, "Teaching Geography in the Christian School." <u>On Teaching</u>, Dec., 1982.

"How singular, and yet how simple, the philosophy of rain; . . . Who but the Omniscient one could have devised such an admirable arrangement for watering the earth?"
                              Andrew Ure, 1778-1857.

"The bee, though it finds every rose has a thorn, comes back loaded with honey, and why should not other tourists do the same?"
                              --Thomas C. Haliburton, 1796-1864.

"The world is a great book, of which those who never stir from home read only a page."
                              --St. Augustine, died in 604.

"The heavens and the earth alike speak of God, and the great natural world is but another Bible, which clasps and binds the written one; for nature and grace are one --grace the heart of the flower, and nature its surrounding petals."
                              --Henry Ward Beecher, 1813-1887.

"The Bible is the chief moral cause of all that is good, and the best corrector of all that is evil, in human society; the best book for regulating the temporal concerns of men, and the only book that can serve as an infallible guide to future felicity."
                              --Noah Webster, 1758-1843.

3

Economics

BIBLICAL CONCEPTS

I. **Attitudes toward money and possessions**

   1. Whatever good things we have are gifts from God.

   2. Believers are stewards over God's possessions, not independent owners.

   3. Material things should not be a goal in life.

   4. Money is entrusted to believers for use as God purposes.

   5. God is the supplier of material needs for those who trust Him.

   6. Money will not buy spiritual blessings.

   7. Attitude toward money is an index of one's general attitude.

   8. True prosperity depends on obedience to God and favor from Him.

II. **Giving to God and to people**

   1. The tithe is God's minimum, taught by the Law, by practice, and by New Testament approval.

   2. God blesses those who are generous with Him.

   3. Giving to God should be in proportion to the way God has prospered us.

   4. Giving to the Lord should be a private matter based on one's own decisions.

   5. God considers our giving an investment; He keeps accounts.

6. Offerings to God should be honestly and fairly handled.
7. Those who serve the Lord full-time should also give of their substance to the Lord.
8. God expects both individuals and churches to be generous with those in need.
9. God's way of providing for needs is through the gifts of His people.

III. Financial matters and men's relationships.
1. Those who are sent out by God to serve Him can expect Him to supply their material needs.
2. God, in some cases, directs a believer to support himself in doing the Lord's work.
3. That which is valuable must sometimes be destroyed because of the danger of its leading into sin.
4. Believers should not expect unbelievers to understand or follow Biblical standards in handling money or possessions.
5. Believers may rightfully give special consideration to other believers.
6. Believers are not to base their respect for people on their wealth.
7. Lending and borrowing money are connected with freedom for a nation or a person.

IV. Property ownership
1. Property rights are to be protected.
2. An owner has a right to buy, sell, or otherwise dispose of his own property.
3. The right to privacy in one's home, or freedom from unlawful search, is a God-given right.
4. Property ownership is to pass from one generation to another.
5. Though voluntary communal ownership has Scriptural precedent for believers, it must be done honestly and out of love for one another; the fact that such ownership created problems and is never recommended in the Epistles is doubtless significant.
6. Women as well as men have property rights.
7. One who invests money has a right to a return on his

investment, providing that return is not gained by taking advantage of the poor.

V. Problems related to money and property
  1. The <u>love</u> of material things leads to problems.
  2. Wealth and prosperity themselves can lead to problems.
  3. Poverty may result from several causes about which God warns us.
  4. One who is security for another's debts is courting trouble.

VI. Work and our attitude toward it
  1. Work is part of God's plan for man.
  2. Honest work results in personal satisfaction.
  3. God approves of and rewards diligence.
  4. One who looks for excuses not to work will accomplish little.
  5. Men are to plan ahead, but also consider God's will in their planning.

VII. Business principles
  1. Business must be conducted honestly.
  2. Business should be conducted with proper safeguards.
  3. An employer must be fair to his workers.
  4. Employees are to serve their employers faithfully and as unto the Lord.
  5. A break in the work week is God's plan, in remembrance of God's rest at the end of the creation week, and in response to the needs of men and animals.
  6. The terms of any business deal should be based on the needs of both parties.

WHAT IS WEALTH?

"Riches are not an end of life, but an instrument of life." -- Henry Ward Beecher, 1813-1887.

"The wealth of a state consists not in great treasures, solid walls, fair palaces, weapons, and armor; but its best and noblest wealth, and its truest safety, is in having learned, wise, honorable, and well-educated citizens."
                                                                      -- Epicurus, 342-270 B.C.

"I cannot call riches by a better name than the baggage of virtue; the Roman word is better, <u>impediment</u>. For as the baggage is to an army, so are riches to virtue. It cannot be spared or left behind, and yet it <u>hindereth</u> the march; yea, and the care of it sometimes loseth or disturbeth the victory. Of great riches there is no real use, except in the distribution; the rest is but conceit." -- Francis Bacon, 1561-1626.

BIBLICAL BACKGROUND

I. Attitudes toward money and possessions
1. Whatever good things we have are gifts from God.

For example:

Deuteronomy 8:17, 18 - Wealth, and power to get it.
God to Israel: *17 And thou say in thine heart, My power and the might of mine hand hath gotten me this wealth. 18 But thou shalt remember the Lord thy God: for it is he that giveth thee power to get wealth . . . .*

1 Chronicles 29:11-16 - Riches, honor, strength, building materials. David praying just before Solomon's accession to the throne: *11 . . . All that is in the heaven and in the earth is thine; thine is the kingdom, O Lord, and thou art exalted as head above all. 12 Both riches and honour come of thee . . . and in thine hand it is to make great, and to give strength unto all. 14 But who am I, and what is my people, that we should be able to offer so willingly after this sort? for all things come of thee, and of thine own have we given thee. 16 . . . All this store that we have prepared to build thee an house . . . cometh of thine hand, and is all thine own.*

Ecclesiastes 5:18-20 - Wealth and good health to eat and enjoy life. Solomon speaking in his old age: *19 Every man also to whom God hath given riches and wealth, and hath given him power to eat thereof, and to take his portion, and to rejoice in his labour; this is the gift of God.*

1 Timothy 4:3-5 - All kinds of food.
3 . . . Meats, which God hath created to be received with thanksgiving of them which believe and know the truth. 4 For every creature of God is good, and nothing to be refused, if it be received with thanksgiving.

1 Timothy 6:17 - All things to enjoy.
Charge them that are rich in this world, that they be not highminded, nor trust in uncertain riches, but in the living God, who giveth us richly all things to enjoy.

James 1:17 - Everything good that we have.
Every good gift and every perfect gift is from above, and cometh down from the Father of lights . . . .

"To value riches is not to be covetous. They are the gift of God, and, like every gift of his, good in themselves, and capable of a good use. But to overvalue riches, to give them a place in the heart which God did not design them to fill, this is covetousness." -- Herman Wayland, 1830-1893.

2. Believers are stewards over God's possessions, not independent owners.

Leviticus 19:23-25
God directed Israel about when they were free to eat the fruit of the land because it was His.

Leviticus 25:1-7
The land which I give you was to be rested every seventh year for the Lord.

Leviticus 25:8-31
The land was God's (v. 23), therefore to be rested and returned to original owner every fiftieth year; all sales to be reckoned until the year of jubilee.

Leviticus 25:35-38
Usury was not to be charged to a poor brother -- i.e., since it was all God's.

Leviticus 25:39-46
A poor man could not become a bond-servant to another Jew, since they were all God's servants (v. 42, 43)

Leviticus 25:47-55
An Israelite bought by a Gentile could be redeemed by a relative; if not, he was to be set free at the jubilee, since he was God's servant (v. 55).

1 Chronicles 29:14-16
David acknowledged that all the materials he had gathered for the temple-building belonged to God.

Ezekiel 7:20, 21
God condemned Israel for using their silver and gold to make images for worship.

Haggai 2:8
The silver is mine and the gold is mine, saith the Lord of hosts.

Matthew 22:21
Render unto Caesar the things that are Caesar's and unto God the things that are God's.

Matthew 25:14-29
Parable of the talents, illustrating the responsibility of servants for possessions, and our responsibility as God's stewards.

Acts 2:44, 45
Believers in Jerusalem gave up private ownership out of love. Also 4:32-35.

1 Corinthians 6:19, 20
What? know ye not that your body is the temple of the Holy Ghost which is in you, which ye have of God, and ye are not your own? For ye are bought with a price . . . .

3. Material things should not be a goal in life.

1 Chronicles 1:11, 12
11 And God said to Solomon, Because this was in thine heart, and thou hast not asked riches, wealth, or honour . . . but hast asked wisdom and knowledge for thyself, that thou mayest judge my people . . .; 12 Wisdom and knowledge is granted unto thee; and I will give thee riches, and wealth, and honour, such as none of the kings have had that have been before thee . . . .

Job 31:24-28
Job recognized that pride in wealth is denial of God. He says: *24 If I have made gold my hope, or have said to the fine gold, Thou art my confidence; 25 If I rejoiced because my wealth was great, and because mine hand had gotten much; 27 And my heart hath been secretly enticed . . . 28 This also were an iniquity to be punished by the judge: for I should have denied the God that is above.*

Proverbs 10:2
Treasures of wickedness profit nothing: but righteousness delivereth from death.

Proverbs 11:4
Riches profit not in the day of wrath: but righteousness delivereth from death.

Proverbs 13:7
There is that maketh himself rich, yet hath nothing: there is that maketh himself poor, yet hath great riches.

Proverbs 15:16
Better is little with the fear of the Lord than great treasure and trouble therewith. Also 28:6.

Proverbs 22:1, 2
A good name is rather to be chosen than great riches, and loving favour rather than silver and gold. The rich and poor meet together: the Lord is the maker of them all.

Proverbs 23:4, 5
Labour not to be rich: cease from thine own wisdom. Wilt thou set thine eyes upon that which is not? for riches certainly make themselves wings; they fly away . . . .

Zephaniah 1:18
Neither their silver nor their gold shall be able to deliver them in the day of the Lord's wrath . . . .

Matthew 4:8-10
Jesus refused to worship Satan even when He was offered all the kingdoms of the earth, and the glory that went with them.

Matthew 6:19-34

We are not to worry about material things as the unsaved do, but seek God's will first and He will care for our needs. Also Luke 12:22-34.

Matthew 16:26

For what is a man profited, if he shall gain the whole world, and lose his own soul? or what shall a man give in exchange for his soul?

Luke 12:15

Take heed, and beware of covetousness: for a man's life consisteth not in the abundance of the things which he possesseth.

Luke 12:16-21

Parable of bigger barns.

1 Timothy 3:3, 8

A bishop (pastor) or deacon must be one who is *not*

greedy of filthy lucre.

1 Timothy 6:6-8

But godliness with contentment is great gain. For we brought nothing into this world, and it is certain we can carry nothing out. And having food and raiment let us be therewith content.

Hebrews 10:34

Persecuted believers are commended for taking joyfully the spoiling of their goods, knowing that they have better possessions in heaven.

Hebrews 13:5

Let your conversation [way of life] be without covetousness; and be content with such things as ye have: for he hath said, I will never leave thee, nor forsake thee.

4. Money is entrusted to believers for use as God purposes.

Three uses seem to be especially emphasized in Scripture: (1) the care of one's family, (2) the needs of others, (3) the furtherance of the Gospel message. Note the following, but also consider many other passages included in this chapter.

Mark 7:9-13 - family

Jesus rebuking the Pharisees for giving their traditions first place over God's commands: *10 For Moses said, Honour thy father and thy mother . . . 11 But ye say, if a man shall say to his father or mother, It is Corban . . . a gift [to God], by whatsoever thou mightest be profited by me; he shall be free. 12 And ye suffer him no more to do ought for his father or his mother; 13 Making the word of God of none effect through your traditions . . . .* In other words, the Lord was saying that giving to God what should go to parents was sin.

1 Timothy 5:4, 8, 16 - family

8 But if any provide not for his own, and specially for those of his own house, he hath denied the faith, and is worse than an infidel.

Deuteronomy 15:10, 11 - others

10 Thou shalt surely give him [i.e., thy poor brother], and thine heart shall not be grieved when thou givest unto him: because that for this thing the Lord thy God shall bless thee in all thy works, and in all that thou puttest thine hand unto. 11 For the poor shall never cease out of the land . . . open thine hand wide unto thy brother, to thy poor, and to thy needy, in thy land.

Ephesians 4:28 - others

Let him that stole steal no more: but rather let him labour, working with his hands the thing which is good, that he may have to give to him that needeth.

Philippians 4:10-19 - the ministry of the Word

Paul expresses appreciation for the support of the Philippian church for his ministry.

Matthew 6:19, 33 - the accomplishment of God's will

19 Lay not up for yourselves treasures upon earth . . . 20 But lay up for yourselves in heaven . . . . 33 But seek ye first the kingdom of God, and his righteousness . . . .

5. God is the supplier of material needs for those who trust Him.

2 Chronicles 31:5, 10

There was plenty to eat when Israel turned to the Lord, bringing their tithes and offerings. Also Ecc. 3:13.

Ezra 8:21-23

God provided protection from enemies and safety in travel when His people asked, in preparation for their

return to the land. Also Ps. 37:25.

Psalm 128

To those that fear the Lord, God promises food, happiness, a fruitful wife and wholesome children.

Matthew 6:25-34

33 But seek ye first the kingdom of God, and his righteousness; and all these things shall be added unto you. Also Luke 12:22-34.

Hebrews 13:5,6

Be content with such things as ye have, for he hath *said, I will never leave thee nor forsake thee. So that* *we may boldly say, The Lord is my helper, and I will* *not fear what man shall do unto me.*

6. Money will not buy spiritual blessings.

Isaiah 55:1-3

Ho, everyone that thirsteth, come ye to the waters, *and he that hath no money; come ye, buy, and eat....*

Ezekiel 7:19

Their silver and their gold shall not be able to deliver *them in the day of the wrath of the Lord: they shall* *not satisfy their souls ....*

Matthew 19:21-24

A rich man shall hardly enter into the kingdom of *heaven ....*

Acts 8:18-22

But Peter said to him [Simon]: Thy money perish with *thee because thou hast thought that the gift of God* *may be purchased with money ... thy heart is not* *right with God ... Repent therefore ....*

1 Peter 1:18, 19

18 ... Ye were not redeemed with corruptible things, *as silver and gold ... 19 But with the precious blood* *of Christ, as of a lamb without blemish and without* *spot.*

7. Attitude toward money is an index of one's general attitude.

Haggai 1:2-4

God reprimands Israel for building beautiful private homes and neglecting God's house and worship.

Matthew 6:19-21

Lay not up for yourselves treasures on earth ... But *lay up ... treasures in heaven ... For where your* *treasure is, there will your heart be also.*

Matthew 18:23-35 (esp. v. 33)

The story of the servant for whom much was forgiven, but who refused to forgive others what they owed.

Luke 12:33,34

Sell that ye have, and give alms; provide yourselves *bags which wax not old, a treasure in the heavens* *that faileth not, where no thief approacheth, neither* *moth corrupteth. For where your treasure is, there* *will your heart be also.*

Luke 16:10,11

He that is faithful in that which is least is faithful also *in much: and he that is unjust in the least is unjust also* *in much. If therefore ye have not been faithful in the* *unrighteous mammon, who will commit to your trust* *the true riches?* Also v. 12.

2 Corinthians 8:3-5

Paul speaking of the churches of Macedonia: *They were* *willing of themselves; Praying us with much entreaty* *that we would receive the gift ... And this they did,* *not as we hoped, but first gave their own selves to the* *Lord, and unto us by the will of God.*

8. True prosperity depends on obedience to God and favor from Him.

Genesis 39:2-5

2 And the Lord was with Joseph, and he was a pros- *perous man ... 3 And his master saw that the Lord* *was with him, and that the Lord made all that he did* *to prosper in his hand. 4 And Joseph found grace in* *his sight, and he served him: and he made him over-* *seer over his house, and all that he had he put into* *his hand. 5 ... the Lord blessed the Egyptian's house* *for Joseph's sake ....* Also 21-23.

Deuteronomy 28:1-13

1 ... If thou shalt hearken diligently unto the voice *of the Lord thy God, to observe and to do all his com-* *mandments ... that the Lord thy God will set thee on* *high above all nations of the earth: 2 And all these* *blessings shall come on thee ...* (Verses 3-13 describe the blessings promised). Also 30:1,2,9,10,15,16.

Joshua 1:8

This book of the law shall not depart out of thy mouth; *but thou shalt meditate therein day and night, that* *thou mayest observe to do according to all that is* *written therein: for then thou shalt make thy way* *prosperous, and then thou shalt have good success.*

Psalm 1:1-3

1 Blessed is the man that walketh not in the counsel of the ungodly . . . 2 But his delight is in the law of the Lord; and in his law doth he meditate day and night. 3 And he shall be like a tree planted by the rivers of water, that bringeth forth his fruit in his season; his leaf also shall not wither; and whatsoever he doeth shall prosper.

Psalm 73

Here Asaph tells how he was envious of the wicked in their seeming prosperity (v. 2-16) until he saw how slippery was their hold (17-22); then he saw the blessings of the righteous (23-28) -- true prosperity! Also Psalm 37:34-40.

Philippians 4:19

God promises through the Apostle Paul that, since the Philippi church has given so generously to him in the Lord's work, God will supply all their need.

II. Giving to God and to people

1. The tithe is God's minimum, taught by the Law, by practice, and by New Testament approval.

Genesis 14:20

Before the Law was given, Abraham gave tithes of all that he gained in battle. He gave them to Melchizedek, recognizing him as a representative of God.

Genesis 28:22

Jacob too promised a tenth to God at Bethel.

Leviticus 27:30-34

The details of the tithe for Israel are given here: *30 And all the tithe of the land, whether of the seed of the land, or of the fruit of the tree, is the Lord's: it is holy unto the Lord.*

Numbers 18:24-29

24 But the tithes of the children of Israel . . . I have given to the Levites to inherit: therefore I have said unto them, Among the children of Israel they shall have no inheritance. 26 Thus speak unto the Levites, . . . When ye take of the children of Israel the tithes . . . then ye shall offer up . . . for the Lord, even a tenth part of the tithe. Also Deuteronomy 12:6, 7; Malachi 3:8-10.

2 Chronicles 31:5-14

When King Hezekiah initiated the keeping of the passover once again, and with it other reforms, he commanded that once again the people should bring in their tithes and offerings. They did so abundantly. *5 And as soon as the commandment came abroad, the children of Israel brought in abundance the firstfruits of corn, wine, and oil, and honey, and of all the increase of the field; and the tithe of all things brought they in abundantly.*

Matthew 23:23

Jesus condemns the Pharisees as hypocrites, saying that though they tithed, they were not consistent in their actions in other matters of the law which were even more crucial. *23 . . . These* [other responsibilities] *ought ye to have done, and not to leave the other* [the tithe] *undone.* Here is His approval of the tithe.

Hebrews 7:4-10

In the discussion here concerning Abraham's giving of the tithe to Melchizedek, the importance of the tithe as a recognition of one who is greater and to be honored is recognized.

2. God blesses those who are generous with Him.

Proverbs 3:9, 10

9 Honour the Lord with thy substance, and with the firstfruits of all thine increase: 10 So shall thy barns be filled with plenty, and thy presses shall burst out with new wine.

Proverbs 11:24, 25

24 There is that scattereth, and yet increaseth; and there is that withholdeth more than is meet, but it tendeth to poverty. 25 The liberal soul shall be made fat: and he that watereth shall be watered himself.

Malachi 3:8-10

10 Bring ye all the tithes . . . and prove me . . . if I will not open you the windows of heaven, and pour you out a blessing . . . .

Matthew 6:31-34

33 Seek ye first the kingdom of God, and his righteousness; and all these things shall be added unto you. Also Deuteronomy 28:11, 12; 30:9, 10.

Matthew 26:7-13

Lavish giving to the Lord is not wasted. The precious ointment was an act of worship from one who loved Him.

Mark 10:29, 30

No man leaves house or brethren . . . for my sake . . . But he shall receive an hundredfold.

Mark 12:41-44

Jesus commended the widow for giving all she had into the treasury. Also Luke 21:3, 4.

Luke 6:38

Give and it shall be given unto you . . . for with the same measure . . . it shall be measured to you again.

2 Corinthians 9:6-12

He which soweth bountifully shall reap also bountifully . . . God loveth a cheerful giver.

Philippians 4:14-19

No church communicated with me as concerning giving and receiving, but ye only . . . ye sent once and again . . . but my God shall supply all your need . . . .

3. Giving to God should be in proportion to the way God has prospered us.

Deuteronomy 16:17

Every man shall give as he is able, according to the blessing of the Lord thy God which he hath given thee.

Ezra 2:68, 69

And some of the chief of the fathers, when they came to the house of the Lord . . . offered freely for the house of God . . . They gave after their ability unto the treasure . . . .

Malachi 3:8

Will a man rob God? Yet ye have robbed me. But ye say, Wherein have we robbed thee? In tithes and offerings.

Mark 12:41-44

The significance of the gift given by the poor widow was based on her attitude and the proportion of her gift to her total assets, not on the amount itself.

1 Corinthians 16:2

Upon the first day of the week let every one of you lay by him in store, as God hath prospered him . . . .

2 Corinthians 8:12

For if there be first a willing mind, it is accepted according to that a man hath, and not according to that he hath not.

"I never knew a child of God being bankrupted by his benevolence. What we keep we may lose, but what we give to Christ we are sure to keep."

-- Theodore L. Cuyler, 1822-1909.

4. Giving to the Lord should be a private matter based on one's own decisions.

Exodus 25:1, 2

Speak unto the children of Israel, that they bring me an offering: of every man that giveth it willingly with his heart ye shall take my offering. Also 35:5.

Exodus 35:21-29

And they came, every one whose heart stirred him up and every one whom his spirit made willing and they brought the Lord's offering to the work of the tabernacle (v. 21). A description of the abundance offered so willingly follows in the next verses.

Ezra 2:68, 69

And some of the chief of the fathers . . . offered freely . . . They gave after their ability . . . .

Matthew 6:1-4

Take heed that ye do not your alms before men, to be seen of them . . . let not thy left hand know what thy right hand doeth: That thine alms may be in secret . . . .

Acts 5:1-5

Peter reminds Ananias that after his land was sold, the money was his to control. He need not have given all or part of it, but what he gave should be done willingly and honestly.

2 Corinthians 8:1-5

In giving to the poor saints at Jerusalem, the Macedonian churches *were willing of themselves, praying us with much entreaty that we should receive the gift . . .* (v. 3, 4).

2 Corinthians 9:7

Every man according as he purposeth in his heart,

so let him give; not grudgingly, or of necessity: for God loveth a cheerful giver.

5. God considers our giving an investment; He keeps accounts.

Matthew 6:20 21
But lay up for yourselves treasures in heaven, where neither moth nor rust doth currupt, and where thieves do not break through nor steal; For where your treasure is, there will your heart be also.

Matthew 19:27-30
God promises reward to those who make sacrifices on earth. *29 And everyone that hath forsaken houses, or brethren, or sisters, or father, or mother, or wife, or children, or lands, for my sake, shall receive an hundredfold, and shall inherit everlasting life.*

Philippians 4:17
Paul, commending the Philippians for their gifts: *Not because I desire a gift: but I desire fruit that may abound to your account.*

6. Offerings to God should be honestly and fairly handled.

Exodus 22:29, 30
Offerings should not be delayed, but given promptly.

Deuteronomy 23:18
Offering money should be that which is gained honestly and honorably. Also 2 Sam. 24:24.

2 Corinthians 8:18-22
Proper precautions should be taken that the money given is administered properly. Also 1 Cor. 16:2, 3.

7. Those who serve the Lord full-time should also give of their substance to the Lord.

Numbers 18:26-32
The Levites were to tithe the offerings that were given to them, giving the best to God.

"There is no portion of money that is our money, and the rest God's money. It is all His; He made it all, gives it all, and He has simply trusted it to us for His service. A servant has two purses, the master's and his own, but we have only one."   -- Adolphe Monod

8. God expects both individuals and churches to be generous with those in need.

Deuteronomy 15:7-11
If there be among you a poor man of one of thy brethren . . . thou shalt open thine hand wide unto him . . . Thou shalt surely give him . . . for this thing the Lord thy God shall bless thee . . . . Also Lev. 19:9, 10, 33, 34; 23:22; 25:35-38.

Psalm 41:1
Blessed is he that considereth the poor; the Lord will deliver him in time of trouble. Also Prov. 28:27.

Proverbs 19:17
He that hath pity upon the poor lendeth unto the Lord and that which he hath given will he pay him again. Also 22:9.

Matthew 5:42
Give to him that asketh thee, and from him that would borrow of thee turn not thou away.

Matthew 25:40
Inasmuch as ye have done it unto one of the least of these my brethren, ye have done it unto me.

Acts 20:35
. . . Laboring, ye ought to support the weak, and to remember the words of the Lord Jesus, how he said, It is more blessed to give than to receive.

2 Corinthians 8:1-5
The example of the Macedonian churches who out of poverty gave *beyond their power*, after they *first* gave their own selves to the Lord. Also 12-15.

Ephesians 4:28
Let him labour working with his hands the thing which is good, that he may have to give to him that needeth. A somewhat surprising reason for working!

1 Timothy 6:17-19

Charge them that are rich . . . that they be rich in good works, ready to distribute . . . . Also Heb. 13:16.

1 John 3:17

But whoso hath this world's good, and seeth his brother have need, and shutteth up his bowels of compassion from him, how dwelleth the love of God in him?

"Riches without charity are nothing worth. They are a blessing only to him who makes them a blessing to others." --Henry Fielding, 1707-1754.

"Serving God with our little, is the way to make it more; and we must never think that wasted with which God is honored, or men are blest." -- John Hall, 1829-1898.

9. God's way of providing for needs is through the gifts of His people.

Exodus 25:1-9

The people were instructed to bring materials for the tabernacle-building -- i.e., specified items. Also 35:21-29, the people willingly gave; in 36:5-7, more than enough was given.

Numbers 7:1-8

The 12 princes who had been in charge of taking the census brought as gifts for the Lord six covered wagons and 12 oxen. This was God's way of providing for the transporting of the tabernacle and the court -- i.e., boards, sockets, bars, hangings, etc.

Deuteronomy 18:1-5

The Levites . . . shall have no part nor inheritance with Israel: they shall eat the offerings of the Lord . . . . In other words it was the offerings of others that were to provide for these needs.

Ezra 1:4-6; 2:68, 69

The method of voluntary gifts for a particular need was recognized even by a heathen king, Cyrus, when he made proclamation concerning Jews returning to Jerusalem to build a temple. *4 Whosoever remaineth in any place where he sojourneth, let the men of his place help him with silver, and with gold, and with goods, and with beasts, beside the freewill-offering for the house of God that is in Jerusalem.*

2 Corinthians 8:13, 14

13 For I mean not that other men be eased, and ye burdened: 14 But by an equality . . . your abundance may be a supply for their want . . . .

James 2:15

If a brother or sister be naked, and destitute of daily food, and one of you say unto them, Depart in peace . . . notwithstanding ye give them not those things which are needful to the body, what doth it profit?

III. Financial matters and men's relationships

1. Those who are sent out by God to serve Him can expect Him to supply their material needs.

Leviticus 2:3, 10

A major portion of certain offerings in the tabernacle was to go to Aaron and his sons, or to the priest who offered it. Also 6:16, 17, 26; 7:6-15; 22:10-13.

Numbers 18:21, 24, 31

The Levites received the tithes of Israel. They also received towns and pasture lands. Also 35:1-8 and Deut. 14:27.

Matthew 10:7-12

Jesus sent out the twelve without provision, expecting their needs to be supplied as they went. Also Luke 9:3-5.

Luke 10:1-11

Jesus sent out the seventy without purse or extra clothing, expecting them to be cared for as they went.

1 Corinthians 9:6-16

Paul shows the reasonableness of support at the hands of others -- the soldier, the farmer, the cattle-raiser, the ox that treads the grain, those who minister in the Jewish temple. The climax in v. 14: *Even so hath the Lord ordained that they which preach the Gospel should live of the Gospel.*

2. God, in some cases, directs a believer to support himself in doing the Lord's work.

Acts 20:33, 34

Paul: *I have coveted no man's silver, or gold, or apparel, Yea, ye yourselves know, that these hands have ministered unto my necessities, and to them that were with me.* Also v. 35.

1 Corinthians 9:14, 15

Even so hath the Lord ordained that they which preach the gospel should live of the gospel. But I have used

none of these things: neither have I written these things that it should be done unto me . . . . Also 2 Cor. 11:7-12.

1 Thessalonians 2:9

For ye remember, brethren, our labor and travail: for laboring night and day, because we would not be chargeable unto any of you, we preached unto you the gospel of God.

3. That which is valuable must sometimes be destroyed because of the danger of its leading into sin.

Deuteronomy 7:25

As Israel captured villages, they were to destroy utterly the graven images, not even saving the silver and gold, *lest thou be snared therein.* They were expressly told not to bring an image into the house *lest thou be a cursed thing like it* (v. 26). Also 13:16, 17.

Deuteronomy 20:16-18

16 But of the cities of these people, which the Lord thy God doth give thee for an inheritance, thou shalt save alive nothing that breatheth: 17 But thou shalt utterly destroy them: . . . as the Lord thy God hath

commanded thee: 18 That they teach you not to do after all their abominations, which they have done unto their gods; so should ye sin against the Lord your God.

Matthew 18:8, 9

The same principle reiterated by the Lord Jesus: *8 Wherefore if thy hand or thy foot offend thee, cut them off, and cast them from thee: it is better for thee to enter into life halt or maimed, rather than having two hands or two feet to be cast into everlasting fire.*

4. Believers should not expect unbelievers to understand or follow Biblical standards in handling money or possessions.

Two examples:

Genesis 14:22-24

Though Abraham refused to take goods offered by the king of Sodom lest that heathen king declare, *I have made Abraham rich,* he let his confederates take their portion (v. 13, 24).

Genesis 23:7-16

Abraham insisted on paying for the field and cave of Machpelah as a burying place for his family, even though Ephron the Hittite was insistent that he accept it without payment.

5. Believers may rightfully give special consideration to other believers.

Deuteronomy 15:1-3

In giving the law concerning the sabbatic year, God directed that Israelites make a difference in their handling of loans made to fellow-Jews and those made to foreigners. *2 . . . Every creditor that lendeth ought unto his neighbour shall release it; he shall not exact it of his neighbour, or of his brother; because*

it is called the Lord's release. 3 Of a foreigner thou mayest exact it again: but that which is thine with thy brother thine hand shall release.

Deuteronomy 23:19, 20

The law in Israel: *19 Thou shalt not lend upon usury to thy brother; usury of money, usury of victuals, usury of any thing that is lent upon usury: 20 Unto a stranger thou mayest lend upon usury; but unto thy brother thou shalt not lend upon usury; that the Lord thy God may bless thee . . . .*

Galatians 6:10

As we have therefore opportunity, let us do good unto all men, especially unto them who are of the household of faith.

6. Believers are not to base their respect for people on their wealth.

James 2:1-9

God's condemnation for basing respect on the amount of one's possessions is summarized in v. 9: *But if ye have respect to persons, ye commit sin, and are convinced of the law as transgressors.* In addition, other logical reasons for not giving favored treatment to wealthy persons are given: (1) by doing so, one makes himself a judge of the thought life of another (v. 2-4): (2) God has shown special concern for the poor, in making many of them rich in faith (v. 5, 6); (3) the rich more than the poor often blaspheme God and oppress believers (v. 6, 7); (4) God's law is summed up in loving of one's neighbor, whether rich or poor (v. 8, 9).

7. Lending and borrowing money are connected with freedom for a nation or a person.

Deuteronomy 15:6

Spoken to Israel: *For the Lord thy God blesseth thee, as he promised thee: and thou shalt lend unto many nations, but thou shalt not borrow; and thou shalt reign over many nations, but they shall not reign over thee.*

Also 28:12, 13.

Proverbs 22:7

The rich ruleth over the poor, and the borrower is servant to the lender.

IV. Property ownership

1. Property rights are to be protected.

Exodus 20:15, 17

Thou shalt not steal . . . thou shalt not covet . . . .
Also Lev. 19:11, 13; Prov. 28:24.

Exodus 21:33-36

Negligence that causes loss to another person must be paid for; it is also considered sin. Also 22:5-15; Lev. 6:1-7.

Exodus 22:1-15

Such actions as stealing, burglarizing, permitting a straying animal to damage property, not giving proper protection to money or goods left in one's care and borrowing an animal and letting it die demand restitution.

Leviticus 24:18, 21

One who kills a beast must make good to its owner.

Deuteronomy 22:1-3

Lost property or straying animals are to be returned.

Deuteronomy 23:24, 25

A person was permitted to eat grapes or corn from his neighbor's crop, but not to harvest and take home any.

Joshua 13-19

Each tribe of Israel was to own certain land, according as the Lord commanded Moses to divide it (14:5). Also Ezekiel 47:13, 14.

1 Kings 21:17-19

Elijah was sent by God to reprimand King Ahab for killing Naboth in order to take possession of his vineyard.

Proverbs 22:28

Markers designating property boundaries were not to be removed. Also 23:10, 11; Deut. 19:14.

Ezekiel 46:18

God forbids a ruler from confiscating property to provide an inheritance for his sons.

Ezekiel 47:22, 23

God makes clear His concern for Gentiles as well as Jews. Here He gives direction concerning the dividing of the land, but specifically commands that *strangers that sojourn among you, which shall beget children among you* shall be included in the inheritance, in the tribes in which they live.

2. An owner has a right to buy, sell, or otherwise dispose of his own property.

Proverbs 31:16, 24

A woman, described as buying a field, planting a vineyard, making fine linen, selling it, and delivering girdles unto the merchant, is called virtuous.

Matthew 20:1-16

Parable of the man who paid the same wage for different hours of work. *15 Is it not lawful for me to do what I will with mine own?*

Acts 5:3, 4

Peter reminded Ananias concerning the sale of his property: *While it remained, was it not thine own? And after it was sold, was it not in thine own power?*

3. The right to privacy in one's home, or freedom from unlawful search, is a God-given right.

Deuteronomy 24:10, 11

Under God's law, a man who lent money to a fellow-citizen, with the loan guaranteed by a pledge of some sort, had no right to enter the house of the borrower to search out the article pledged. He must wait for the owner to bring the article out to him.

"Property is dear to men . . . because it is the bulwark of all they hold dearest on earth, and above all else, because it is the safeguard of those they love." -- William G. Sumner, 1840-1910.

4. Property ownership is to pass from one generation to another.

Numbers 27:8-11

In Israel under the Law, when a man died his property was to go to his sons, daughters, or nearest relatives.

Numbers 36

Each tribe's inheritance was to remain the property of that tribe; this regulation was so important that freedom to marry outside the tribe had to be forefeited to carry it out.

Deuteronomy 21:15-17

Property rights of the first born were to be protected in case a man later had sons by a second wife.

Ezekiel 46:16-18

Even in the future, property is to be kept within the families of Israel's princes.

5. Though voluntary communal ownership has Scriptural precedent for believers, it must be done honestly and out of love for one another; the fact that such ownership created problems and is never recommended in the Epistles is doubtless significant.

Acts 2:44, 45

And all that believed were together, and had all things common; And sold their possessions and goods, and parted them to all men, as every man had need. Also 4:32-37.

Acts 5:1-11

The dishonesty of Ananias and Sapphira, and God's judgment of them.

6. Women as well as men have property rights.

Numbers 27:1-9 Cf. Job 42:15.

God approved the request of the daughters of Zelophehad for an inheritance in Israel, since they did not have brothers (v. 8). Also 36:5-12; Joshua 17:3, 4.

Proverbs 31:16, 18, 24

A virtuous woman considers a field and buys it; she knows her merchandise is good; she makes fine linen and sells it, along with finished garments.

Acts 5:7-10

Sapphira, as well as Ananias, was considered responsible for the disposition of their property; she too was judged for the dishonesty.

7. One who invests money has a right to a return on his investment, providing that return is not gained by taking advantage of the poor.

Exodus 22:25

If thou lend money to any of my people that is poor by thee, thou shalt not be to him as a usurer, neither shalt thou lay upon him usury.

Deuteronomy 24:6

No man shall take the nether or the upper millstone to pledge: for he taketh a man's life to pledge. The millstones were essential for meal preparation.

Proverbs 28:8

He that by usury and unjust gain increaseth his substance, he shall gather it for him that will pity the poor.

Matthew 25:15-30

The parable of the talents. The condemnation of the man who did not invest his money for gain is expressed in v. 27, 28: *27 Thou oughtest therefore to have put my money to the exchangers, and then at my coming I should have received mine own with usury. 28 Take therefore the talent from him, and give it unto him which hath ten talents . . . 30 And cast ye the unprofitable servant into outer darkness . . . .* The application which the Lord makes here indicates approval, or at least recognition of the legitimacy of gain.

Luke 19:11-25

The parable of the ten pounds. *23 Wherefore then gavest not thou my money into the bank, that at my coming I might have required mine own with usury?* Here also the application is similar. Also Mark 12:1-9.

V. Problems related to money and property

1. The love of material things leads to problems.

Proverbs 15:27 - trouble in the home

He that is greedy of gain troubleth his own house . . . .

Proverbs 22:16 - poverty

He that oppresseth the poor to increase his riches, and he that giveth to the rich, shall surely come to want.

Proverbs 28:20-22 - sin, poverty

20 . . . He that maketh haste to be rich shall not be innocent. 22 He that hasteth to be rich hath an evil eye, and considereth not that poverty shall come upon him.

Ecclesiastes 5:10-16 - lack of anticipated satisfaction

10 He that loveth silver shall not be satisfied with silver; nor he that loveth abundance with increase: this is also vanity. 11 When goods increase, they are increased that eat them: and what good is there to the owners thereof, saving the beholding of them with their eyes? 13 There is a sore evil which I have seen under the sun, namely, riches kept for the owners thereof to their hurt. Surely King Solomon was well acquainted with the results of a lust for riches!

Isaiah 56:9-12 - selfishness, blindness to real issues, drunkenness

God describing Israel: *9 . . . beasts . . . come to devour . . . 10 . . . watchmen are blind . . . all ignorant . . . dumb dogs, they cannot bark; sleeping, lying down, loving to slumber . . . 11 . . . greedy dogs which can never have enough . . . shepherds that cannot understand: they all look to their own way, every one for his gain, from his quarter 12 . . . we will fill ourselves with strong drink . . . .* See also Ezekiel 22:12, 13, 25-29.

Matthew 13:22 - choking of the Word, unfruitfulness

He also that received seed among the thorns is he that heareth the word; and the care of this world, and the deceitfulness of riches, choke the word, and he becometh unfruitful.

Matthew 19:21-24; Mark 10:21-25 - forfeiting eternal life

21 Jesus said unto him, . . . Sell that thou hast, and give to the poor, and thou shalt have treasure in heaven . . . 22 But when the young man heard that saying, he went away sorrowful: for he had great possessions.

Luke 12:13-34 - an empty life, worry

The parable of the rich man who built bigger and better barns, but failed to seek after God.

1 Timothy 6:9, 10 - temptation, lusts, all kinds of evil

9 But they that will be rich fall into temptation and a snare, and into many foolish and hurtful lusts, which drown men in destruction and perdition. 10 For the love of money is the root of all evil . . . .

James 4:1-3 - lust, wars, fighting

1 From whence come wars and fightings among you? come they not hence, even of your lusts that war in your members? Also 5:1-6; 1 John 2:15, 16.

2. Wealth and prosperity themselves can lead to problems.

Deuteronomy 8:11-18 - forgetting the Lord; taking undue credit

God warns Israel before they enter the Land: *11 Beware that thou forget not the Lord thy God . . . 12 Lest when thou hast eaten and art full, and hast built goodly houses, and dwelt therein; 13 And when thy herds and thy flocks multiply, and thy silver and thy gold is multiplied, and all that thou hast is multiplied; 14 Then thine heart be lifted up, and thou forget the Lord thy God, which brought thee forth out . . . of Egypt . . . 15 Who led thee . . . 16 Who fed thee . . . 17 And thou say in thine heart, My power and the might of mine hand hath gotten me this wealth.*

Proverbs 19:6 - false friends

Many will entreat the favour of the prince: and every man is a friend to him that giveth gifts.

Ecclesiastes 5:10-16 - a variety of problems

Solomon, out of his experience with great riches, is used by the Lord to issue some warnings concerning the problems wealth brings: he cites covetousness, expense, worry, insomnia, losses, lack of permanence after this life. Also Proverbs 20:21.

1 Timothy 6:17-19 - pride, trust in wealth, hoarding

A warning to New Testament believers about special dangers to those who were rich in the things of the world.

3. Poverty may result from several causes about which God warns us.

Proverbs 11:24 - hoarding

. . . There is that withholdeth more than is meet, but it tendeth to pverty.

Proverbs 13:18 - refusing instruction

Poverty and shame shall be to him that refuseth instruction: but he that regardeth reproof shall be honoured.

Proverbs 14:23 - talking too much

. . . The talk of the lips tendeth only to penury.

Proverbs 20:13 - laziness

Love not sleep, lest thou come to poverty; open thine eyes, and thou shalt be satisfied with bread.

Proverbs 22:16 - taking advantage of the poor; catering to the rich

He that oppresseth the poor to increase his riches, and he that giveth to the rich, shall surely come to want.

Proverbs 23:20, 21 - drunkenness, overeating, oversleeping

20 Be not among winebibbers; among riotous eaters of flesh: 21 For the drunkard and the glutton shall come to poverty: and drowsiness shall clothe a man with rags.

Proverbs 28:19, 22 - bad friends, being in a hurry to be rich

19 . . . He that followeth after vain persons shall have poverty enough. 22 He that hasteth to be rich . . . considereth not that poverty shall come upon him. Also v. 20.

Jeremiah 17:11 - getting riches by wrong methods

. . . He that getteth riches, and not by right, shall

leave them in the midst of his days, and at his end shall be a fool.

Isaiah 65:12, 13 - refusing to hear and obey God

12 . . . When I called, ye did not answer; when I spake, ye did not hear; but did evil before mine eyes, and did choose that wherein I delighted not. 13 Therefore thus saith the Lord God, Behold, my servants shall eat, but ye shall be hungry . . . shall drink, but ye shall be thirsty: . . . shall rejoice, but ye shall be ashamed.

4. One who is security for another's debts is courting trouble.

Proverbs 6:1-5

1 My son, if thou be surety for thy friend, if thou hast stricken thy hand with a stranger, 2 Thou art snared with the words of thy mouth, thou art taken with the words of thy mouth. The following verses urge immediate extracting of oneself from the agreement, before sleeping!

Proverbs 11:15

He that is surety for a stranger shall smart for it: and he that hateth suretiship is sure.

Proverbs 17:18

A man void of understanding striketh hands, and becometh surety in the presence of his friend.

Proverbs 22:26, 27

26 Be not thou one of them that strike hands, or them that are sureties for debts. 27 If thou hast nothing to pay, why should he take away thy bed from under thee?

VI. Work and our attitude toward it

1. Work is part of God's plan for man.

Genesis 1:26, 28

26 And God said, Let us make man in our image . . . and let them have dominion . . . over all the earth . . . 28 And God said . . . subdue it and have dominion over . . . every living thing . . . .

Genesis 2:15

And the Lord God took the man, and put him in the garden of Eden to dress and keep it.

Genesis 3:19

After the Fall: *In the sweat of thy face shalt thou eat bread, till thou return unto the ground . . . .*

Exodus 20:9

Six days shalt thou labour, and do all thy work. Also 23:12; Deut. 5:13.

Proverbs 14:23

In all labour there is profit: but the talk of the lips tendeth to penury.

Proverbs 28:19

He that tilleth his land shall have plenty of bread . . . .

Proverbs 31:10-27

A virtuous woman is described as a busy woman who *eateth not the bread of idleness* (v. 27).

Acts 20:34, 35

Paul labored with his hands and instructed thus: *35 I have showed you all things how that so labouring, ye ought to support the weak . . . .*

Ephesians 4:28

Let him that stole steal no more, but rather let him labour, working with his hands the thing which is good, that he may have to give to him that needeth.

1 Thessalonians 4:11, 12

11 Study to be quiet, and to do your own business, and to work with your own hands as we commanded you: 12 That ye may walk honestly toward them that are without, and that ye may have lack of nothing.

2 Thessalonians 3:10-13

10 . . . This we commanded you, that if any would not work, neither should he eat. 11 For we hear that there are some . . . working not at all, but are busybodies. 12 Now them that are such we command . . . that with quietness they work and eat their own bread.

"There are two things needed in these days; first, for rich men to find out how poor men live; and second, for poor men to know how rich men work."
-- Edward Atkinson, 1827-1905.

2. Honest work results in personal satisfaction.

Psalm 128:2 - happiness

For thou shalt eat the labour of thine hands: happy shalt thou be, and it shall be well with the.. Also Proverbs 31:25.

Proverbs 12:11 - adequate food

He that tilleth his land shall be satisfied with bread....

Proverbs 31:21 - warmth and security in winter

She [the virtuous woman] is not afraid of the snow for her household: for all her household are clothed with scarlet.

Proverbs 31:28-31-appreciation from family and the Lord

28 Her children rise up, and call her blessed; her husband also, and he praiseth her. 30 ... A woman that feareth the Lord, she shall be praised. 31 Give

her of the fruit of her hands; and let her own works praise her in the gates.

Ecclesiastes 5:12 - sweet sleep

The sleep of a labouring man is sweet, whether he eat little or much ....

Ephesians 4:28 - ability to give to those in need

Let him that stole steal no more: but rather let him labour, working with his hands the thing which is good, that he may have to give to him that needeth.

1 Thessalonians 4:11, 12 - an honest reputation; lack of nothing

11 ... Study to be quiet, and to do your own business, and to work with your own hands, as we commanded you; 12 That ye may walk honestly toward them that are without, and that ye may have lack of nothing.

3. God approves of and rewards diligence.

Proverbs 10:4, 5

... The hand of the diligent maketh rich. He that gathereth in summer is a wise son: but he that sleepeth in harvest is a son that causeth shame. Also 12:11.

Proverbs 13:4

The soul of the sluggard desireth, and hath nothing: but the soul of the diligent shall be made fat. Also v. 11.

Proverbs 20:13

Love not sleep, lest thou come to poverty; open thine eyes, and thou shalt be satisfied with bread. Also 27:23; 28:19.

Proverbs 31:27

A virtuous woman is commended because she looketh

well to the ways of her household, and eateth not the bread of idleness.

Ecclesiastes 9:10

Whatsoever thy hand findeth to do, do it with thy might; for there is no work ... in the grave whither thou goest.

Ezekiel 34:2-6

The shepherds of Israel were rebuked by God for failure to fulfill their responsibilities to their flocks.

Romans 12:11

Believers are to be *Not slothful in business: but fervent in spirit; serving the Lord.* Also Eph. 4:28; 2 Thes. 3:8-12; 2 Tim. 2:15.

4. One who looks for excuses not to work will accomplish little.

Proverbs 26:13-16

The slothful man saith, There is a lion in the way; a lion is in the streets. As the door turneth upon his hinges, so doth the slothful upon his bed (v. 13, 14).

Proverbs 27:1

Boast not thyself of tomorrow; for thou knowest not what a day may bring forth.

Ecclesiastes 11:4

He that observeth the wind shall not sow; and he that regardeth the clouds shall not reap.

"God never goes to the lazy or the idle when He needs men for His service.

**Moses was busy with his flock at Horeb;
Gideon was threshing wheat by the winepress;
Saul was searching for his father's donkeys;
Elisha was plowing with his oxen;
Nehemiah was bearing the king's winecup;
Amos was following the flock;
Peter and Andrew were casting a net;
James and John were mending their nets;
Matthew was collecting customs;
Saul was persecuting friends of Jesus."**

--Author unknown.

5. Men are to plan ahead, but also consider God's will in their planning.

Proverbs 6:6-11
> The example of the ant that provides in summer for the winter.

Proverbs 30:25-28
> Examples of the ant, the cony, the locust and the spider.

Proverbs 31:16, 21, 27
> The virtuous woman is one who considers a field, then buys it and plants a vineyard; who clothes her family for winter.

Matthew 25:1-13
> The parable of the wise and foolish virgins.

Luke 14:28-32
> The man who builds a tower but who first plans and counts the cost; the king who plans his battle before entering into it.

James 4:13-15
> Believers are warned about planning without considering God's will.

VII. Business principles

1. Business must be conducted honestly.

Leviticus 19:35-37
> *35 Ye shall do no unrighteousness in judgment, in meteyard, in weight, or in measure. 36 Just balances, just weights, a just ephah, and a just hin, shall ye have: I am the Lord your God . . . . 37 Therefore shall ye observe all my statutes, and all my judgments and do them; I am the Lord.* Also Deut. 25:13-16; Ezek. 45:10.

Proverbs 11:1
> *A false balance is abomination to the Lord: but a just weight is his delight.* Also 16:11; 20:23.

Ezekiel 18:5-9
> In God's description of a just man, many details are mentioned; among them are these: *7 . . . Hath not oppressed any, but hath restored to the debtor his pledge . . . 8 . . . Hath not given forth upon usury . . . hath executed true judgment between man and man.* See also Ezekiel 22:12, 13 for God's condemnation of

Israel for some of these same offenses.

Amos 8:4-7
> Again God enumerates Israel's sins. Among them several dishonest business practices and attitudes: overeagerness to sell, skimpy measures, inaccurate balances, overcharging, making people slaves for their indebtedness, selling chaff as wheat.

Acts 5:1-11
> Ananias and Sapphira are judged by the Lord for misrepresenting the proceeds from their sale of property.

Romans 12:17; 13:13
> *17 . . . Provide things honest in the sight of all men. 13 Let us walk honestly, as in the day . . . .*

2 Corinthians 13:7
> *Now I pray to God that ye do no evil . . . that ye should do that which is honest . . . .*

2. Business should be conducted with proper safeguards.

Examples:

Genesis 23:10-20
> Abraham's purchase of the cave of Machpelah: (1) he paid in full; (2) the transaction was carefully witnessed and made sure; (3) the property involved was fully described.

Ezra 1:7-11
> The temple vessels being sent back to Jerusalem from Babylon were weighed and recorded before they were transported.

Ezra 8:24-30, 33, 34
> When these riches were parceled out to the twelve priests they were weighed, and again when they arrived at the temple.

Acts 15:19-31
> After the church council in Jerusalem, the accuracy of the report to the Antioch church was insured by the sending of a written letter and by sending several men to do the reporting orally. *27 We have sent therefore Judas and Silas, who shall also tell you the same things*

by mouth. And this was in addition to Paul and Barnabas.

1 Corinthians 16:1-4

Here the Apostle Paul is instructing the church in Corinth about sending money to help the Jerusalem church. He is very specific about the church's approval of those who should deliver the gift. *3 . . . Whomsoever ye shall approve by your letters, them will I send to bring your liberality unto Jerusalem.*

3. An employer must be fair to his workers.

Exodus 21:20-27

Injury to an employee caused by the employer's action must be paid for.

Leviticus 19:13

Wages must be paid and paid promptly as they are due. Also Deut. 24:15; Jer. 22:13; Mal. 3:5; James 5:1, 4

Leviticus 25:43

Actions toward an employee must not be unduly rigorous or oppressive. Also Deut. 24:14.

Matthew 20:1-16

The employer has a right to pay as he chooses above the agreed wage (Parable of vineyard laborers).

Luke 10:7

The laborer is worthy of his hire. Also Matt. 10:10; 1 Tim. 5:18.

Ephesians 6:5-9

The employer is to remember that he too has a master in heaven who is no respecter of persons. Also Col. 4:1.

4. Employees are to serve their employers faithfully and as unto the Lord.

Matthew 25:45-51

In speaking of the actions of faithful believers in the light of His coming again, Jesus likens their conduct to that of faithful slaves who perform well even when their master is away.

Ephesians 6:5-8

5 Servants, be obedient . . . with fear and trembling, in singleness of your heart, as unto Christ; 6 Not with eyeservice, as menpleasers; but as the servants of Christ, doing the will of God from the heart.

1 Timothy 6:1

Let . . . servants . . . count their own masters worthy of all honor, that the name of God and his doctrine be not blasphemed. Also v. 2.

Titus 2:9, 10

9 Exhort servants to be obedient to their own masters, and to please them well in all things; not answering again; 10 Not purloining [stealing], but showing all good fidelity, that they may adorn the doctrine of God our Saviour in all things.

5. A break in the work week is God's plan, in remembrance of God's rest at the end of the creation week, and in response to the needs of men and animals.

Genesis 2:3

God blessed the seventh day and sanctified it; because that in it he had rested from all his work.

Exodus 20:9-11

Six days shalt thou labour, and do all thy work: but the seventh is the sabbath of the Lord thy God: in it thou shalt not do any work . . . For in six days the Lord made heaven and earth . . . and rested the seventh day . . . .

Exodus 23:12

That thine ox and thine ass may rest, and the son of thy handmaid, and the stranger, may be refreshed. Also Deut. 5:12-14.

Exodus 34:21

In earing time and in harvest thou shalt rest. Even in the busiest times!

Exodus 31:13, 17

However, Sabbath-keeping as the law describes it was made a special sign between Israel and God. See also Deut. 5:15; Ezek. 20:12.

Mark 2:27; 3:4

Jesus made it clear that, though the Sabbath was God-given, it was not merely an arbitrary requirement without regard for man's needs. *27 . . . The sabbath was made for man, and not man for the sabbath.* When citicized for healing, He said, *4 . . . Is it lawful to do good on the sabbath days, or to do evil? to save life or to kill?* Also Matt. 12:1-14; Luke 6:1-11.

Luke 14:1-6

In a similar situation, Jesus answered: . . . *Which of you shall have an ass or an ox fallen into a pit, and will not straightway pull him out on the sabbath day?*

"The Sabbath is God's special present to the workingman, and one of its chief objects is to prolong his life, and preserve efficient his working tone . . . . The savings bank of human existence is the weekly Sabbath."
-- William G. Blaikie,

6. The terms of any business deal should be based on the needs of both parties.

Exodus 22:25

In Israel, people were not to charge interest on loans to poor borrowers, if they were also Jews.

Exodus 22:26, 27

A lender was not to keep clothing overnight as security for a loan, lest the borrower suffer cold during the night. Also Deut. 24:12-16.

Leviticus 25:14-17

Under the Law, people were not to oppress one another in selling or buying.

Deuteronomy 24:6

A lender must not take millstones as a pledge for a loan, since without millstones grain could not be ground for a meal.

Deuteronomy 24:10

A lender was not to enter the house of the borrower to get an article offered as security; he must wait for the borrower to bring it out.

Deuteronomy 24:17

People were commanded not to take advantage of an alien, an orphan, or widow. In particular, they were forbidden to take a widow's clothing as security, even if she had nothing else to offer.

Matthew 18:23-34

Jesus uses an illustration of the forgiving of indebtedness as a picture of the way His followers should forgive one another repeatedly, if necessary. He condemns one who, though forgiven, will not forgive another.

****

"Poverty is very terrible, and sometimes kills the very soul within us; but it is the north wind that lashes men into Vikings; it is the soft, luscious, southwind, which lulls them to lotus dreams." -- Ouida, 1839-1908 (Penname for Louise De la Ramie).

"A friend to everybody is often a friend to nobody; or else, in his simplicity, he robs his family to help strangers, and so becomes brother to a beggar."
-- Charles Haddon Spurgeon, 1834-1892.

"Neither a borrower, nor a lender be; for loan oft loses both itself and friend; and borrowing dulls the edge of husbandry." -- William Shakespeare, 1564-1616.

"No race can prosper 'til it learns that there is as much dignity in tilling the field, as in writing a poem." -- Booker T. Washington, 1859?-1915.

"Work is a great blessing; after evil came into the world, it was given as an antidote, not as a punishment." -- Arthur S. Hardy, 1847-1930

"There are many ways of being frivolous, only one way of being intellectually great; that is honest labor." -- Sidney Smith, 1771-1845.

"Getting into debt is getting into a tanglesome net." -- Benjamin Franklin, 1706-1790.

"To possess money is very well; it may be a most valuable servant; to be possessed by it, is to be possessed by a devil, and one of the meanest and worst kind of devils."
-- Tryon Edwards, 1809-1894, great grandson of Jonathan Edwards.

4

Government

BIBLICAL CONCEPTS

I. **The basis of government**
1. God is the supreme ruler, controlling nations and rulers.
2. Human government was established by God as a means of controlling sinful man.
3. The powers that be are ordained of God.
4. Civil authorities are a deterrent to evil, not to good.
5. The basis of good government and political stability is personal integrity and strong family life.
6. The actions of believers, even few in number, can change the direction of government.

II. **Nations, governments and God**
1. God holds nations accountable for their actions.
2. When men refuse God's rule, He lets them rule themselves.
3. When a godly city or nation turns from God, her sins are often more serious than those of the heathen, and her condemnation greater.
4. God has often used war to accomplish His purposes.
5. God at times has had a specific hand in warfare, giving directions, insuring victory, causing others to recognize Him.

III. Personal citizenship responsibilities of believers
1. Governments and government officials are to be respected for their position and obeyed.
2. God expects submission to God-ordained leaders; He condemns rebellion and rioting.
3. Obedience to God comes before obedience to men when the two conflict.
4. Love of country and concern for her welfare is natural, and is encouraged by example and exhortation.
5. Believers are responsible to pay their share for the support of government.
6. Believers must pray for their leaders, in order that there may be peaceful living.

GOD OR GOVERNMENT?

1. The midwives refused to obey the law of Pharaoh to kill all male Hebrew children. As a result, Moses was protected and became the deliverer of the Hebrew nation.

2. Rahab refused to obey the king's order to reveal the spies that came to spy out the land of Jericho. As the result, she and her family were saved.

3. Daniel refused to obey the king's order to eat his meat and drink his wine and God blessed him greatly.

4. The three Hebrew children refused to obey the king's command to worship the golden image and were thrown into the fiery furnace.

5. Daniel refused to obey the king's command that no one should pray for 30 days and was thrown in the lion's den.

6. The apostles refused to obey the "law" that forbade them from preaching the Gospel and were persecuted, beaten, imprisoned and killed.

Would it have been better for all these to have obeyed the law?
Adapted from Frank Gaydosh.

"Our Constitution was made only for a moral and religious people. It is wholly inadequate to the government of any other." -- President James Madison, as quoted in "The Firm Foundation for a New Beginning" (Plymouth Rock Foundation).

". . . The purpose of a devout and united people was set forth in the pages of the Bible: Moses led his people out of slavery toward the Promised Land. Their purpose was three-fold: (1) to live in freedom, (2) to work in a prosperous land 'flowing with milk and honey,' and (3) to obey the commandments of God -- within their own country and in their dealings with other nations.

"This Biblical story of the Promised Land inspired the founders of America. It continues to inspire us, and we are privileged to hand it down, bright and strong, to every generation."
-- President Dwight D. Eisenhower.

BIBLICAL BACKGROUND

I. The basis of government

1. God is the supreme ruler, controlling nations and rulers.

See Chapter one on history, noting especially Section II, entitled "God's Relationship to the Events of History."

2. Human government was established by God as a means of controlling sinful man.

Genesis 9:5, 6

5 And surely your blood of your lives will I require; at the hand of every beast . . . and at the hand of every man; at the hand of every man's brother will I require the life of man. 6 Whoso sheddeth man's blood, by man shall his blood be shed: for in the image of God made he man. See also footnote in *Scofield Reference Bible*, where the relationship between capital punishment and human government is explained more fully.

See also Romans 13:3, 4, where government is spoken of as a minister of God.

3. The powers that be are ordained of God.

Romans 13:1, 2, 4

1 . . . For there is no power but of God: the powers that be are ordained of God. 2 Whosoever therefore resisteth the power, resisteth the ordinance . . . . 4 For he is the minister of God to thee for good . . . a revenger to execute wrath upon him that doeth evil.

"As are families, so is society . . . . If well-ordered, well-instructed, and well-governed, they are the springs from which go forth the streams of national greatness and prosperity, of civil order and public happiness."
-- William M. Thayer, 1820-1898.

4. Civil authorities are a deterrent to evil, not to good.

Romans 13:3, 4

3 For rulers are not a terror to good works, but to the evil. Wilt thou then not be afraid of the power? do that which is good, and thou shalt have praise of the same: 4 For he is the minister of God to thee for good. But if thou do that which is evil, be afraid; for he beareth not the sword in vain: for he is the minister of God, a revenger to execute wrath upon him that doeth evil.

1 Timothy 2:1, 2

1 I exhort . . . that . . . prayers be made . . . 2 . . . for all that are in authority; that we may lead a quiet and peaceable life in all godliness and honesty.

1 Peter 2:13, 14

13 Submit yourself to every ordinance of man for the Lord's sake: whether it be to the king as supreme; 14 Or unto governors, as unto them that are sent by him for the punishment of evildoers, and for the praise of them that do well.

5. The basis of good government and political stability is personal integrity and strong family life.

Exodus 20:12

Honor thy father and thy mother: that thy days may be long upon the land which the Lord thy God giveth thee.

Deuteronomy 21:18-21

In Israel, a rebellious son who would not obey his parents was to be stoned by the elders of the city. *So shalt thou put evil away from among you: and all Israel shall hear, and fear* (v. 21).

Proverbs 11:10, 11

When it goeth well with the righteous, the city rejoiceth: and when the wicked perish, there is shouting. 11 By the blessing of the upright the city is exalted: but it is overthrown by the mouth of the wicked.

Proverbs 14:34

Righteousness exalteth a nation: but sin is a reproach to any people.

1 Timothy 3:4, 5, 12

The qualification described for a bishop or deacon in these verses is that he must be one whose own home is in order, else *How shall he take care of the church of God?* The same principle of leadership without doubt can be applied to civil government.

6. The actions of believers, even few in number, can change the direction of government.

Examples:

Genesis 39-50

Repeatedly, it is said that the Lord was with Joseph, even in Potiphar's house as a slave, and later in prison unjustly. In God's time, Joseph was brought to the palace to interpret the dream. Here too he gave credit to God (41:16, 25, 28, 32) and Pharaoh chose him as the wise man to take charge and save Egypt and the surrounding areas.

Esther 1-10

Esther, a Jewess, became queen in the heathen palace of Ahasuerus at a time when the kingdom extended from India to Ethiopia, over 127 provinces. Mordecai, her uncle, saved the king's life. Their trust in God and willingness to risk their lives to do what was right were used by God to reverse the king's decree that would have destroyed the captive Jews. Mordecai finally was rewarded with the position of prime minister.

Daniel 2:46-49

Daniel, acknowledging God, rehearsed and interpreted Nebuchadnezzar's forgotten dream. As a result the king declared the lordship of God, promoted Daniel, and gave leadership positions to his friends.

Daniel 3:28-30; 4:1-3

Shadrach, Meshech and Abednego refused to bow to Nebuchadnezzar's image, went through the fiery furnace. The king reversed his position and honored them, forbidding anyone to speak evil of them, and proclaiming Jehovah as Lord. See also 4:18-27, 34-37.

Daniel 6:10, 25-28

Daniel refused to cease praying to God when King Darius so decreed. God delivered him from the lions; Darius proclaimed Daniel's God as the eternal God to be worshipped.

"Let the ground of all religious actions be obedience; examine not why it is commanded, but observe it because it is commanded. True obedience neither procrastinates nor questions." -- Francis Quarles, 1592-1644

II. Nations, governments and God

1. God holds nations accountable for their actions.

See many references in Chapter 1, dealing with history.

For example, God condemns nations for specific sins:

Jeremiah 46. Egypt for her pride.

Jeremiah 48:1-8. Moab for trust in her works and treasures

Jeremiah 49:1-6. Ammon for glorying in her own resources

Jeremiah 49:7-22. Edom for dependence on her rocky refuge

Jeremiah 50:1-29. Babylon and Chaldea for gloating over Israel's downfall

2. When men refuse God's rule, He lets them rule themselves.

Numbers 22:4-20

When Balaam refused to accept God's answer, God directed him to go, as he insisted on doing anyway.

1 Samuel 8:5-9, 19-22

When Israel insisted on a king, in order to be like other nations, God said to Samuel: *22 . . . Hearken unto their voices and make them a king.*

Psalm 81:11, 12

11 But my people would not hearken to my voice; and Israel would none of me. 12 So I gave them up unto their own hearts' lust: and they walked in their own counsels.

Ezekiel 20:39

O house of Israel, thus saith the Lord God, Go ye, *serve ye every one his idols . . . if ye will not hearken unto me . . . .*

Romans 1:21-28

21 Because that when they knew God, they glorified him not as God, neither were thankful . . . 24 Wherefore God also gave them up to uncleanness through the lusts of their own hearts . . . 25 Who changed the truth of God into a lie, and worshipped and served the creature more than the Creator . . . 26 For this cause God gave them up unto vile affections: 28 . . . And even as they did not like to retain God in their knowledge, God gave them over to a reprobate mind, to do those things which are not convenient [or fitting] . . . .

3. When a godly city or nation turns from God, her sins are often more serious than those of the heathen, and her condemnation greater.

Ezekiel 16:48-54

God compares Jerusalem with Sodom and Samaria. *51 Neither hath Samaria committed half of thy sins; but thou hast multiplied thine abominations more than they . . . .*

Matthew 10:15

Jesus speaking to the Twelve concerning cities which would not receive them: *15 . . . It shall be more tolerable for the land of Sodom and Gomorrah in the day of judgment, than for that city.*

Matthew 11:20-24

Then began he to upbraid the cities wherein most of his mighty works were done, because they repented not. Jesus pronounces woe upon Chorazin, Bethsaida, and Capernaum, saying that if Tyre, Sidon and Sodom had heard and seen what they had seen they would have repented and been saved from destruction.

Luke 12:48

A general principle: *48 . . . For unto whomsoever much is given, of him shall be much required: and to whom men have committed much, of him they will ask the more.*

4. God has often used war to accomplish His purposes.

a. He commanded Israel to go to war against other nations. Some examples from the conquest of Canaan:

Numbers 31:1-20

He commanded Israel to war against Midian to avenge Himself because of Balaam's sin (v. 2, 3, 14-16).

Numbers 33:50-56

The Lord directed that in Canaan they were to *drive out all the inhabitants . . . destroy all their pictures . . . images . . . high places . . . dispossess the inhabitants of the land and dwell therein . . .* (v. 52, 53).

Deuteronomy 2:24-36

God commanded that they war against the Amorites and take their land (v. 17, 24).

b. He stirred up Israel's enemies to bring His people to repentance. Examples:

Judges 3:8, 9

8 . . . [God] sold them unto the hand of Cushan-rishathaim, king of Mesopotamia . . . 9 And when the children of Israel cried unto the Lord, the Lord raised up a deliverer . . . who delivered them, even Othniel . . . .

Judges 3:12

The children of Israel did . . . evil . . . and the Lord strengthened Eglon, king of Moab, against Israel . . . See also 4:1-3, 23; 6:1, 6, 7; 10:6, 7, 10; 13:1.

2 Chronicles 33:9-13

9 So Manasseh made Judah and the inhabitants of Jerusalem to err, and to do worse than the heathen, whom the Lord had destroyed before the children of Israel. 10 And the Lord spake . . . but they would not hearken. 11 Wherefore the Lord brought upon them . . . Assyria, which took Manasseh . . . and carried him to Babylon. 12 And when he was in affliction, he besought the Lord . . . .

c. He prophesied war and destruction upon nations that mistreated Israel, and that refused to recognize Him as God. These events came to pass. For examples, see Ezekiel 25, 29, 30, and many of the O.T. prophetic books.

5. God at times has had a specific hand in warfare, giving directions, insuring victory, causing others to recognize Him.

Examples:

Joshua 1:1-6

God promised the land to Israel.

Joshua 2:9-11

Rahab, speaking also for other inhabitants, recognized God's promise to Israel, as well as Israel's recent victories. Also 5:1.

Joshua 6:2, 20, 21

God promised them Jericho and gave victory.

Joshua 8:1, 2, 8, 28

God promised and gave victory over Ai.

Joshua 9:24, 25

The inhabitants of Gibeon recognized God's plan.

Joshua 10:8

God promised victory over the alliance of five Amorite kings; He defeated them sending huge hailstones. See v. 10, 11, 42; 11:8, 19, 20, 23.

Joshua 21:43, 44

43 And the Lord gave unto Israel all the land which he sware to give unto their fathers . . . 44 . . . And there stood not a man of all their enemies before them; the Lord delivered all their enemies into their hand.

Joshua 23:9, 10

Joshua's testimony: *9 For the Lord hath driven out from before you great nations and strong: but as for you, no man hath been able to stand before you unto this day . . . . 10 . . . For the Lord your God, he it is that fighteth for you as he hath promised you.*

Judges 1:19-36

In many cases Israel did not destroy the inhabitants completely as God had directed. God rebuked them for this failure. See also 2:1-5, 20-23.

1 Samuel 30

After the Amalekites had burned Ziklag, David inquired of the Lord whether he should attack them.

David obeyed, had victory and recognized God's hand in the victory. See especially v. 1, 8, 10, 22-25.

III. Personal citizenship responsibilities of believers

1. Governments and government officials are to be respected for their position and obeyed.

Exodus 22:28

Thou shalt not revile the gods, nor curse the ruler of thy people. Note that the word here translated *gods* is *Elohim.* The *New Scofield Reference Bible* renders it as *God;* the Berkeley Version as *judges.*

Proverbs 25:6, 7

6 Put not forth thyself in the presence of the king, and stand not in the place of great men: 7 For better it is that it be said unto thee, Come up hither; than that thou shouldest be put lower in the presence of the prince whom thine eyes have seen.

Romans 13:1-7

1 Let every soul be subject unto the higher powers. For there is no power but of God: the powers that be are ordained of God. 2 Whosoever therefore resisteth the power resisteth the ordinance of God . . . .4 For he is the minister of God to thee for good . . . . 5 Wherefore ye must needs be subject . . . for conscience sake. 6 For this cause pay ye tribute also: for they are God's ministers . . . . 7 Render therefore to all their dues; tribute . . . custom . . . fear . . . honour.

Titus 3:1, 2

1 Put them in mind to be subject to principalities and powers, to obey magistrates, to be ready to every good work, 2 To speak evil of no man, to be no brawlers, but gentle, shewing all meekness unto all men.

1 Peter 2:12-20

Here is instruction to submit for the Lord's sake, in order that unbelievers may see a right attitude and action and so be silenced. Believers, by their actions, are to recognize their freedom in Christ, but not to use that freedom to cover maliciousness.

Examples:

1 Samuel 24:6, 7; 26:8-11

In spite of all that Saul had done in an effort to kill David, David recognized the fact that God had ordained Saul; he therefore refused to take his life when he had opportunity.

1 Samuel 31:8-13

When the Philistines had multilated the body of King Saul, the men of Jabesh-Gilead rescued it and buried it and mourned his death, in recognition of his position.

2 Samuel 1:14-16

David condemned the Amalekite who came to him boasting of having killed Saul. He said, *How wast thou not afraid to stretch forth thine hand to destroy the Lord's anointed?* (v. 14)

2 Samuel 4:5-12

David did not commend Rechab and Baanah for killing Saul's son Ishbosheth and bringing his head; instead, he had the two men executed.

Matthew 17:24-27; also 22:15-22; Mark 12:13-17; Luke 20:20-26

In the question of the tribute money, Jesus directed that it should be paid *lest we offend them* (v. 27). He was also careful to point out that some things belong to Caesar, and some to God. See also 23:1-7.

Acts 23:2-5

Here the Apostle Paul expresses his recognition of the place of government, in this case that of the high priest, saying: *5 . . . I wist not, brethren, that he was the high priest: for it is written, Thou shalt not speak evil of the ruler of thy people.*

2. God expects submission to God-ordained leaders; He condemns rebellion and rioting.

Exodus 32

The golden calf incident and God's judgment.

Numbers 11:1-3

Judgment for murmuring; God sent fire. Also Psa. 78:18-31.

Numbers 11:12

Judgment upon Miriam for leading in complaining against Moses.

Numbers 14:1-4, 20-35

Forty years of wandering because of rebellion against

entering the land; death by sudden plague for the 10 spies who led in that rebellion (v. 36-38).

Numbers 16:1-35

God opened up the earth to swallow Korah, Dathan and Abiram and their families because of rebellion against Moses and Aaron; He sent fire to consume their 250 followers (v. 35).

Numbers 16:41-50

God destroyed 14,700 by a plague because they accused Moses and Aaron of killing the Lord's people when it was God who had done it.

Numbers 21:4-9

Griping about the route and about the manna, after 40 years of wandering, brought fiery serpents from God. Also Psa. 106:15.

Numbers 27:12-14

God judged Moses, even after a long history of faithfulness, *for ye rebelled against my commandment in the desert . . . to sanctify me at the water before their eyes . . .* (v. 14).

Deuteronomy 17:12

A man who refused to hearken to a priest or judge

was to be put to death -- to rid Israel of this kind of evil.

Deuteronomy 21:18-21

A rebellious son was to be turned over, by his parents, to the city elders for stoning.

Ezra 7:26

Artaxerxes decreed that anyone who would not submit to God and the king should be judged speedily. Ezra praised God for the king's decree, recognizing God's hand (v. 27, 28).

Romans 13:1-7

Emphasis on submission, not rebellion.

Jude 6, 7

The rebellious angels are reserved in chains until judgment; Sodom and Gomorrah were destroyed for their refusal to obey God.

Jude 4, 8-10

Jude warns of men who refuse godly teaching, who despise dominion, and speak evil or dignities -- i.e., are rebellious.

3. Obedience to God comes before obedience to men when the two conflict.

Acts 4:18-20

The men of the Sanhedrin in Jerusalem commanded Peter and John: *18 . . . not to speak at all nor teach in the name of Jesus. 19 But Peter and John answered and said unto them, Whether it be right in the sight of God to hearken unto you more than unto God, judge ye. 20 For we cannot but speak the things which we have seen and heard.*

Acts 5:28-33

Once again Peter and the other apostles were reprimanded for their preaching. Their answer: *29 . . . We ought to obey God rather than men.*

4. Love of country and concern for her welfare is natural, and is encouraged by example and exhortation.

1 Chronicles 19:10-13

In war with an alliance of Ammon and Syria, Joab, the commander under David, planned his strategy and then said: *13 Be of good courage, and let us behave ourselves valiantly for our people, and for the cities of our God: and let the Lord do that which is good in his sight.*

Ezra 1:5

When God stirred the heart of Cyrus of Persia to send an expedition of Jews back to Jerusalem to build a temple there, there was no lack of Jews willing to go. When the worship was reestablished there was great

rejoicing (3:10-13). Likewise when the Passover was reinstituted (6:19.22).

Nehemiah 1:2-11; also 2:1-20.

Nehemiah describes his feelings and his prayer after hearing the report from the remnant in Jerusalem. God honored his request and turned the heart of the king.

Psalm 137:1-6

Here is a description of Israel's longing for their homeland when they were captive in Babylon. *5 If I forget thee, O Jerusalem, let my right hand forget her cunning. 6 If I do not remember thee, let my tongue cleave to the roof of my mouth; if I prefer not Jerusalem above my chief joy.*

Consider also the song of Deborah in Judges 5.

In addition, consider passages in the next sections which instruct believers to pray for their country and its rulers. Prayer is one of the truest expressions of concern.

5. Believers are responsible to pay their share for the support of government.

Exodus 38:25-28

Though much of the metal used for the Tabernacle was part of a great free-will offering, every man was also taxed a specific amount towards the materials needed. Here is Old Testament precedent.

Nehemiah 10:32

Again, after the rebuilding under Nehemiah, the temple was to be supported by a specific tax: *32 Also we made ordinances for us, to charge ourselves yearly with the third part of a shekel for the service of the house of our God.* In Israel civil and religious government were one.

1 Kings 9:15

Under Solomon, a tax was levied to build the house of the Lord, the king's palace, the wall of Jerusalem, and several cities.

Matthew 17:24-27

When the tax-collector asked Peter if his master paid tribute, Peter said *yes*, but did not understand the significance of paying tribute. Nevertheless, Jesus directed that he pay the tax in order not to be misunderstood.

Matthew 22:17-21; Mark 12:13-17; Luke 20:21-26

When the Herodians tried to entangle Jesus, they asked: *17 What thinkest thou? Is it lawful to give tribute unto Caesar, or not?* Though He knew they were trying to trick Him, He used the illustration of the coin with Caesar's superscription on it to make his point that they did owe something to Caesar. He was careful also to set some limits, recognizing the fact that some things are God's and do not belong to the government.

Romans 13:6-8

6 For this cause pay ye tribute also: for they are God's ministers . . . . 7 Render therefore to all their dues . . . . 8 Owe no man anything but to love one another . . . .

6. Believers must pray for their leaders, in order that there may be peaceful living.

Jeremiah 29:7

Jeremiah's directions to Israel at a time when they were a captive people in Babylon: *7 Seek the peace of the city whither I have caused you to be carried away captives, and pray unto the Lord for it; for in the peace thereof ye shall have peace.*

1 Timothy 2:1-3

1 I exhort therefore, that . . . supplications, prayers, intercessions, and giving of thanks, be made for all men; 2 For kings, and for all that are in authority; that we may lead a quiet and peaceable life in all godliness and honesty. 3 For this is good and acceptable in the sight of God our Saviour.

"Congress has no right to give charity. Individual members may give as much of their own money as they please, but they have no right to touch a dollar of the public money for that purpose . . . . The people have delegated, by the Constitution, the power to do certain things. To do these, it is authorized to collect and pay moneys, and for nothing else. Everything beyond this is usurpation, and a violation of the Constitution." -- Horatio Bunce, in conversation with Colonel David Crockett. From *The Life of Colonel David Crockett*, Edward S. Ellis, compiler, 1884, as excerpted in *CLA Defender*, Vol. 4, Issue 9.

"Whatever makes men good Christians makes them good citizens." -- Daniel Webster, 1782-1852.

"Modern politics is, at bottom, a struggle not of men but of forces." -- Henry Brooks Adams, 1838-1918.

5

Leadership and Administration

BIBLICAL CONCEPTS

I. **Leaders and leadership**

1. Good leadership is of extreme importance to the welfare of any people.

2. Leaders should be chosen on the basis of qualifications.

3. Leadership responsibility carries with it high demands in personal living, often higher than is expected of others.

4. Leaders must be concerned for the unity of God's people.

5. Leaders must be faithful in carrying out responsibilities and keeping promises.

6. Godly leaders place God's honor above their own.

7. True leadership is servanthood, not lordship.

8. God must be recognized as the one who promotes and gives victories.

9. An effective leader is concerned about an orderly transfer of leadership when his term is completed.

10. Even in corrupt times, it is possible to serve God faithfully.

11. Inconsistency in a leader confuses his followers and causes loss of respect.

II. **Administrative principles**

1. Responsibility should be distributed in order that work be done effectively.

2. Individual gifts should be recognized in the delineation of responsibilities; each person should concentrate in specific areas of work.

3. Delegation of responsibility must include delegation of authority to act (within set limits).

4. Job descriptions should be clearly delineated.

5. Unity within an organization, and appreciation for one another, are essential to the stability of the group.

6. Various segments of a group should be fairly represented, to lessen the danger of partiality.

7. Adequate preparation should precede a major change.

8. Projects should be completed in an orderly fashion.

9. Provision must be made for irregularities, human error and sin.

10. Decision by lot has Scriptural precedent and, done in recognition of God's sovereignty, can indicate God's will.

11. Decisions and judgments must be consistent, not based on personalities, preconceived notions or hearsay.

12. Gifts to those in office endanger justice and are therefore not to be received.

13. The benefits from any project should be shared with those behind the scenes.

14. The separation of religious and civil responsibilities and decisions has a long history, even in a theocracy.

15. Administrative policies and procedures must avoid injustices of all kinds.

$$* * * * *$$

"Do not think of waiting until you can do some great thing for God: do little things, and then the Master will bid you go up higher. Eleven years ago I was addressing Sunday school children, and these alone . . . . Nine years ago I was preaching in little insignificant rooms here and there, generally going out and coming back on foot, and occasionally getting a lift in a cart . . . .

"Now, I am perfectly sure that, if I had not been willing to preach to those small gatherings of people in obscure places, I should never have had the privilege of preaching to thousands of men and women in large buildings all over the land. If one wishes to be a steward in God's house, he must first be prepared to serve as a scullion, in the kitchen, and be content to wash out the pots and clean the boots. Remember our Lord's rule: *Whosoever exalteth himself shall be abased; and he that humbleth himself shall be exalted.*"

--C. H. Spurgeon, in his *Autobiography*, as quoted in *Christian Education Trends*, Feb. 10, 1983.

BIBLICAL BACKGROUND

I. Leaders and leadership

1. Good leadership is of extreme importance to the welfare of any people.

a. Leaders set the pattern for the whole group: they lead people to sin or to righteousness.

Proverbs 28:2

> *. . . By a man of understanding and knowledge the state thereof shall be prolonged.*

Proverbs 29:4

> *The king by judgment establisheth the land; but he that receiveth gifts overthroweth it.*

Proverbs 29:8, 12, 14

> *8 Scornful men bring a city into a snare; but wise men turn away wrath. 12 If a ruler hearken unto lies, all his servants are wicked. 14 The king that faithfully judgeth the poor, his throne shall be established forever.*

Isaiah 9:16

> *For the leaders of the people cause them to err; and they that are led of them are destroyed.*

Jeremiah 22:21, 22

> *21 I have not sent these prophets . . . I have not spoken to them, yet they prophesied. 22 But if they had stood in my counsel and had caused my people to hear my words, then they should have turned them*

from their evil way and from the evil of their doings. See also 23:11-15; Ezekiel 44:10-16.

b. The absence of good leadership following the removal of a strong leader often results in people's turning away from the standards previously set. Examples:

Exodus 32

> Moses, though he had not died, was away at God's command. Without his leadership Aaron and the people worshipped the golden calf.

Judges 2:16-19

> A general statement concerning the sequence of judges: *18 . . . The Lord raised them up judges, then the Lord was with the judge and delivered them . . .*

all the days of the judge: 19 . . . When the judge was dead, . . . they ceased not from their own doings, nor from their stubborn way.

Judges 8:33-35

33 . . . As soon as Gideon was dead . . . the children of Israel turned, and went whoring after Baalim, and made Baal-berith their god. 34 And . . . remembered not the Lord their God, who had delivered them . . . 35 Neither showed they kindness to the house of . . . Gideon.

2. Leaders should be chosen on the basis of qualifications.

Genesis 41:33

Joseph's advice to Pharaoh in a crisis: . . . *Let Pharaoh look out a man discreet and wise, and set him over the land of Egypt.*

Exodus 18:21, 22

Jethro to Moses: *21 . . . Provide . . . able men, such as fear God, men of truth, hating coveteousness: and place such over them, to be rulers of thousands . . . 22 And let them judge the people . . .* (This is rehearsed again in Deut. 1:13-15).

Deuteronomy 17:14, 15

God, anticipating Israel's future desire for a king: *15 Thou shalt in any wise set him king over thee, whom the Lord thy God shall choose: one from among thy brethren shalt thou set king over thee: thou mayest not set a stranger over thee, which is not thy brother.*

Acts 6:3

The Twelve to the church at Jerusalem, when there was a need: *Wherefore, brethren, look ye out among you seven men of honest report, full of the Holy Ghost and wisdom, whom we may appoint over this business.*

1 Timothy 3:1-7

Qualifications for pastor or bishop: *2 . . . Blameless, the husband of one wife, vigilant, sober, of good behavior, given to hospitality, apt to teach, 3 Not given to wine, no striker, not greedy of filthy lucre; but patient, not a brawler, not covetous; 4 One that ruleth well his own house, having his children in subjection with all gravity . . . 6 Not a novice . . . 7 . . . He must have a good report of them that are without . . .* See also Titus 1:5-9.

1 Timothy 3:8-13

Qualifications of a deacon: serious, not two-faced, not a drinker, not greedy for money, with honest convictions, mature in the things of the Lord, with exemplary wife, with children under control.

3. Leadership responsibility carries with it high demands in personal living, often higher than is expected of others.

Leviticus 4:22-26

When a ruler sinned, even through ignorance, he too was obligated to bring an offering and be forgiven.

Leviticus 10:1-3

Nadab and Abihu; the fact that one had a position given by God brought no exemption from the need for obedience to God.

Leviticus 16:6, 11

Even Aaron must offer sacrifices for his own sins first, and then for those of the people.

Deuteronomy 17:16-20

God made several special requirements of the man who should at a later date become Israel's king:

-- he was not to send to Egypt to buy horses;
-- he was not to multiply wives or riches, lest he be turned from God;

-- he was to make his own copy of the Law, so that he could meditate on it all the days of his life, that he might keep the Law, that he might not become proud, and that he might therefore prolong his life and the reign of himself and his sons.

Joshua 1:7, 8

God speaking to Joshua after the death of Moses: *7 Only be thou strong and very courageous that thou mayest observe to do according to all the law, which Moses my servant commanded thee: turn not from it to the right hand or to the left, that thou mayest prosper whithersoever thou goest. 8 This book of the law shall not depart out of thy mouth; but thou shalt meditate therein day and night, that thou mayest observe to do according to all that is written therein: for then thou shalt make thy way prosperous, and then thou shalt have good success.*

2 Samuel 12:13, 14

Though David was called *a man after God's own heart,*

when he sinned with Bathsheba, God punished, as well as forgave him. The reason: *14 Because . . . thou hast given great occasion to the enemies of the Lord to blaspheme . . . .* See also 1 Chron. 21:1-17.

Proverbs 31:4, 5

4 It is not for kings, O Lemuel, it is not for kings to drink wine; nor for princes strong drink: 5 Lest they drink, and forget the law and pervert the judgment of any of the afflicted.

Ecclesiastes 10:16, 17

16 Woe to thee, O land, when thy king is a child, and thy princes eat in the morning! 17 Blessed art thou, O land, when thy king is the son of nobles, and thy princes eat in due season, for strength, and not for drunkenness!

Amos 3:10

For they know not to do right, saith the Lord, who store up violence and robbery in their palaces.

Ezekiel 44:17-31

Stricter regulations and higher standards were re-

quired for the Levites in such areas as clothing, hair, strong drink, marriage relationship, pollution, possessions, food.

Malachi 2:1-10

The priests were expected by God to hear God's word and lay it to heart; priests unfaithful to God were judged by Him.

Matthew 23

Christ, speaking to the multitude and to his disciples, urges them to observe what the Pharisees teach out of the Law, but not to pattern their lives after them. He especially condemns these leaders for the following:

-- teaching what they do not practice   1-4
-- seeking honor and position   5-15
-- pretense   14, 15
-- putting emphasis on the wrong things in serving God   16-24
-- attention to outward appearance   25-28
-- assuming they had not committed the sins of their fathers   29-35

4. Leaders must be concerned for the unity of God's people.

Numbers 32:1, 5-7, 20-27

Moses' concern for the unity of Israel when the tribes of Reuben and Gad wanted to settle east of Jordan. He insisted that these too participate in conquering Canaan.

Romans 12:4-13

Paul's concern for believers in Rome, that they see themselves as one body with many members, each with its function: *4 For as we have many members in one body, and all members have not the same office: 5 So we, being many, are one body in Christ, and every one members one of another. 6 Having then gifts differing according to the grace that is given to us, whether prophecy, let us prophesy according to the proportion of faith; 7 Or ministry, let us wait on our ministering: or he that teacheth, on teaching: 8 Or he that exhorteth, on exhortation: he that giveth, let him do it with simplicity; he that ruleth, with diligence; he that showeth mercy, with cheerfulness.*

1 Corinthians 12:4-31

Paul's discussion of spiritual gifts majors on one Spirit, one Lord, one God, one body, with diversity in gifts, administrations, members.

In v. 14-24 he uses the example of the human body to show the necessity for members with different

functions, and the absurdity of insisting that all be alike, or that they part company because all members were not alike. *12 For as the body is one, and hath many members, and all the members of that one body, being many, are one body, so also is Christ. 13 For by one Spirit are we all baptized into one body, whether we be Jews or Gentiles, whether we be bond or free; and have been all made to drink into one Spirit. 14 For the body is not one member, but many . . . 24 . . . God hath tempered the body together . . . 25 That there should be no schism in the body; but that the members should have the same care one for another.*

Ephesians 4:1-16

1 I therefore the prisoner of the Lord, beseech you that ye walk worthy of the vocation wherewith ye are called . . . 3 Endeavouring to keep the unity of the Spirit in the bond of peace. Note in v. 4-6 the many things that believers have in common. Verse 11 lists leaders Christ gave to churches for the perfecting of the saints (or for maturing them). Pick out of verses 13-16 expressions which indicate a concern for unity.

1 Thessalonians 3:6-12; 4:11-15; 2 Thessalonians 1:3, 4

Note in these passages how the Apostle expresses his appreciation for the believers in Thessalonica, and how he encourages them to love and appreciate one another

5. Leaders must be faithful in carrying out responsibilities and keeping promises.

Jeremiah 23:1, 11-15

God holds prophets and priests responsible: *1 Woe be unto the pastors that destroy and scatter the sheep of my pastures! saith the Lord.* In v. 11-15, God describes the failures of these leaders. Also Ezekiel 34:1-10.

Ezekiel 17:13-19

God condemns the breaking of covenants. Note especially v. 18, 19.

Ezekiel 33:1-6

God holds watchmen responsible: *6 But if the watchman see the sword come, and blow not the trumpet, and the people be not warned; if the sword come, and take any person from among them, he is taken away in his iniquity; but his blood will I require at the watchman's hand.*

Ezekiel 33:7-9

God holds prophets responsible: *7 So thou, O son of man, I have set thee a watchman unto the house of Israel; therefore thou shalt hear the word at my mouth, and warn them from me. 8 When I say unto the wicked, O wicked man, thou shalt surely die; if thou dost not speak to warn the wicked from his way, that wicked man shall die in his iniquity; but his blood will I require at thine hand.*

Malachi 1:6-9, 12-14; 2:1-9; 3:14, 15

God condemns the priests of Israel for offering polluted sacrifices, for making light of God's worship, for exalting those who work wickedness.

Romans 12:8

God holds New Testament leaders responsible. Paul speaks of the responsibility to use leadership gifts properly: *8 . . . He that ruleth, [let him do it] with diligence . . . .*

Titus 1:13; also 2:1, 15

Paul to Titus, speaking of his responsibility as a pastor: *13 . . . Wherefore rebuke them sharply, that they may be sound in the faith.*

Hebrews 13:17

Obey them that have the rule over you, and submit yourselves; for they watch for your souls as they that must give account. Note that one reason for obedience to spiritual leaders is that they are accountable.

Examples:

Genesis 39

Joseph was responsible in the house of Potiphar and in the prison, even as a slave and then a prisoner.

1 Samuel 13:9, 11-14

The prophet Samuel faithfully rebuked King Saul for offering the burnt offering when he should have waited.

1 Samuel 15:1-3, 7-26

Again, Samuel dares to face Saul and deliver a rebuke from the Lord, this time saying that the Lord was taking the kingdom from him.

1 Chronicles 21:1-4

Joab protests the proposal to count the people, even though it was king David who proposed it.

6. Godly leaders place God's honor above their own.

Genesis 41:16, 25

Joseph repeatedly gave credit to God for showing Pharaoh what He was about to do, refusing to take credit himself: *16 And Joseph answered Pharaoh, saying, It is not in me: God shall give Pharaoh an answer of peace . . . . 25 And Joseph said unto Pharaoh, The dream of Pharaoh is one: God hath showed Pharaoh what he is about to do . . . . 28 This is the thing which I have spoken unto Pharaoh: What God is about to do he showeth unto Pharaoh . . . 32 And for that the dream was doubled unto Pharaoh twice; it is because the thing is established by God, and God will shortly bring it to pass.* See also v. 31, 39.

Genesis 45:4-8; 50:15-21

So also when he revealed himself to his brothers, Joseph recognized the Lord's hand in his exaltation, and was not concerned with getting even or proving his own greatness.

Exodus 32:9-14

When God threatened to consume Israel because of the golden calf incident and make of Moses a great nation, Moses remonstrated, pleading rather for the reputation of God.

Numbers 14:11-19

When, after Israel's insistence on following the ten

spies, God again threatened to destroy Israel and begin a new nation from Moses, Moses pled for God's honor among the nations.

Daniel 2:28-30

Daniel refused to take credit for the interpretation of the king's dreams: *28 But there is a God in heaven that revealeth secrets, and maketh known to the king Nebuchadnezzar what shall be in the latter days. . . . 30 But as for me, this secret is not revealed to me for any wisdom that I have more than any living . . . .*

7. True leadership is servanthood, not lordship.

In contrast to the concept of leadership among unbelievers, the Christian concept is service and humility, as shown in these passages and others:

Matthew 20:20-28

25 But Jesus called them unto him, and said, Ye know that the princes of the Gentiles exercise dominion over them, and they that are great exercise authority upon them. 26 But it shall not be so among you: but whoever will be great among you, let him be your minister; 27 And whosoever will be chief among you, let him be your servant: 28 Even as the Son of man came not to be ministered unto, but to minister, and to give his life a ransom for many. Also Mark 10:35-45; Luke 22:24-30.

Matthew 23:1-12

8 But be not ye called Rabbi: for one is your Master, even Christ; and all ye are brethren . . . . 10 Neither be ye called masters: for one is your Master, even Christ. 11 But he that is greatest among you shall be your servant. 12 And whosoever shall exalt himself shall be abased; and he that shall humble himself shall be exalted.

1 Peter 5:2, 3

Elders or pastors are exhorted: *2 Feed the flock of God which is among you, taking the oversight thereof, not by constraint, but willingly; not for filthy lucre, but of a ready mind; 3 Neither as being lords over God's heritage, but being ensamples to the flock.*

8. God must be recognized as the one who promotes and gives victories.

Genesis 39-41

Over and over again: *The Lord was with Joseph,* or something equivalent.

2 Samuel 7:8-17

God instructs Nathan the prophet to tell David how He has been with him and established his house.

2 Samuel 7:18-29

David's response to God's rehearsal is one of worship and acknowledgment of all that God has done.

2 Samuel 8:6, 14

. . . And the Lord preserved David whithersoever he went.

2 Samuel 8:11

As God gave victories, kings brought him gifts, *Which also king David did dedicate unto the Lord, with the silver and gold that he had dedicated of all nations which he subdued . . . .*

Psalm 75:5-7

5 Lift not up your horn on high: speak not with a stiff neck. 6 For promotion cometh neither from the east, nor from the west, nor from the south. 7 But God is the judge: he putteth down one, and setteth up another.

Daniel 1:17

As for these four children, God gave them knowledge and skill in all learning and wisdom: and Daniel had understanding in all visions and dreams. See also 1 Cor. 4:7.

Matthew 20:20-28; Mark 10:35-40

Jesus responded to the request for an honored position for James and John by saying: *23 . . . To sit on my right hand, and on my left, is not mine to give, but it shall be given to them for whom it is prepared of my Father.*

✳ ✳ ✳

"True statesmanship is the art of changing a nation [or organization] from what it is into what it ought to be."
--William R. Alger, 1822-1905.

"He that cannot obey, cannot command."
--Poor Richard, 1774.

9. An effective leader is concerned about an orderly transfer of leadership when his term is completed.

Numbers 27:15-23

When God told Moses his leadership was ending, Moses was greatly concerned about his successor. *15 And Moses spake unto the Lord, saying, 16 Let the Lord, the God of the spirits of all flesh, set a man over the congregation, 17 Which may go out before them, and which may lead them out, and which may bring them in; that the congregation of the Lord be not as sheep which have no shepherd.*

Numbers 27:18-23

God too is concerned about his successor and instructs Moses in order that Joshua be accepted by the people. Therefore God said,

-- *Take thee Joshua* - one known for his leadership.
-- *Lay thine hand on him* - put your approval on him.
-- *Give him a charge in their sight* - make sure the people know his responsibility and position.
-- *Put some of thine honour upon him* - so the people will accept him and obey him.

-- *He shall stand before Eleazar the priest, who shall ask counsel for him . . . before the Lord* - so his instructions will come from God, and the people will know it.

Deuteronomy 34:9

Joshua had worked with Moses and had been so authenticated as his successor that after Moses died, *the children of Israel hearkened unto him, and did as the Lord commanded Moses.*

Joshua 1:16-18

People responded to Joshua: *17 According as we hearkened unto Moses in all things, so will we hearken unto thee: only the Lord thy God be with thee, as he was with Moses. 18 Whosoever he be that doth rebel against thy commandment, and will not hearken unto thy words in all that thou commandest him, he shall be put to death: only be strong and of a good courage.*

10. Even in corrupt times, it is possible to serve God faithfully.

Genesis 6:1-22

8 But Noah found grace in the eyes of the Lord. 9 . . . Noah was a just man and perfect in his generations, and Noah walked with God . . . 22 Thus did Noah; according to all that God commanded him, so did he. See also 7:5; 8:1, 20-22; 9:1, etc. Consider also Joseph

and Daniel.

Hebrews 11:4-38

A list of persons who took responsibilities, each in a difficult time, and in faith served God. Many others in the prophetic books.

11. Inconsistency in a leader confuses his followers and causes loss of respect.

2 Samuel 18, 19

Absalom was disloyal to his father, King David. He won the people to himself and sought to kill David (15:1-12; 17:1-4). In spite of these facts David wanted him spared (18:5). As a result David's leaders were confused and so were the people. This fact is shown in Joab's rebuke to David in verses 19:5-9: *5 And Joab came into the house of the king, and said, Thou hast shamed this day the faces of all thy servants, which this day have saved thy life, and the lives of thy sons and of thy daughters, and the lives of thy wives, and the lives of thy concubines; 6 In that thou lovest thine enemies, and hatest thy friends. For thou hast declared this day, that thou regardest neither princes nor servants: for this day I perceive, that if Absalom had*

lived, and all we had died this day, then it had pleased thee well.

Malachi 2:17

Leaders who confuse evil and good are condemned by God. *17 Ye have wearied the Lord with your words. Yet ye say, Wherein have we wearied him? When ye say, Everyone that doeth evil is good in the sight of the Lord, and he delighteth in them; or, Where is the God of judgment?*

Matthew 23:1-7, 13-33

Jesus, here and in other instances, condemns the Pharisees and scribes for their hypocrisy and pride. On occasion, He tells people to obey their regulations, but not pattern their lives after them.

II. Administrative principles

1. Responsibility should be distributed in order that work be done effectively.

Exodus 18:13-27

Jethro's advice to Moses when he saw that Moses was doing all the counseling, attempting to settle all the difficulties and teaching the people God's laws: *21 . . . provide out of the people able men . . . 22 And let them judge . . . .* The results Jethro predicted: *22 . . . It shall be easier for thyself, and they shall bear the burden with thee. 23 . . . Thou shalt be able to endure, and all this people shall also go to their place in peace.*

Numbers 1:1-19

In taking the census of men eligible for army service, Moses was directed by God to use one leader from each tribe. God considered these men important enough to be named (5-16).

Numbers 4:1-33

Responsibility for packing up and transporting the tabernacle was to be divided among the sons of Aaron, with specific responsibilities assigned. Summarized in v. 15, 16, 19, 27, 28, 33.

Numbers 11:11-17

When Moses complained to God about his heavy responsibility for Israel, God directed him to choose 70 men respected by the people with whom He would share His Spirit, and who would share the responsibility. Also v. 24, 25.

Numbers 34:16-29

God directed Moses to choose specific men to divide the inheritance--and their names are listed.

Nehemiah 3:1-32

The wall of Jerusalem was rebuilt because each group of Jews built one portion; the result was that the enemies saw that this accomplishment was wrought by God (6:15, 16).

Matthew 9:36-38

36 But when he saw the multitudes, he was moved with compassion on them, because they fainted, and were scattered abroad, as sheep having no shepherd. 37 Then saith he unto his disciples, The harvest truly is plenteous, but the laborers are few; 38 Pray ye therefore the Lord of the harvest, that he will send forth laborers into his harvest.

Matthew 10:1-6

1 And when he had called unto him his twelve disciples, he gave them power against unclean spirits, to cast them out, and to heal all manner of sickness and all manner of disease. 2 Now the names of the twelve apostles are these . . . 5 These twelve Jesus sent forth and commanded them . . . .

Matthew 14:19

When Jesus fed the 5,000, *He blessed, and brake, and gave the loaves to his disciples, and the disciples to the multitude.* See also 15:32-39, the feeding of the 4,000.

Matthew 28:18-20

The Great Commission -- not a one-man job.

Acts 6:1-8

1 . . . When the number of the disciples was multiplied, there arose a murmuring of the Grecians against the Hebrews, because their widows were neglected . . . . 2 Then the twelve called the multitude of the disciples unto them, and said, It is not reason that we should leave the word of God, and serve tables. 3 Wherefore, brethren, look ye out among you seven men of honest report, full of the Holy Ghost and wisdom, whom we may appoint over this business. 4 But we will give ourselves continually to prayer, and to the ministry of the word. 5 And the saying pleased the whole multitude: and they chose Stephen . . . .

2. Individual gifts should be recognized in the delineation of responsibilities; each person should concentrate in specific areas of work.

Romans 12:6-8

6 Having then gifts differing according to the grace that is given to us, whether prophecy, let us prophesy according to the proportion of faith; 7 Or ministry, let us wait on our ministering: or he that teacheth, on teaching; 8 Or he that exhorteth, on exhortation: he that giveth, let him do it with simplicity; he that ruleth, with diligence; he that sheweth mercy, with

cheerfulness.

1 Corinthians 12:4-29

8 For to one is given by the Spirit the word of wisdom; to another the word of knowledge by the same Spirit; 9 To another faith . . . to another . . . healing . . . 10 To another the working of miracles; to another prophecy; to another discerning of spirits; to another

divers kinds of tongues; to another the interpretation of tongues: 11 But all these worketh that one and the selfsame Spirit, dividing to every man severally as he will. 29 Are all apostles? are all prophets? are all teachers? are all workers of miracles? 30 Have all the gifts of healing? do all speak with tongues? do all interpret?

3. Delegation of responsibility must include delegation of authority to act (within set limits).

Matthew 10:1-42; Mark 6:7-13; Luke 9:1-6

When Jesus sent out the Twelve, He gave power to *8 Heal the sick, cleanse the lepers, raise the dead, cast out devils . . .* He also promised the Holy Spirit's work in their behalf when they would be persecuted (v. 18-20); and assurance that they really·represented Him. *40 He that receiveth you receiveth me . . . .*

Luke 10:1-12

So also when He sent out the Seventy.

4. Job descriptions should be clearly delineated.

Numbers 4:1-33

God spelled out very carefully the specific responsibilities of the Kohathites, Gershonites and Merarites in the dismantling and transporting of the tabernacle, as Israel moved from place to place. He also indicated which things they were not to do but which were to be done only by Aaron and his sons (v. 15-20).

Deuteronomy 1:15-18

Moses, in telling the new generation of Israelites in the wilderness how God had led them, rehearses what was done (Exodus 18:13-27): *15 So I took the chief of your tribes, wise men, and known, and made them heads over you, captains over thousands, and captains over hundreds, and captains over fifties, and captains over tens, and officers among your tribes. 16 And I charged your judges . . . Hear the causes . . . judge righteously . . . Ye shall not respect persons in judgment; but ye shall hear the small as well as the great; ye shall not be afraid of the face of man . . . the cause that is too hard for you, bring it to me, and I will hear it.*

Matthew 10:5-14, 17-23, 28; Luke 10:2-12

In these accounts of our Lord sending out the Twelve and then the Seventy, He was specific in what He wanted them to do.

Acts 6:1-8

In this passage, quoted under Concept 1, the differences between the duties of the apostles and the deacons are clear.

5. Unity within an organization, and appreciation for one another, are essential to the stability of the group.

Mark 3:22-26

When the scribes accused Jesus of casting out demons by the power of Satan, He pointed out the incongruity of their accusation, saying: *24 And if a kingdom be divided against itself, that kingdom cannot stand. 25 And if a house be divided against itself, that house cannot stand.*

Romans 12:4-16

The picture is given of one body with many members, with those members having differing gifts and responsibilities. Paul urges: love without dissimulation (v. 9); kind affection, brotherly love, and preferring one another (v. 10); sympathy and understanding (v. 11-15); and being of one mind (v. 16).

1 Corinthians 3:3-10

The Apostle, writing to a church divided on several serious issues, reminds them that he cannot give them deeper truth since they are so divided. *3 For ye are yet carnal: for whereas there is among you envying, and strife, and divisions, are ye not carnal, and walk as men?* Using the garden to illustrate, he shows the necessity of working together if there is to be accomplishment (5-8). *9 For we are labourers together with God: ye are God's husbandry, ye are God's building.*

1 Corinthians 12:4-31

Several related points are made here: the diversities of gifts among the group, the one body with all its necessary parts, the absurdity of any one part's minimizing the others, the recognition that one member's

suffering hurts others, the variety within the body of Christ, and the fact that no one person holds all the offices.

Ephesians 4:1-16

Again, an emphasis on unity, on varied gifts, on the overall goal that, whatever the gift, all are concerned with edifying the body and developing mature believers.

6. Various segments of a group should be fairly represented, to lessen the danger of partiality.

Numbers 1:1-16

1 And the Lord spake unto Moses . . . 2 Take ye the sum of all the congregation of the children of Israel . . . 3 . . . All that are able to go forth to war in Israel: thou and Aaron shall number them by their armies. 4 And with you there shall be a man of every tribe; every one head of the house of his fathers. 5 And these are the names of the men that shall stand with you . . . . 16 These were the renowned of the congregation, princes of the tribes of their fathers, heads of thousands in Israel.

Numbers 7:1, 2, 10-84

A prince from each tribe made an offering at the dedication of the tabernacle.

Numbers 13:1-16

God commanded Moses to send one from each tribe to

spy out the land. Each was to be a ruler in his tribe.

Numbers 34:16-29

One prince from each tribe was to be involved in portioning out the land.

Joshua 4:1-9

God told Joshua to use twelve men, one from each tribe, to take twelve stones for a memorial to the crossing of the Jordan River.

Joshua 18:4

Three men from each tribe were to describe the land and bring the description to Joshua, with a division into seven parts, for the tribes who had not yet received their portion.

7. Adequate preparation should precede a major change.

Exodus 24-40

The preparation for the establishment of the tabernacle included the following:

-- commitment to the Lord to do what He instructed (24:7, 8)
-- instruction concerning the materials needed (25:2-8)
-- details of construction (25:10-Ch. 30)
-- appointment and enabling of skilled leadership to do the actual work and to teach others (31:1-11)
-- assurance that, in spite of the sin of the golden calf, God would still go with His people (Ch. 35, 36).

Numbers 9:17 through 10:10

An adequate communications system was established so that all would understand: the pillar of cloud to

indicate whether they were to stay or move on (9:15-23), and two trumpets to signal the congregation for assembly, war, or victory celebration (10:1-10).

Joshua 1:1-18

Though Israel had looked forward to entering Canaan for forty years, immediate preparation included:

-- God's command and encouragement to Joshua as the leader (1:1-9)
-- communication to all the people through their officers (v. 10, 11)
-- preparation for physical needs (v. 11)
-- reminder of the Lord's promises that had been given earlier (v. 11-15)
-- getting a response from the people in terms of their readiness to participate (16-18)

8. Projects should be completed in an orderly fashion.

Many examples and some admonitions are given in Scripture. Here are a few:

Numbers 1:17-19

The numbering of the Israelites was to be done tribe by tribe, and family by family as the Lord commanded Moses.

Numbers 2:1-34

God commanded a specific arrangement of the tribes of Israel around the tabernacle when they camped, and a specific order as they moved on.

Luke 14:28-33

Jesus uses the illustrations of the man building the tower, and the king going to war. In each case He shows the importance of planning ahead and counting the cost if the projects are to be properly completed.

John 6:10-14

In distributing the food to the 5000 and collecting the left-overs, there was orderliness. In addition, there was care that nothing be lost. No littering!

Acts 6:1-7

Deacons were appointed to see that the widows were properly cared for, so that the ministry of the word and prayer should not suffer. Here is the provision of adequate personnel for the work to be done.

1 Corinthians 11:18-34

Here are instructions for an orderly observance of the Lord's Supper to replace the disorders which had developed in this church.

1 Corinthians 14:33, 40

33 For God is not the author of confusion, but of peace, as in all churches of the saints. 40 Let all things be done decently and in order. The whole chapter deals with the need for orderliness in the church services, in the light of the controversy over speaking in tongues

9. Provision must be made for irregularities, human error and sin.

Leviticus 4:2-13, 22, 27, etc.

Under the Law, God made provision for sins of ignorance. They were not to be ignored, but there was special provision for forgiveness.

Numbers 9:10-13

God made provision for one who was unavoidably detained from keeping the Passover on the usual date; he was to do it a month later. Note however that this provision was not for one who was merely careless (v. 13).

Deuteronomy 19:1-10

Six cities of refuge were to be set aside for the protection of those who unintentionally killed someone.

Mark 3:9; 4:1

Jesus directed his disciples to have a boat ready, since great crowds were following Him.

Romans 14

Believers are not to judge one another in details that are not specified in Scripture. *13 Let us not therefore judge one another any more: but judge this rather, that no man put a stumblingblock or an occasion to fall in his brother's way.*

Galatians 6:1

Brethren, if a man be overtaken in a fault, ye which are spiritual restore such an one in the spirit of meekness, considering thyself, lest thou also be tempted.

10. Decision by lot has Scriptural precedent and, done in recognition of God's sovereignty, can indicate God's will.

Proverbs 16:33

The lot is cast into the lap; but the whole disposing thereof is of the Lord.

Proverbs 18:18

The lot causeth contentions to cease, and parteth between the mighty.

Numbers 26:55, 56

The land was to be distributed by lot to the tribes of Israel. See also 33:54; 34:13; 36:2. Josh. 13:6; 14:1, 2; 15:1; 16:1; 17:1, 14; 18:11; 19:1-40; 21:4-10. Acts 13:19.

1 Samuel 14:41-44

King Saul prayed the Lord would show His will by the way the lot fell, and God did so.

1 Chronicles 6:63-65

The distribution of the cities to the sons of Levi was to be by lot.

1 Chronicles 24:1-31

The division of the descendents of Aaron into 24 groups for service on a rotating basis was to be by lot. Also Luke 1:8, 9.

Nehemiah 11:1

After the return of the Jews from Babylon, they cast lots to determine the one tenth of the men who should live in Jerusalem.

Ezekiel 47:12, 22

The Israel of the future is to be divided by lot. Also 48:29.

Jonah 1:7

God guided the casting of lots, even by the unbelieving ship's crew, to designate Jonah as the offending person on board.

11. Decisions and judgments must be consistent, not based on personalities, preconceived notions or hearsay.

Leviticus 19:15

Ye shall do no unrighteousness in judgment: thou shalt not respect the person of the poor, nor honour the person of the mighty: but in righteousness shalt thou judge thy neighbor. Also Ex. 23:3, 7, 9. Lev. 24:22. Deut. 27:19. 2 Chron. 19:5-7. Prov. 18:5. Zech. 7:9, 10.

Leviticus 24:10-23

The Israelite and the stranger were to be treated alike when they were guilty of the same crimes. *16 And he that blasphemeth the name of the Lord, he shall surely be put to death . . . as well the stranger as he that is born in the land . . . . 22 Ye shall have one manner of law, as well for the stranger as for one of your own country: for I am the Lord your God.*

Deuteronomy 13:12-15

The facts should be checked carefully before action is taken on an evil report. *12 If thou shalt hear say in one of thy cities . . . 14 Then thou shalt inquire, and make search, and ask diligently; and behold, if it be truth and the thing certain, that such abomination is wrought among you; 15 Thou shalt surely smite the inhabitants . . . .*

Deuteronomy 16:18, 19

18 Judges and officers . . . shall judge the people with judgment. 19 Thou shalt not wrest judgment; thou shalt not respect persons, neither take a gift . . . . Also 27:19; 2 Sam. 23:3; Prov. 24:23-26.

Joshua 20:1-6

Cities of Refuge were provided to protect the unintentional slayer.

Joshua 22:10-34

An example. Israel almost had civil war over a misunderstanding. Premature judgment, or the judging of motives easily leads to strained relationships.

Proverbs 28:21

To have respect of persons is not good: for for a piece of bread that man will transgress.

John 7:24, 51

24 Judge not according to the appearance, but judge righteous judgment. 51 Doth our law judge any man before it hear him and know what he doeth?

12. Gifts to those in office endanger justice and are therefore not to be received.

Exodus 23:8

And thou shalt take no gift: for the gift blindeth the wise, and perverteth the words of the righteous. Also Deuteronomy 16:19.

1 Samuel 8:1-6

When Samuel was old, he made his sons judges. However they were ungodly and took bribes and perverted judgment. As a result, the elders of Israel were dissatisfied and demanded a king.

Proverbs 17:23

A wicked man taketh a gift out of the bosom to pervert the ways of judgment.

Isaiah 1:23

Thy princes are rebellious, and companions of thieves: everyone loveth gifts, and followeth after rewards: they judge not the fatherless, neither doth the cause of the widow come unto them.

Isaiah 5:22, 23

22 Woe unto them . . . 23 Which justify the wicked for reward, and take away the righteousness of the righteous from him!

Micah 7:3

That they may do evil with both hands earnestly, the prince asketh, and the judge asketh for a reward.

13. The benefits from any project should be shared with those behind the scenes.

Joshua 22:8

When Joshua sent the soldiers of Reuben, Gad and the half tribe of Manasseh back home after victory in Canaan, he said, *8 Return with much riches . . . cattle . . . silver . . . gold . . . brass . . . iron . . . raiment:*

divide the spoil of your enemies with your brethren.

1 Samuel 30:22-31

24 . . . But as his part is that goeth down to the battle, so shall his part be that tarrieth by the stuff: they shall part alike.

14. The separation of religious and civil responsibilities and decisions has a long history, even in a theocracy.

Exodus 18:13-26

Describes the setting up of judges to decide many cases, relieving Moses from some of his work.

Deuteronomy 17:8-13

God, just before the entrance to Canaan, describes the responsibility of judges as well as priests, in deciding cases of disagreement.

2 Chronicles 19:8-11

Jehoshaphat stationed not only priests and Levites, but *of the chief of the fathers of Israel, for the judgment of the Lord, and for the controversies* (v. 8). Verse 11 specifies: *Amariah the chief priest is over you in all matters of the Lord, and Zebadiah . . . for all the king's matters.*

15. Administrative policies and procedures must avoid injustices of all kinds.

Accounts of God's condemnation of various kinds of injustice are plentiful in the Bible. See Chapter 8, on social problems, and Chapter 1, on history. Two examples:

Ezekiel 45:9-12

Future princes of Israel are commanded to be concerned for right dealings with the people, avoiding violence and destruction, injustice, overtaxation, dishonest practices.

Habakkuk 2:12, 17

God pronounces judgment on those who build a city on violence and bloodshed.

AN EXAMPLE OF LEADERSHIP
1 Thessalonians 2, 3

1. Paul's willingness to serve even in the light of opposition and previous mistreatment, v. 2
2. His honesty, v. 3
3. His recognition of his responsibility to God, v. 4
4. His refusal to seek glory from men, or to use flattery, v. 5, 6
5. His gentle concern, rather than dictatorialness, v. 6, 7, 11
6. His willingness to give of his own life, in addition to teaching and preaching, v. 8
7. His consideration and concern about his own example, v. 9, 10
8. His keeping in contact with those who have been his responsibility, 3:1-10

"I find the doing of the will of God leaves me no time for disputing about His plans."

--George MacDonald, 1824-1905.

6

Social Relationships

BIBLICAL CONCEPTS

I. **Scriptural principles governing social relationships**
   1. Love is to characterize godly people.
   2. Ministry to others should be an expression of love.
   3. The basis for consideration of others is God's kindness to us.
   4. Christian character is the product of the Holy Spirit's work in us.
   5. God is interested in individuals, both weak and mature.
   6. Believers do not have the same understanding on every point; each is to live as unto God and respect others.
   7. Loyalty to Christ will result in our being misunderstood by others.
   8. The sin of one person affects the lives of others.
   9. God holds us responsible for what He has given us - both in abilities and possessions.
   10. Others are likely to treat us the way we treat them.
   11. God's people are meant to be a blessing even to unbelievers with the hope that they too will glorify God.

II. **Responsibilities of believers in relation to others**
   1. Every person must accept individual responsibility; ultimate responsibility is to God.
   2. People must submit to one another in order to live and work together happily.

3. Each person must respect the rights and property of others.
4. Within our limitations, we are to do good to others, and especially to other believers.
5. A believer is responsible to rebuke sin in another believer but with the purpose of restoring him, if possible.
6. Believers are to show a distinctive attitude toward enemies -- one of love and concern.
7. God forbids meddling in the affiars of other people; He condemns busybodies.
8. God expects honesty in our dealings with one another.
9. God encourages hospitality that is not limited to close friends.
10. It is right to give honor to those whose lives and/or work commend them.
11. Believers should choose carefully those with whom they fellowship, lest they learn the ways of sin, and lest they give approval to sin.
12. True friendship depends on a number of friendly actions.

III. Prevention of strife and settling of disagreements
1. God's people are responsible to avoid strife in as many ways as possible.
2. A believer should correct his own life before he attempts to correct others.
3. God forbids believers to go to law against other believers before a court made up of unsaved persons.
4. Disagreements should be settled quickly and directly between the persons involved.
5. When two believers cannot resolve their disagreement. they should involve witnesses; they may need to involve the church, or some larger group of Christians.

FRIENDS AND FRIENDSHIP

"A true friend is the gift of God, and he only who made hearts can unite them."
-- Robert South, English clergy, 1634-1716.

"All men have their frailties; and whoever looks for a friend without imperfections, will never find what he seeks. We love ourselves notwithstanding our faults, and we ought to love our friends in like manner."
-- Cyrus the Great, founder of the Persian empire.

"That friendship will not continue to the end which is begun for an end."
-- Francis Quarles, English author, 1592-1644.

BIBLICAL BACKGROUND

I. Scriptural principles governing social relationships

1. Love is to characterize godly people.

Leviticus 19:18, 34

18 Thou shalt love thy neighbor as thyself: I am the Lord. 34 But the stranger that dwelleth with you shall be unto you as one born among you, and thou shalt love him as thyself; for ye were strangers in Egypt. God's law in Israel. Also Matt. 19:19; 22:39; Gal. 5:14.

Psalm 133:1-3

1 Behold, how good and how pleasant it is for brethren to dwell together in unity! 2 It is like the precious ointment . . . 33 As the dew of Hermon . . . .

John 13:35

By this shall all men know that ye are my disciples, if ye have love one to another.

Romans 12:10

Be kindly affectioned one to another with brotherly love; in honour preferring one another.

1 Corinthians 13:1-3, 13

1 Though I speak with the tongues of men and of angels, and have not charity, I am become as sounding brass, or a tinkling cymbal. 2 And though I have the gift of prophecy . . . all faith . . . 3 . . . bestow all my goods to feed the poor, and . . . give my body to be burned, and have not charity, it profiteth me nothing. 13 And now abideth faith, hope, charity, these three;
but the greatest of these is charity.

Philippians 1:9

. . . I pray, that your love may abound yet more and more in knowledge and in all judgment.

1 Thessalonians 3:12

The Lord make you to increase and abound in love one toward another, and toward all men, even as we do toward you.

See also 1 John 3:11-18 and many other passages.

PROJECT: Using a concordance, or a topical Bible, look up references to love, especially as it relates to people loving one another. Try also to find Scriptural examples in which love was shown. How important is love in the Christian life? This study by students could be the basis for an essay assignment.

✱ ✱ ✱

"Love is an image of God, and not a lifeless image, but the living essence of the divine nature which beams full of all goodness." -- Martin Luther, 1483-1546.

2. Ministry to others should be an expression of love.

Matthew 25:40

Verily I say unto you, Inasmuch as ye have done it unto one of these my brethren, ye have done it unto me.

Luke 10:30-37

The Good Samaritan parable.

Acts 2:44, 45

44 And all that believed were together, and had all things common; 45 And sold their possessions and goods and parted them to all men, as every man had need. Also 4:34, 35.

2 Corinthians 8, 9

Gifts from the Asian and European churches to the saints at Jerusalem. See especially 8:2-9; 9:7-8.

Philippians 4:15-19

The example of the church at Philippi in giving to Paul.

1 Timothy 5:10

An older widow, without family to care for her, was to be cared for by the church as an expression of love and appreciation for her good works for others.

James 1:27

Pure religion and undefiled before God and the Father is this, To visit the fatherless and widows in their affliction, and to keep himself unspotted from the world. Also 2:14-20.

1 John 3:16-18

17 But whoso hath this world's good, and seeth his brother have need, and shutteth up his bowels of compassion from him, how dwelleth the love of God in him?

3. The basis for consideration of others is God's kindness to us.

Luke 6:35, 36

35 But love ye your enemies, and do good . . . and ye shall be the children of the Highest: for he is kind unto the unthankful and to the evil. 36 Be ye therefore merciful, as your Father also is merciful.

John 13:34

A new commandment I give unto you, That ye love one another; as I have loved you, that ye also love one another. Also 15:12.

Ephesians 4:32

Be ye kind one to another, tenderhearted, forgiving one another, even as God for Christ's sake hath forgiven you.

Ephesians 5:2, 25

2 Walk in love, as Christ also hath loved us, and hath

given himself for us an offering and a sacrifice to God . . . . 25 Husbands, love your wives, even as Christ also loved the church, and gave himself for it.

Colossians 3:12, 13

13 Forbearing one another, and forgiving one another, if any man have a quarrel against any: even as Christ forgave you, so also do ye.

1 John 3:16 and 4:11

16 Hereby perceive we the love of God, because he laid down his life for us: and we ought to lay down our lives for the brethren. 11 Beloved, if God so loved us, we ought also to love one another.

4. Christian character is the product of the Holy Spirit's work in us.

Matthew 12:35

A good man out of the good treasure of the heart bringeth forth good things: and an evil man out of the evil treasure bringeth forth evil things. In other words, actions come out of our inner being, our thought-life, and whatever controls it.

John 15:5

We are told here that it is the One who is in us that

brings forth fruit. *5 I am the vine, ye are the branches: He that abideth in me and I in him, the same bringeth forth much fruit: for without me ye can do nothing.*

Romans 5:5

. . . The love of God is shed abroad in our hearts by the Holy Ghost which is given unto us.

Galatians 2:20

I am crucified with Christ: nevertheless I live; yet

not I, but Christ liveth in me: and the life which I now live in the flesh I live by the faith of the Son of God, who loved me, and gave himself for me. The Apostle is saying that what he is results from the Lord's working, not himself.

Galatians 5:22, 23

These are perhaps the key verses: 22 But the fruit of the Spirit is love, joy, peace, longsuffering, gentle-

ness, goodness, faith[fulness], 23 Meekness, temperance: against such there is no law. How do these character traits come? By the Holy Spirit's indwelling and ruling in our hearts. Also Ephesians 5:9.

Philippians 2:13

For it is God which worketh in you both to will and to do of his good pleasure.

5. God is interested in individuals, both weak and mature.

Genesis 6:8, 9

8 But Noah found grace in the eyes of the Lord. 9 . . . Noah was a just man and perfect in his generations, and Noah walked with God. God took note of one man in the midst of a sinful society.

Exodus 30:12-16

God was concerned with the action of each Jewish man, or family. 12 . . . Then shall they give every man a ransom . . . 13 This they shall give, every one . . . half a shekel. . . . 15 The rich shall not give more, and poor shall not give less . . . .

Numbers 7:12-83

Twelve princes presented identical gifts, yet God recorded the description of each one.

PROJECT: Find others who stood for God in the midst of sin and ungodliness, and for whom God

did something special. Prepare a chart, with columns labelled: Scripture reference, Person's name, Situation, How the person differed, What God did.

Mark 9:36-42; 10:13-16; Matthew 18:1-10

Jesus placed a child in His arms and explained the importance of a little child.

Romans 14:1

God exhorts similar concern on our part: 1 Him that is weak in the faith receive ye, but not to doubtful disputations.

Romans 14:21

It is good neither to eat flesh, nor to drink wine, nor anything whereby thy brother stumbleth, or is offended, or is made weak. Also 1 Cor. 8:8, 13.

6. Believers do not have the same understanding on every point; each is to live as unto God and respect others.

John 4:36-38

Jesus points out that one sows and another reaps, and that we enter into the labors of others. We do not engage in the same ministries, yet we all count.

1 Corinthians 4:7

After a discussion about the dangers of judging one another, Paul records: 7 For who maketh thee to differ from another? and what hast thou that thou didst not receive? Now if thou didst receive it, why dost thou glory as if thou hadst not received it?

1 Corinthians 8:4-13

Here the Corinthians are warned against judging others about their eating of food that had first been offered to idols, when not all believers agreed as to the significance of the act. Also 10:23-33.

Galatians 5:13-15

13 For brethren, ye have been called unto liberty; only use not liberty for an occasion to the flesh, but by love serve one another.

Colossians 1:11

Here is part of Paul's prayer: 11 Strengthened with all might according to his glorious power, unto all patience and longsuffering with joyfulness. Note for what purpose Paul wants them and us to be strengthened.

Romans 14:1-23

The same principle of allowing others to differ with us on some matters, yet still respecting them, is applied to kinds of foods to be eaten and observance of special days. The principle is liberty under God, yet concern not to cause others to stumble in their faith.

7. Loyalty to Christ will result in our being misunderstood by others.

Matthew 5:10-12

11 Blessed are ye, when men shall revile you and persecute you and shall say all manner of evil against you falsely, for my sake. 12 Rejoice, and be exceeding glad: for great is your reward in heaven: for so persecuted they the prophets which were before you. Also Matthew 10:12-37.

2 Timothy 3:12

All that will live godly in Christ Jesus shall suffer persecution.

2 Timothy 4:3-5

3 For the time will come when they will not endure sound doctrine . . . 4 And they shall turn away their ears from the truth . . . 5 But watch thou in all things, endure afflictions, do the work of an evangelist, make full proof of thy ministry.

1 Peter 3:16

16 Having a good conscience; that, whereas they speak evil of you, as of evildoers, they may be ashamed that falsely accuse your good conversation [way of life] in Christ.

1 Peter 4:3-5

4 Wherein they think it strange that ye run not with them to the same excess of riot, speaking evil of you. See also Heb. 10:32-34; 11:36-40; 2 Tim. 4:16.

8. The sin of one person affects the lives of others.

Exodus 20:5

For I the Lord thy God am a jealous God, visiting the iniquity of the fathers upon the children unto the third and fourth generation of them that hate me. Also Jer. 32:18.

Deuteronomy 28:15, 32, 41

God promised that Israel's refusal to hearken unto Him would result in their children's being given to another people (32); also in their begetting children who would go into captivity (41).

Numbers 14:33

The new generation of Israel was to wander 40 years, until the older generation had died -- all because of the sins of the older generation.

Numbers 16:31-33

The families of Dathan and Abiram were swallowed up with them.

Numbers 26:11

So also with part of Korah's family.

Joshua 7:24, 25

So with Achan's sons, daughters and animals.

Proverbs 17:25

A foolish son is a grief to his father, and bitterness to her that bare him. Also 19:13; 28:7.

Romans 5:12

Wherefore, as by one man [Adam] sin entered into the world, and death by sin; and so death, passed upon all men, for that all have sinned. Also vs. 15-21.

9. God holds us responsible for what He has given us-both in abilities and possessions.

Matthew 25:15-30

Parable of the talents; also Luke 19:13-26, parable of the pounds.

Luke 16:10-12

10 He that is faithful in that which is least is faithful also in much: and he that is unjust in the least is unjust also in much. 11 If ye therefore have not been faithful in the unrighteous mammon, who will commit to your trust the true riches? 12 And if ye have not been faithful in that which is another man's, who shall give you that which is your own?

1 Timothy 6:17, 18

17 Charge them that are rich in this world, that they be not high-minded, nor trust in uncertain riches, but in the living God, who giveth us richly all things to enjoy; 18 That they do good, that they be rich in good works, ready to distribute, willing to communicate.

"The feeling of a direct responsibility of the individual to God is almost wholly a creation of Protestantism."
-- John Stuart Mill, 1806-1873.

10. Others are likely to treat us the way we treat them.

Matthew 7:2
For with what judgment ye judge, ye shall be judged: and with what measure ye mete, it shall be measured to you again.

Matthew 7:12
Therefore all things whatsoever ye would that men should do to you, do ye even so to them: for this is the law and the prophets.

11. God's people are meant to be a blessing even to unbelievers with the hope that they too will glorify God.

Genesis 30:27, 28
Laban said to Jacob, *I have learned by experience that the Lord hath blessed me for thy sake.*

Genesis 39:2-5
2 And the Lord was with Joseph . . . 3 And his master saw that the Lord was with him, and that the Lord made all that he did to prosper in his hand . . . . 5 . . . The Lord blessed the Egyptian's house for Joseph's sake . . . .

Daniel 1
Daniel and his friends purposed in their hearts not to defile themselves -- God gave them knowledge and skill -- the king communed with them -- none like them -- *in all matters of wisdom and understanding that the king enquired of them he found them ten times better.*

Daniel 2
Nebuchadnezzar dreamed -- Daniel answered with counsel and wisdom -- Daniel made the thing known to his companions -- the secret was revealed unto Daniel -- Daniel blessed God -- he said, *There is a God in heaven that revealeth secrets* -- he interpreted the dream to Nebuchadnezzar -- verse 47: *The king answered . . . Of a truth it is, that your God is a God of gods, and a Lord of kings, and a revealer of secrets, seeing thou couldest reveal this secret.* Also Daniel 3:28, 29; 6:3, 26-28.

Matthew 5:13-16
16 Let your light so shine before men, that they may see your good works and glorify your Father which is in heaven.

1 Peter 2:11-17
12 Having your conversation [or way of life] *honest among the Gentiles: that, whereas they speak against you as evildoers, they may by your good works, which they shall behold, glorify God . . . 13 Submit yourselves to every ordinance of man for the Lord's sake . . . 15 For so is the will of God, that with well doing ye may put to silence the ignorance of foolish men.*

II. Responsibilities of believers in relation to others.

1. Every person must accept individual responsibility; ultimate responsibility is to God.

Proverbs 20:11
Even a child is known by his doings, whether his work be pure and whether it be right.

Isaiah 3:10, 11
10 Say ye, to the righteous, that it shall be well with him: for they shall eat the fruit of their doings. Woe unto the wicked! 11 It shall be ill with him: for the reward of his hands shall be given him.

Jeremiah 17:10
I the Lord search the heart, I try the reins, even to give every man according to his ways, and according to the fruit of his doings. Also 32:19; Mal. 3:16-18; 4:1-3.

Ezekiel 18:1-4
Note the emphasis on individual responsibility -- not the children suffering for their fathers' sins, but the *soul that sinneth, it shall die.* Also Deut. 24:16; Ex. 32:31-33.

Luke 19:11-27
Parable of the pounds -- each man responsible for what he did with his.

Luke 20:9-16
Parable of the husbandman and vineyard. The husbandmen were to be destroyed for their mistreatment of the servants and the son.

Romans 14:12

Every one of us shall give account of himself to God.
Also 1-23.

2 Corinthians 5:10

For we must all appear before the judgment seat of Christ; that everyone may receive the things done in his body, according to that he hath done, whether it be good or bad.

Colossians 3:23-25

23 Whatsoever ye do, do it heartily, as to the Lord, and not unto men; 24 Knowing that of the Lord ye shall receive the reward of the inheritance: for ye serve the Lord Christ. 25 And he that doeth wrong shall receive for the wrong which he hath done: and there is no respect of persons. Also 4:1; 2 Thes. 3:10; 1 Tim. 5:8, 16.

2. People must submit to one another in order to live and work together happily.

Romans 13:1

Let every soul be subject unto the higher powers.

Ephesians 5:18, 21, 22

Be filled with the Spirit . . . submitting yourselves one to another in the fear of God. Wives, submit yourselves unto your husbands, as unto the Lord. Also Col. 3:18.

Colossians 3:20

Children, obey your parents in all things: for this is

well-pleasing unto the Lord. Also Eph. 6:1.

1 Peter 2:13-23

Submit yourselves to every ordinance of man for the Lord's sake . . . for so is the will of God . . . Servants, be subject to your masters with all fear; not only to the good and gentle but also to the froward (13, 15, 18). Also Heb. 13:17.

3. Each person must respect the rights and property of others.

Exodus 20:15-17

The ten commandments forbid stealing, killing, adultery, coveting of another's property, wife or servants.

Leviticus 19:13

Defrauding a neighbor is forbidden; wages are not to

be withheld beyond the day they are due.

1 Timothy 5:18

The laborer is worthy of his hire.

For a fuller treatment of this concept, see chapter on Economics, the section dealing with property ownership.

4. Within our limitations, we are to do good to others, and especially to other believers.

Numbers 32

The tribes of Reuben and Gad could not be concerned only with their own needs, but must help the other tribes fight their battles.

Proverbs 3:27, 28

27 Withhold not good from them to whom it is due, when it is in the power of thine hand to do it. 28 Say

not unto thy neighbor, Go, and come again, and tomorrow I will give thee; when thou hast it by thee. Also 28:27.

Galatians 6:10

As we have therefore opportunity, let us do good unto all men, especially unto them who are of the household of faith. Also Matt. 19:21, 22; Luke 6:32-34; 1 Cor. 10:24; Gal. 6:2; Phil. 2:4; James 2:15, 16; 1 Jn. 3:17.

"I expect to pass through life but once . . . . If therefore, there be any kindness I can show, or any good thing I can do to any fellow-being, let me do it now, and not defer or neglect it, as I shall not pass this way again." -- William Penn, 1644-1718.

5. A believer is responsible to rebuke sin in another believer, but with the purpose of of restoring him, if possible.

Leviticus 5:1

A witness to an alleged crime who fails to tell what he knows is considered guilty himself. See also Berkeley version; also 20:4, 5.

Leviticus 19:17

Thou shalt not hate thy brother in thine heart: thou shalt in any wise rebuke thy neighbor, and not suffer sin upon him. In other words, to refuse to rebuke when needed is to hate.

1 Corinthians 5:1, 2, 11, 12

Paul takes to task the church in Corinth because they did not rebuke and excommunicate one of their members guilty of fornication. *11 But now I have written unto you not to keep company, if any man that is called a brother be a fornicator, or covetous, or an idolator, or a railer, or a drunkard, or an extortioner; with such an one no not to eat. 13 . . . Therefore put away from among yourselves that wicked person.*

2 Thessalonians 3:6

Now we command you . . . that ye withdraw yourselves from every brother that walketh disorderly.

2 Thessalonians 3:14, 15

14 If any man obey not our word . . . note that man, and have no company with him, that he may be ashamed, 15 Yet count him not as an enemy, but admonish him as a brother.

Also Matthew 18:15-17; Galatians 6:1; Titus 1:13; James 5:19, 20.

6. Believers are to show a distinctive attitude toward enemies -- one of love and concern.

Proverbs 24:17, 18

17 Rejoice not when thine enemy falleth, and let not thine hand be glad when he stumbleth: 18 Lest the Lord see it, and it displease him . . . .

Proverbs 25:21, 22

21 If thine enemy be hungry, give him bread to eat; and if he be thirsty, give him water to drink: 22 For thou shalt heap coals of fire upon his head, and the Lord shall reward thee.

Job 31:29, 30

Job recognized the sin of cursing an enemy.

Matthew 5:38-48

But I say unto you, Love your enemies, bless them that curse you, do good to them that hate you, and pray for them which despitefully use you and persecute you (v. 44). Also Luke 6:27-36.

Luke 23:34

Jesus forgave those who crucified Him.

Acts 7:60

Stephen prayed for those who stoned him.

Romans 12:17-21

17 Recompense to no man evil for evil . . . 19 Dearly beloved, avenge not yourselves, but rather give place unto wrath: for it is written, Vengeance is mine; I will repay, saith the Lord. 20 Therefore if thine enemy hunger, feed him; if he thirst, give him drink: for in so doing thou shalt heap coals of fire on his head. 21 Be not overcome of evil, but overcome evil with good. Also verse 14.

7. God forbids meddling in the affairs of other people; He condemns busybodies.

Leviticus 19:16

Thou shalt not go up and down as a talebearer among the people . . . .

Proverbs 20:3

It is an honour for a man to cease from strife: but every fool will be meddling.

2 Thessalonians 3:11, 12

11 For we hear that there are some which walk among you disorderly, working not at all, but are busybodies. 12 Now them that are such we command . . . that with quietness they work . . . .

1 Peter 4:18

But let none of you suffer as a . . . busybody in other men's matters.

1 Timothy 5:13

Here is part of the reasoning behind the admonition that the church should not provide for younger widows.

There was the danger that *13 . . . They learn to be idle, wandering about from house to house, and not only idle but tattlers also, and busybodies, speaking things which they ought not.* Instead, they were encouraged to remarry, and thus have their own household responsibilities.

8. God expects honesty in our dealings with one another.

Leviticus 19:11, 13

11 Ye shall not steal, neither deal falsely, neither lie one to another. 13 Thou shalt not defraud thy neighbor, neither rob him . . . .

Psalm 12:2, 3

David describing the ungodliness around him: *2 . . . With flattering lips and with a double heart do they speak. 3 The Lord shall cut off all flattering lips, and the tongue that speaketh proud things.*

Psalm 55:21-23

A description of a betrayer: *21 The words of his mouth were smoother than butter, but war was in his heart: his words were softer than oil, yet they were drawn swords . . . 23 But thou, O God, shalt bring them down into the pit of destruction: bloody and deceitful men shall not live out half their days . . . .*

Proverbs 12:22

Lying lips are abomination to the Lord: but they that deal truly are his delight.

Proverbs 13:5; 14:5

5 A righteous man hateth lying . . . . 5 A faithful

witness will not lie: but a false witness will utter lies. Also 14:25; 19:5.

Proverbs 26:28

. . . A flattering mouth worketh ruin.

Proverbs 28:23

He that rebuketh a man afterwards shall find more favour than he that flattereth with his tongue.

Ephesians 4:25, 28

25 Wherefore putting away lying, speak every man truth with his neighbour: for we are members one of another. 28 Let him that stole steal no more . . . .

Colossians 3:9

Lie not one to another, seeing that ye have put off the old man with his deeds.

Revelation 21:8

. . . All liars shall have their part in the lake which burneth with fire and brimstone: which is the second death.

See also Economics section, on honesty in business relationships.

9. God encourages hospitality that is not limited to close friends.

Leviticus 19:10

And thou shalt not glean thy vineyard, neither shalt thou gather every grape of thy vineyard; thou shalt leave them for the poor and stranger. Also v. 33, 34.

Deuteronomy 10:19

Love ye therefore the stranger for ye were strangers in the land of Egypt.

Luke 14:12-14

12 . . . When thou makest a dinner or a supper, call not thy friends nor thy brethren, . . . lest they bid thee again . . . 13 But . . . call the poor, the maimed, the lame, the blind: 14 And thou shalt be blessed; for they cannot recompense thee . . . .

Romans 12:13

[Be] distributing to the necessity of the saints; given to hospitality. Also 16:12.

1 Timothy 3:2; Titus 1:8

A bishop or pastor is to be *given to hospitaltiy*, or *a lover of hospitality*.

1 Timothy 5:10

A widow, if she was to be cared for by the church, was to be one who had *lodged strangers*, and *washed the saints' feet*.

Hebrews 13:2; 1 Peter 4:9, 10; 3 John 5, 6

All believers are encouraged in hospitality.

10. It is right to give honor to those whose lives and/or work commend them.

Examples:

Matthew 11:7-15

Jesus gives honorable recognition to John the Baptist before His own multitude of followers.

John 1:26, 27

John the Baptist gives honor to the Lord, saying: *26 . . . There standeth one among you, whom ye know not; 27 He it is, who coming after me is preferred before me, whose shoe's latchet I am not worthy to unloose.* Also 30-34.

Romans 13:7, 8

Here a principle is stated: *7 Render therefore to all their dues: tribute to whom tribute is due; custom to whom custom; fear to whom fear; honour to whom honour. 8 Owe no man any thing, but to love one another: for he that loveth another hath fulfilled the law.*

Romans 16:1-16, 21-23

Here the Apostle mentions specific saints to whom he wants greetings conveyed. In many cases he mentions some characteristic which he appreciates in them. So also in the second list, of those whose greetings he wishes to include. He does not hesitate to honor others.

11. Believers should choose carefully those with whom they fellowship, lest they learn the ways of sin, and lest they give approval to sin.

Exodus 23:24-33

As Israel entered the land, God was specific in commanding them not to associate with the heathen in the land, but rather to destroy them, *lest they make thee sin against me, for if thou serve their gods, it will surely be a snare unto thee* (v. 33). Also 34:13-16; Num. 16:26; 25:1-5; Josh. 23:12, 13; Ezra 10:11.

Psalm 1:1

Blessed is the man that walketh not in the counsel of the ungodly, nor standeth in the way of sinners, nor sitteth in the seat of the scornful.

Proverbs 4:14

Enter not into the path of the wicked, and go not in the way of evil men.

Proverbs 19:27

Cease, my son, to hear the instruction that causeth to err from the words of knowledge. Also 14:7.

Proverbs 28:19

. . . He that followeth after vain persons shall have poverty enough.

1 Corinthians 5:11

Believers are commanded by Paul not to keep company, or even to eat, with another believer known to be living in sin.

2 Corinthians 6:14-17

14 Be ye not unequally yoked together with unbelievers: for what fellowship hath righteousness with unrighteousness? and what communion hath light with darkness? 15 And what concord hath Christ with Belial? or what part hath he that believeth with an infidel? 16 And what agreement hath the temple of God with idols? for ye are the temple of the living God . . . 17 Wherefore come out from among them, and be ye separate, saith the Lord, and touch not the unclean thing . . . .

Ephesians 5:11

And have no fellowship with the unfruitful works of darkness, but rather reprove them.

Also 2 Thess. 3:6, 14, 15; 1 Tim. 6:3-5; 2 Tim. 3:2-5; 2 John 10, 11.

12. True friendship depends on a number of friendly actions.

Proverbs 17:9. Keeping confidences.
Proverbs 18:24. Being friendly.
Proverbs 25:17. Going home soon enough.
Proverbs 27:6, 9. Wholehearted counsel, even when it hurts.

Proverbs 27:17. Stimulating one another toward right action and attitude.
Ecclesiastes 4:9-12. Helping one another.
Amos 3:3. Being in agreement.

III. Prevention of strife and settling of disagreements

1. God's people are responsible to avoid strife in as many ways as possible.

Some Biblical instruction about how to avoid quarrels:

Genesis 13:8-11

The example of Abraham's offer to Lot, with the result that the two men and their herdsmen separated.

Genesis 26:17-35

Isaac's repeated digging of wells in new places in order to get away from strife with other herdsmen.

Proverbs 3:30

Be sure there is adequate reason before speaking. *30 Strive not with a man without a cause, if he have done thee no harm.*

Proverbs 10:12

Remember the power of love. *12 Hatred stirreth up strifes: but love covereth all sins.*

Proverbs 13:10

Recognize a major cause of strife. *10 Only by pride cometh contention: but with the well-advised is wisdom.*

Some New Testament exhortation to unity and peace:

Romans 12:18; 14:19

18 If it be possible, as much as lieth in you, live peaceably with all men. 19 Let us therefore follow after the things which make for peace, and things wherewith one may edify another.

1 Corinthians 1:10

I beseech you, brethren . . . that ye all speak the

Proverbs 15:18; also 25:8

Be slow to take offense. *18 A wrathful man stirreth up strife: but he that is slow to anger appeaseth strife.*

Proverbs 20:3

Be the first to give in. *3 It is an honour for a man to cease from strife: but every fool will be meddling.*

Proverbs 26:17

Avoid being a busybody. *17 He that passeth by, and meddleth with strife belonging not to him, is like one that taketh a dog by the ears. Also 16:28; 18:6; 22:10; 23:29, 30; 28:25; 29:9.*

Proverbs 26:20, 21

Don't add fuel to the fire. *20 Where no wood is, there the fire goeth out: so where there is no tale-bearer, the strife ceaseth. 21 As coals are to burning coals, and wood to fire; so is a contentious man to kindle strife.*

same thing, and that there be no divisions among you; but that ye be perfectly joined together in the same mind and in the same judgment.

Also Phil. 2:2-5; 1 Cor. 3:1-4; 4:7; 2 Tim. 2:14, 23, 24; James 3:14, 16; 4:1, 2.

2. A believer should correct his own life before he attempts to correct others.

Matthew 7:3-5

Jesus speaking: *3 Why beholdest thou the mote that is in thy brother's eye, but considerest not the beam that is in thine own eye? 4 Or how wilt thou say to thy brother, Let me pull out the mote out of thine eye; and behold a beam is in thine own eye? 5 Thou hypocrite, first cast out the beam out of thine own eye; then shalt thou see clearly to cast out the mote*

out of thy brother's eye.

Galatians 6:1

Brethren, if a man be overtaken in a fault, ye which are spiritual, restore such an one in the spirit of meekness, considering thyself, lest thou also be tempted.

> **"A hypocrite makes a sober jest of God and religion; he finds it easier to be upon his knees than to rise to a good action; like an impudent debtor, who goes every day to talk familiarly to his creditor, without ever paying what he owes."**
> **-- Alexander Pope, 1688-1744.**

3. God forbids believers to go to law against other believers before a court made up of unsaved persons.

1 Corinthians 6:1-7
Since in the future believers will judge the world, and will judge angels, they surely should be able to settle differences among themselves without going to law. Better to suffer wrong than to win before unbelievers in court.

4. Disagreements should be settled quickly and directly between the persons involved.

Genesis 4
Cain and Abel failed to settle their differences. The result was murder and loss of life.

Genesis 13
Abraham, who was older and more mature, took the initiative in solving the difficulty with Lot and his servants. See also 26:17-25, the example of Isaac.

Proverbs 25:9
Debate thy cause with thy neighbor himself; and discover not a secret to another . . . .

Matthew 5:23-26
23 If thou bring thy gift to the altar and there remember that thy brother hath ought against thee; 24 Leave there thy gift before the altar, and go thy way; first, be reconciled to thy brother, and then come back and offer thy gift. 25 Agree with thine adversary quickly. Also Matt. 18:15.

5. When two believers cannot resolve their disagreement, they should involve witnesses; they may need to involve the church, or some larger group of Christians.

Matthew 18:15-17
15 Moreover if thy brother shall trespass against thee, go and tell him his fault between thee and him alone; if he shall hear thee, thou hast gained thy brother. 16 But if he will not hear thee, then take with thee one or two more, that in the mouth of two or three witnesses every word may be established. 17 And if he shall neglect to hear them, tell it unto the church: but if he neglect to hear the church, let him be unto thee as an heathen and a publican.

Acts 15:1-35
The council at Jerusalem. Here is an example of a disagreement between believers, the resolution of which finally came in the church in Jerusalem, where all those involved were free to explain their views and seek the counsel of the larger group.

See also Joshua 22:11-34 for an interesting Old Testament example of settling a difficulty between two groups.

****

BIBLE STUDIES IN SOCIAL RELATIONSHIPS

1. Study the life of Joseph in Genesis 37-50. Watch for his attitudes in different situations -- with his father, brothers, Potiphar and his wife, fellow-prisoners, the prison-keeper, Pharaoh, brothers in later life, father in later life. Repeatedly the record says *The Lord was with Joseph.* What are the results?

2. Compare the character traits which Joseph showed with those listed in 2 Peter 1:3-7.

3. God called David *a man after mine own heart* (Acts 13:22). Study David's life to find out what attitudes he displayed, and what he did that could have brought this testimony. David was not perfect, yet God speaks highly of him in several places. Why?

7

Social Institutions - Family

BIBLICAL CONCEPTS

I. **General principles related to the family**
   1. God originated marriage and the family to accomplish His purpose and to meet man's needs.
   2. Relationship to God and obedience to Him must have priority over family relationships.
   3. Right attitude toward God results in right family relationships.
   4. One godly person in a household may bring God's blessing on that home.
   5. A peaceful, quiet atmosphere is characteristic of a godly home.
   6. When strife is continuous between family members, agreement to part company may be the only peaceful solution.
   7. Marriage is not essential to living a godly and useful life; God has a place for single people.

II. **The relationships of marriage**
   1. The marriage relationship is designed to picture the union of Christ and the church.
   2. The marriage relationship is to take precedence over the parent-adult-child relationship.

3. Marriage is meant by God to be permanent -- until the death of one partner.

4. Husband and wife are one in God's eyes, and should be in their own eyes.

5. Husbands and wives are heirs together of God's grace -- equal in importance and potential.

6. The choice of a suitable marriage partner is a matter for prayer and concern, whether for oneself, or for one's children.

7. Family relationships are of special importance to leaders.

III. The responsibilities and privileges of marriage

1. Husbands and wives are expected to enjoy one another.

2. Spouses are to respect one another and consider one another's needs.

3. The headship of the home belongs to the husband and father.

4. The woman in the home is praised by God and appreciated by her husband and family as she develops godly qualities in her life.

5. A man should have only one wife.

6. Sexual activity outside of marriage is condemned by God, and brings with it serious problems within the home.

IV. God's plan for children

1. God's plan is that most couples will have children.

2. Children are a gift from God and therefore to be appreciated.

3. Children are sources of great joy and grief to parents and grandparents.

4. Children are important to God.

5. It is possible to rear children for God, even in a sinful day.

V. Parental responsibility for children

1. God holds parents responsible for their children -- to teach them, to provide for them, to control them, to correct them.

2. Parents and children must have a mutual respect for one another.

3. Parents must be fair in their dealings with their children, not showing favoritism.

4. The lives of parents affect their children and future generations.

VI. Children's responsibility to parents

1. Children are responsible to God, especially as they come to maturity.

2. Children must obey or submit to their parents.

3. Children must accept responsibility for their parents as they grow older.

* * * * * * * *

THE FAMILY: HOW IMPORTANT?

"Civilization varies with the family, and the family with civilization. . . . . Its highest and most complete realization is found where enlightened Christianity prevails; where woman is exalted to her true and lofty place as equal with the man; where husband and wife are one in honor, influence, and affection, and where children are a common bond of care and love . . . . This is the idea of a perfect family."

--William Aikman, 1682-1731.

"We are not born as the partridge in the wood, or the ostrich of the desert, to be scattered everywhere; but we are to be grouped together, and brooded by love, and reared day by day in that first of churches, the family."

--Henry Ward Beecher, 1813-1887.

"As are families, so is society . . . . If well ordered, well instructed, and well governed, they are the springs from which go forth the streams of national greatness and prosperity, of civil order and public happiness."

--William Makepeace Thayer, 1820-1898.

"A hundred men may make an encampment, but it takes a woman to make a home."

--A Chinese Proverb.

"It was the policy of the good old gentleman to make his children feel that home was the happiest place in the world; and I value this delicious home-feeling as one of the choicest gifts a parent can bestow."

--Washington Irving, 1783-1859.

"He is the happiest, be he king or peasant, who finds peace in his home."

--Johann Wolfgang von Goethe, 1749-1832.

"Eighty per cent of our criminals come from unsympathetic homes."

--Hans Christian Andersen, 1805-1875.

BIBLICAL BACKGROUND

I. General principles related to the family

1. God originated marriage and the family to accomplish His purpose and to meet man's needs.

Genesis 1:26, 28; 2:15 - God's purpose

26 And God said, Let us make man in our image, after our likeness: and let them have dominion over the fish . . . fowl . . . cattle . . . all the earth, and over every creeping thing that creepeth upon the earth. 28 And God . . . said unto them, Be fruitful, and multiply, and replenish the earth, and subdue it: and have dominion . . . . 15 And the Lord God took the man, and put him into the garden of Eden to dress it and to keep it.

Genesis 2:18, 20-25 - Man's need

18 And the Lord God said, It is not good that the man should be alone; I will make him an help meet for him. 19 And out of the ground the Lord God formed every beast . . . 20 . . . but for Adam there was not found an help meet for him. 21 And the Lord God caused a deep sleep to fall upon Adam . . . 22 And the rib, which the Lord God had taken from the man, made he

a woman, and brought her unto the man. 23 And Adam said, This is now bone of my bones, and flesh of my flesh . . . . 24 Therefore shall a man leave his father and his mother, and shall cleave unto his wife: and they shall be one flesh.

Psalm 68:6

God setteth the solitary in families . . . .

Proverbs 18:22; 19:14

22 Whoso findeth a wife findeth a good thing, and obtaineth favour of the Lord. 14 . . . A prudent wife is from the Lord.

1 Corinthians 11:8, 9

8 For the man is not of the woman; but the woman of the man. 9 Neither was the man created for the woman; but the woman for the man.

See also Matthew 19:5, 6 and Mark 10:7-9.

2. Relationship to God and obedience to Him must have priority over family relationships.

Genesis 12:1-3

God called Abram to leave his family and homeland to go to a new location unknown to him.

Genesis 22:1-14

For many years God had promised Abraham a son through whom should come One who was to bless all the earth. Now the son, Isaac, had grown to teen-age years, when God called on Abraham to offer him as a sacrifice. Abraham obeyed and God intervened in his behalf.

Deuteronomy 13:6-11

Under the Law, God commanded: *6 If thy brother, the son of thy mother, or thy son, or thy daughter, or the wife of thy bosom, or thy friend . . . entice thee secretly, saying, Let us go and serve other gods . . . 8 Thou shalt not consent . . . neither shall thine eye pity him, neither shalt thou spare, neither shalt thou conceal him: 9 But thou shalt surely kill him; thine hand shall be first upon him to put him to death, and afterwards the hand of all the people.*

Matthew 10:34-37

37 He that loveth father or mother more than me is not worthy of me: and he that loveth son or daughter more than me is not worthy of me.

Matthew 12:46-50; also Mark 3:31-35; Luke 8:19-21

When Jesus' mother and brothers wished to speak to the Lord, He said: *48 . . . Who is my mother? and who are my brethren? 49 . . . Behold my mother and my brethren! 50 For whosoever shall do the will of my Father which is in heaven, the same is my brother, sister, and mother.* These words were spoken as He stretched out His hand toward his disciples.

Matthew 19:29

Every one that hath forsaken houses, or brethren, or sisters, or father, or mother, or wife, or children, or lands, for my name's sake, shall receive an hundred-fold, and shall inherit everlasting life.

Luke 14:26

The love of a disciple for the Lord is meant to be so great that, in comparison, love for family members seems like hate.

3. Right attitude toward God results in right family relationships.

Leviticus 19:2, 3

Showing proper respect for parents is part of being set apart for God. *2 . . . Ye shall be holy: for I the Lord your God am holy. 3 Ye shall fear every man his mother, and his father, and keep my sabbaths . . . .*

Psalm 128:1-6

1 Blessed is every one that feareth the Lord; that walketh in his ways . . . . 3 Thy wife shall be as a fruitful vine by the sides of thine house: thy children *like olive plants round about thy table . . . . 6 Yea, thou shalt see thy children's children, and peace upon Israel.*

Acts 16:30-34

When the Philippian jailor believed on Christ, he and his family ministered to the physical needs of Paul and Silas. There was oneness in the family.

4. One godly person in a household may bring God's blessing on that home.

Genesis 39:5

Joseph was a slave in Potiphar's house, yet he brought blessing. *5 . . . The Lord blessed the Egyptian's house for Joseph's sake; and the blessing of the Lord was upon all that he had in the house, and in the field.*

Exodus 18:9-12

As Jethro, a Midianite priest, observed his son-in-law, Moses, he was convinced of the sovereignty and power of God.

1 Corinthians 7:13, 14

In a divided household, where the wife is a believer and the husband an unbeliever, the woman is told not to leave him, because *14 the unbelieving husband is sanctified by the wife.* Also it is said of the children, *Now are they holy.*

1 Peter 3:1

Wives are commanded to be in subjection to their own husbands so that *1 . . . If any obey not the word, they also may without the word be won by the conversation* [or lifestyle] *of the wives.*

"The words that a father speaks to his children in the privacy of home are not heard by the world, but, as in whispering galleries, they are clearly heard at the end, and by posterity."

--Jean Paul Richter, 1763-1826.

5. A peaceful, quiet atmosphere is characteristic of a godly home.

Genesis 45:4-9; 50:19-21

Willingness to forgive one another, and to see God's hand in the events of life can knit a family together. Joseph refused to blame his brothers for all that they had done to him many years before. Instead he gave God the glory for what He had done, and loaded his brothers with benefits.

Proverbs 11:29; 15:7, 25, 27; 18:19; 19:13; 21:9, 19

Here God through Solomon warns of a number of actions and attitudes which destroy the peaceful atmosphere of a godly home: a troubler, a greedy member, hatred, pride, an offended brother, contentiousness, a brawling woman. Some of the statements are very emphatic; for instance, (19:13) . . . *The contentions of a wife are a continual dropping.* Also, (15:17) *Better is a dinner of herbs where love is than a stalled ox and hatred therewith.* (21:9) *It is better to dwell in a corner of the housetop, than with a brawling woman in a wide house.*

6. When strife is continuous between family members, agreement to part company may be the only peaceful solution.

Genesis 13:5-18; 14:11-16

God blessed Abram after he generously gave Lot first choice of the land and the two men separated, with their shepherds and flocks. Later Abram showed his continued concern for his nephew by rescuing him from his captors. God blessed this attitude and action on Abram's part (14:18-20).

Genesis 21:10-12

God approved of the separation of Hagar and Ishmael from Abraham's household.

Genesis 31:1-3, 13, 17-22

God directed Jacob, with his family, to leave Laban when they could no longer get along together.

7. Marriage is not essential to living a godly and useful life; God has a place for single people.

Isaiah 56:4, 5

God promised special blessing to one group in Isaiah's day: *4 For thus saith the Lord unto the eunuchs that keep my sabbaths, and choose the things that please me, and take hold of my covenant; 5 Even unto them will I give in mine house and within my walls a place and a name better than of sons and of daughters: I will give them an everlasting name, that shall not be cut off.*

Jeremiah 16:1-4

There are times when God directs to a life without a spouse and children. God spoke to Jeremiah: *2 Thou shalt not take thee a wife, neither shalt thou have sons or daughters in this place.* In the following verses He explains of the coming judgment.

Matthew 19:10-12

After Jesus' discussion with the Pharisees about the permanence of marriage: *10 His disciples say unto him, If the case of the man be so with his wife, it is not good to marry. 11 But he said unto them, All men cannot receive this saying, save they to whom it is given. 12 For there are some eunuchs, which were so born from their mother's womb: and there are some eunuchs, which were made eunuchs of men: and there be eunuchs, which have made themselves eunuchs for the kingdom of heaven's sake. He that is able to receive it, let him receive it.*

1 Corinthians 7:7-9, 25-38

In the light of the coming persecution and then the coming of the Lord, Paul urges the unmarried to remain unmarried, even as he is; yet he recognizes that this is not God's will for all. *7 . . . But every man hath his proper gift of God, one after this manner, and another after that.* The same thought occurs in 25-29.

Verses 32-34 show some differences between the single and the married life. *32 . . . He that is unmarried careth for the things that belong to the Lord, how he may please the Lord: 33 But he that is married careth for the things that are of the world, how he may please his wife. 34 There is difference also between a wife and a virgin. The unmarried woman careth for the things of the Lord, that she may be holy both in body and in spirit: but she that is married careth for the things of the world, how she may please her husband. 24 And this I speak for your own profit . . . that ye may attend upon the Lord without distraction.*

1 Corinthians 9:5, 6

Paul points out that both he and Barnabas were unmarried, but other apostles were married. God has a place for both.

Revelation 14:1-5

During the Tribulation period, God has a special work to be done by 144,000 Jews chosen by Him. All will be chaste, unmarried men.

"In full and glad surrender we give ourselves to thee,
Thine utterly and only and evermore to be!
O Son of God, who lovest us, we will be thine alone,
And all we are and all we have shall henceforth
    be thine own."
        --Frances Ridley Havergal.

II. The relationships of marriage

1. The marriage relationship is designed to picture the union of Christ and the church.

Ephesians 5:22-32

Several aspects of the union of Christ and the church are pictured: the submission of the church to Christ its head, the sacrificial love of Christ for the church, the desire of Christ to perfect and sanctify the church, the union between Christ and the church which makes other relationships less important.

2. The marriage relationship is to take precedence over the parent-adult-child relationship.

Genesis 2:24

Adam speaking, just after the creation of the woman: *24 Therefore shall a man leave his father and his mother, and shall cleave unto his wife: and they shall be one flesh.*

Matthew 19:5; Mark 10:6, 7

Jesus answering the Pharisees as they questioned Him about divorce: *6 But from the beginning of the creation God made them male and female. 7 For this cause shall a man leave his father and mother, and cleave to his wife.*

See also Ephesians 5:31.

3. Marriage is meant by God to be permanent -- until the death of one partner.

Matthew 5:32; Luke 16:18

Under the Law, and in the Kingdom, to divorce a wife not guilty of fornication was to make her an adulteress; so also in 19:9. Also, to marry a divorced woman was to commit adultery. In other words, divorce was not approved under the Law.

Matthew 19:5, 6; Mark 10:8, 9

Jesus speaking to the Pharisees: *5 . . . They twain shall be one flesh. 6 Wherefore they are no more twain, but one flesh. What therefore God hath joined together, let not man put asunder.*

Romans 7:2, 3

Here the law concerning the permanence of marriage is used to illustrate the relationship between law and grace. *2 For the woman which hath an husband is bound by the law to her husband so long as he liveth; but if the husband be dead, she is loosed from the law of her husband.*

1 Corinthians 7:10-16

Written to Gentile Christians, three things are said about the permanence of marriage as God intends it: (1) a wife should not depart from her husband, and a husband should not put away his wife; (2) if a wife departs, she should not marry another man; (3) if a believer has an unbelieving spouse who is willing to continue, the believer should not separate.

1 Corinthians 7:39

The wife is bound by the law as long as her husband liveth; but if her husband be dead, she is at liberty to be married to whom she will; only in the Lord.

4. Husband and wife are one in God's eyes, and should be in their own eyes.

Genesis 2:22-25

23 And Adam said, This is now bone of my bones, and flesh of my flesh: she shall be called Woman, because she was taken out of man. 24 . . . They shall be one flesh.

Genesis 3:22-24

When God looked for man in the garden, and later when He expelled Adam and Eve from the garden, He spoke of the man, but obviously meant both of them. *22 And the Lord said, Behold, the man is become as one of us . . . 23 Therefore the Lord God sent him from the garden . . . . 24 So he drove out the man . . . .* In 4:1, they were obviously together.

Matthew 19:5, 6

5 . . . For this cause shall a man leave father and mother, and shall cleave to his wife: and they twain shall be one flesh? 6 Wherefore they are no more twain, but one flesh.

1 Corinthians 11:11, 12

11 Nevertheless neither is the man without the woman, neither the woman without the man, in the Lord. 12 For as the woman is of the man, even so is the man also by the woman; but all things of God.

Ephesians 5:28-31

28 So ought men to love their wives as their own bodies. He that loveth his wife loveth himself.

5. Husbands and wives are heirs together of God's grace -- equal in importance and potential.

Matthew 28:5-10

It was women who were commissioned to go tell the disciples and Peter that He had risen. Note that they were commissioned by both the angel and by the Lord Himself. Also Mark 16:1, 6, 7; Luke 24:10, 11; John 20:11, 17, 18.

Acts 1:13, 14

The women were with the men in the upper room in prayer and later in preaching.

Acts 2:16-18

In Peter's sermon at Pentecost he referred back to Joel 2:28-32 in which the prophecy was made that God would pour out His Spirit on both men and women. In v. 16, he identifies the day of Pentecost with part of the fulfillment of Joel 2.

Acts 8:3, 4

When Saul persecuted the church, men and women went everywhere preaching the Word.

Romans 16:1-15; Hebrews 11:4-40

Note the mixture of names of both sexes; note also the specific commendations.

Galatians 3:26-28

26 For ye are all the children of God by faith in Christ Jesus. 27 For as many of you as have been baptized into Christ have put on Christ. 28 There is neither Jew nor Greek . . . neither male nor female: for ye are all one in Christ Jesus.

1 Peter 3:1, 2

Wives have the privilege of winning their husbands to the Lord by their godly conduct.

1 Peter 3:7

Likewise, ye husbands, dwell with them according to knowledge . . . as being heirs together of the grace of life . . . .

6. The choice of a suitable marriage partner is a matter for prayer and concern, whether for oneself, or for one's children.

a. Specific directions from God

Exodus 34:15, 16

God warned Moses against covenants, marriage, or other relationships with heathen nations. *15 Lest thou make a covenant . . . and they go a whoring after their gods, and do sacrifice unto their gods . . . 16 And thou take of their daughters unto thy sons and their daughters go a whoring after their gods . . . .*

Leviticus 18:6-18

Under the Law, marriage to a near relative was forbidden.

Deuteronomy 7:2-6

God commands Israel not to marry the heathen, nor to allow their children to do so, lest they turn from God. Also Joshua 23:11-13; Judges 3:6, 7.

Ezra 9:12

Ezra reviews God's command which Israel had broken again and again: *12 Now therefore give not your daughters unto their sons, neither take their daughters unto your sons, nor seek their peace or their wealth for ever: that ye may be strong, and eat the good of the land, and leave it for an inheritance to your children for ever.*

1 Corinthians 7:39

The widow is instructed that she is free to marry whomever she wills in the Lord.

2 Corinthians 6:14-18

14 Be ye not unequally yoked together with unbelievers: for what fellowship hath righteousness with unrighteousness?

b. Examples

Genesis 24

Abraham's great care in the choice of a bride for Isaac.

Genesis 38

Judah married a Canaanite. Their firstborn, Er, was so wicked that God slew him (v. 7); the second son, Onan, also was slain by the Lord for spilling sperm cells, refusing to raise up seed for his brother, as the

Law required (8-10). Read the rest of the sordid family account in 11-30. Serious consequences follow disobedience to God.

Judges 14:1-20; 15:1, 2, 6, 12, 13; 16:1

Study the results of Samson's marriage to a Philistine.

1 Kings 11:1-8

1 But king Solomon loved many strange women . . . 2 Of the nations concerning which the Lord said unto the children of Israel, Ye shall not go in to them, neither shall they come in unto you: for surely they will turn away your heart after their gods: Solomon clave unto these in love. Verses 4-8 tell the results.

Nehemiah 13:23-28

Nehemiah rebukes the Jews who had married foreign wives, reminding them of the problems and sins of Solomon from his unbelieving wives. One result was that their children were unable to speak their own language properly (v. 24).

7. Family relationships are of special importance to leaders.

Deuteronomy 17:14-20

God lists here a number of prohibitions for a future king of Israel. Among them: *17 Neither shall he multiply wives to himself, that his heart turn not away . . . .*

Esther 1:10-22

Though godly people would probably agree that Queen Vashti was justified in refusing the king's request, here is recognition on the part of heathen leaders of the power of example, and the importance of the husband-wife relationship for one in charge of a nation.

1 Timothy 3:2, 4, 5, 11, 12; also Titus 1:7

In listing the qualifications for pastors and deacons much is said about their family relationships: *2 A bishop then must be blameless, the husband of one wife . . . 4 One that ruleth well his own house, having his children in subjection with all gravity; 5 (For if a man know not how to rule his own house, how shall he take care of the church of God?) 11 Even so must their* [i.e., deacons] *wives be grave, not slanderers, sober, faithful in all things. 12 Let the deacons be the husbands of one wife, ruling their children and their own houses well.*

III. The responsibilities and privileges of marriage

1. Husbands and wives are expected to enjoy one another.

Genesis 2:23-25

Man and wife, before the entrance of sin, were entirely comfortable in the presence of one another. *25 And they were both naked, the man and his wife, and were not ashamed.*

Deuteronomy 24:5

Under the Law, God directed that a newly married couple were to spend much time together: *5 When a man hath taken a new wife, he shall not go out to war, neither shall he be charged with any business: but he shall be free at home one year, and shall cheer up his wife which he hath taken.*

Proverbs 5:18, 19

18 Let thy fountain be blessed: and rejoice with the

wife of thy youth. 19 Let her be as the loving hind and pleasant roe; let her breasts satisfy thee at all times; and be thou ravished always with her love.

Song of Solomon

Here is a picture of the delight of a bride and groom, or husband and wife, rightly related to one another. Several characteristics are described:

--their desire to be close together (1:2, 7, 13; 2:10, 14, 16, etc.)

--their mutual feelings of unworthiness of the other's love (1:5; 2:2)

--their desire to extol the other's virtues (1:8-10, 15, 16; 2:3, 4, 8; 4:1-16; 5:10-16, etc.)

--their fruitful, fragrant life together (4:11-16)
--their recognition of the headship of the husband (3:6-11)
--their desire to belong to one another. *My beloved is mine, and I am his . . .* (2:16; 6:3, 10).

Ecclesiastes 9:9

Live joyfully with the wife whom thou lovest all the days of the life of thy vanity, which he hath given

thee under the sun . . . .

1 Corinthians 7:2-5

Marriage partners are warned against refusing to satisfy one another, except for brief times of fasting and prayer, and that by agreement.

Hebrews 13:4

Marriage is honourable in all, and the bed undefiled, but whoremongers and adulterers God will judge.

2. Spouses are to respect one another and consider one another's needs.

Genesis 2:18

God's purpose was that the woman should be a help to the man.

Deuteronomy 21:10-14

A man who took a woman captured in war to be his wife, and then found he had no delight in her, was still to be considerate of her.

Deuteronomy 22:13-19

Under the Law, a husband who ruined his wife's reputation morally was to be chastened by the elders of the city, and fined.

Proverbs 12:4

A virtuous woman is a crown to her husband: but she that maketh ashamed is as rottenness in his bones.

Proverbs 14:1

A wise woman buildeth her house: but the foolish plucketh it down with her hands.

Proverbs 18:22; 19:14

22 Whoso findeth a wife findeth a good thing, and obtaineth favour of the Lord. 14 . . . A prudent wife is from the Lord. If these statements are true, it is because the wife contributes to her husband's happiness.

Proverbs 31:10-31

The virtuous wife described here contributes much to the home: her husband can trust her; she will do him good; she is industrious and thrifty; she is considerate of the poor around her; she clothes her family adequately; she speaks with wisdom and kindness; she is respected and appreciated by her husband and children.

1 Corinthians 7:3-5

Marriage partners are to recognize the relationship to one another physically, and to meet one another's

needs, in order that neither may be tempted to seek satisfaction elsewhere.

Ephesians 5:22-33

Husbands are to love their wives as their own bodies, and wives to submit and reverence, or respect, their husbands. Also Col. 3:19.

Titus 2:3-5

One of the important duties of older women is to teach younger women to live holy lives, to love their husbands and their children, to be obedient to their husbands in order that God may be honored.

1 Peter 3:1-7

Believing wives are to be concerned about their unsaved or wayward husbands and live before them in a way that is a good testimony; husbands are to be understanding of their wives, recognizing their limited physical strength, but recognizing their joint heirship in Christ.

Examples:

Genesis 21:10-12

God told Abraham to listen to Sarah when she asked him to cast out Hagar and Ishmael. There must be a mutual respect that leads to listening to the other.

Genesis 20:1-18

Relationships must be honestly represented. Abraham lied about his relationship to Sarah. As a result she became part of a heathen harem, and Abraham was finally rebuked by the Philistine king, Abimelech. A ruined testimony! See also 26:6-32, for Isaac's experience -- like father, like son.

Genesis 27:1-46

Lack of honesty and oneness between Rebekah and Isaac caused disaster in the home -- deceitfulness, hatred, separation. Reconciliation of Jacob and Esau came after many years of mistrust.

"The kindest and the happiest pair will find occasion to forbear; and something, every day they live, to pity and perhaps forgive."

--William Cowper, 1731-1800.

3. The headship of the home belongs to the husband and father.

a. Husbands are responsible for their wives and children.

Genesis 2:20-23

Before the Fall, there are indications of the headship of the man. God made man before woman; He made woman to prevent his loneliness and provide human fellowship for Adam. Also, it was to Adam God spoke when He found them hiding in the garden; He held Adam accountable (3:8, 9, 17). Also 1 Tim. 2:13, 14.

Genesis 3:16

As a result of man's sin, God pronounced that the husband would rule over the wife.

Genesis 18:19

God's testimony concerning Abraham: *19 For I know him, that he will command his children and his household after him, and they shall keep the way of the Lord, to do justice and judgment . . . .* Contrast 1 Samuel 3:13.

Numbers 30:6-8, 10-15

Under the Law, a husband was responsible for the vows his wife might make. He could veto the vow, but if he did not object, he was equally responsible for her keeping the vow. Likewise with a single daughter living at home, her father was responsible.

1 Corinthians 11:3

. . . The head of every man is Christ; and the head of the woman is the man; and the head of Christ is God.

Ephesians 5:22-33

Husbands are to love as Christ loves the church, and give of themselves as He did; they are to be concerned with the nourishing and cleansing of their wives spiritually; they are to give their wives preference over their parents. Also Col. 3:18, 19.

1 Peter 3:7

. . . Ye husbands, dwell with them according to knowledge, giving honour unto the wife, as unto the weaker vessel, and as being heirs together of the grace of life; that your prayers be not hindered.

b. Wives are responsible to submit to their husbands.

Genesis 3:16

God spoke specifically to Eve, saying: *16 . . . Thy desire shall be to thy husband, and he shall rule over thee.*

Esther 1:20-22

Even in the heathen world of Persia, the responsibility of wives to give honor to their husbands was recognized, so much so that disobedience on Vashti's part, even to an unreasonable request, was the basis for her being set aside, and a decree to the whole empire that *all the wives shall give to their husbands honour, both to great and small.*

1 Corinthians 14:34, 35

In the services of the church women are instructed to let the men do the speaking. Wives are to seek further information from their own husbands, rather than asking questions in church. Also 1 Tim. 2:11-14.

Ephesians 5:21-33

Mutual submission is to characterize believers in many relationships, as shown in these verses and in chapter 6. In particular, wives are told: *22 Submit yourselves unto your own husbands, as unto the Lord. 23 For the husband is the head of the wife, even as Christ is the head of the church: and he is the saviour of the body. 24 Therefore as the church is subject unto Christ, so let the wives be to their own husbands in every thing. 33 . . . The wife see that she reverence her husband.* Also Col. 3:18.

1 Peter 3:1-6

1 Likewise, ye wives, be in subjection to your own husbands; that, if any obey not the word, they also may without the word be won by the conversation [or behavior] of the wives. The following verses detail that behavior which will be a testimony to an unsaved husband.

4. The woman in the home is praised by God and appreciated by her husband and family as she develops godly qualities in her life.

Proverbs 11-30

The book of Proverbs provides a rich source of help in determining what qualities a wife and mother should cultivate if she is to be a blessing to her household. Some are quoted here, both negatives and positives:

11:16 A gracious woman retaineth honour. 11:22 As a jewel of gold in a swine's snout, so is a fair woman which is without discretion. 12:4 A virtuous woman is a crown to her husband: but she that maketh ashamed is as rottenness in his bones. 15:17 Better is a dinner of herbs where love is, than a stalled ox and hatred therewith. 19:13 The contentions of a wife are a continual dropping. 14 . . . A prudent wife is from the Lord. 21:9 It is better to dwell in a corner of the housetop, than with a brawling woman in a wide house. 19 It is better to dwell in the wilderness, than with a contentious and an angry woman. 27:15 A continual dropping in a very rainy day and a contentious woman are alike. 30:21, 23 For three things the earth is disquieted, and for four which it cannot bear . . . For an odious woman when she is married . . . .

PROJECT: Study Proverbs 31:10-31. Make a list of all the qualities of womanhood that are here recognized by God and by other members of a family. Also write a paraphrase of this passage, using present-day language and activities. Write it in such a way that it would be suitable for use on an occasion honoring wives or mothers.

1 Timothy 2:9, 10

In like manner also, that women adorn themselves in modest apparel, with shamefacedness and sobriety; not with broided hair, or gold, or pearls, or costly array; 10 But (which becometh women professing godliness) with good works.

PROJECT: Using 1 Timothy 5:3-10, make a list in everyday English of the qualifications of a widow who was to be helped by the early church. What qualities were considered evidence of a woman's genuine love for the Lord?

1 Peter 3:1-4

Note these qualities: *subjection . . . chaste conversation* [way of life] *. . . fear* [or reverence] *. . . whose adorning let it not be that outward adorning of plaiting the hair, and of wearing of gold, or putting on of apparel; But let it be the hidden man of the heart, in that which is not corruptible, even the ornament of a meek and quiet spirit, which is in the sight of God of great price.* Note the example of Old Testament women, in verses 5, 6.

5. A man should have only one wife.

Leviticus 18:18; 20:14

Under the Law, a man was forbidden to marry two sisters, or a woman and her mother. The penalty in the second case is stated as death by burning for all three persons.

Deuteronomy 17:17

A future king of Israel was forbidden to multiply wives, for fear they would lead him away from God.

Matthew 19:4, 5; Mark 10:2-8

Jesus condemns a multiplicity of wives, even when a man puts one away in order to enjoy the next one.

1 Timothy 3:2, 12; Titus 1:6

A pastor or deacon in the New Testament church must not have more than one wife.

Examples:

Genesis 16:1-8; 21:9-11

Abraham's relationship with Hagar as a second wife created a variety of problems and jealousies, some of which are with us today.

See also other accounts of bigamy or polygamy and their results in the following passages: Genesis 29:30-34, Jacob; Judges 8:30 and Chapter 9, Gideon; 1 Samuel 1:4-7, Elkanah; 1 Chronicles 11:21, Rehoboam; 1 Kings 11:1-8, Solomon.

6. Sexual activity outside of marriage is condemned by God, and brings with it serious problems within the home.

Exodus 20:14; Deuteronomy 5:18

The seventh commandment: *14 Thou shalt not commit adultery.*

Leviticus 18:20; 20:10-12

20 Moreover thou shalt not lie carnally with thy neighbor's wife, to defile thyself with her.

2 Samuel 11, and 12:1-23

God condemned David's sin with Bathsheba, though he was the king. David repented and God still used him.

1 Corinthians 5:1-11

Paul instructed the church at Corinth to discipline a man guilty of fornication.

1 Corinthians 6:13-20

13 . . . Now the body is not for fornication, but for the Lord; and the Lord for the body. 16 What? know ye not that he which is joined to an harlot is one body? for two, saith he, shall be one flesh. 18 Flee fornication . . . . 19 What? know ye not that your body is the temple of the Holy Ghost which is in you, which ye have of God, and ye are not your own? 20 ... Therefore glorify God in your body ....

Galatians 5:19-21; Ephesians 5:3, 5; Colossians 3:5; 1 Thessalonians 4:3, 4; Hebrews 13:4, and many other passages.

PROJECT: For a study of the effects of adultery on the home, consult a topical Bible, under the heading Adultery, looking for instances of its occurrence.

Study the passages indicated to determine the results.

NOTE: Irregularities in sexual activity are not usually considered in the social sciences, and are therefore not included here. Biblical teaching related to them, as well as more detail concerning this whole area, is found in Volume 4 of this series, *Fine Arts and Health*, chapter 5, Sex Education.

IV. God's plan for children

1. God's plan is that most couples will have children.

Genesis 1:28; 3:20; 9:1, 7

God's original command was *28 ... Be fruitful, and multiply, and replenish the earth. ... 20 Adam called his wife's name Eve; because she was the mother of all living.* After the Flood, God said to Noah and his sons, *7 And you, be ye fruitful, and multiply; bring forth abundantly in the earth, and multiply therein.*

Psalm 113:9

He [God] maketh the barren woman to keep house, *and to be a joyful mother of children.*

Psalm 127:3-5; 128:3, 6

Children, in Scripture, are everywhere seen as a blessing from the Lord, and much to be desired.

1 Timothy 5:14

Young widows are urged to marry again and bear children.

2. Children are a gift from God and therefore to be appreciated.

Genesis 4:1, 25

Eve recognized that her sons came from the Lord. So did Leah when Reuben was born (29:32) and later as she and Rachel talked about their condition (30:2-24); Esau credited God with his children, as he came to meet Jacob (33:5); Joseph, presenting his sons to his father said, *These are my sons whom God hath given me in this place* (48:9).

Ruth 4:13-17

Boaz and Ruth, Naomi, and the neighbor women recognized God's gift of Obed to the couple and to the grandmother.

Job 1:21; 42:10-16

Job, when stripped of everything, still recognized the fact that it was God who had given both his children and his material goods, and now had taken them away. At the end, he recognized the Lord's goodness as well.

Psalm 127:3-5

3 Lo, children are an heritage of the Lord: and the fruit of the womb is his reward. 4 As arrows are in the hand of a mighty man; so are children of the youth. 5 Happy is the man that hath his quiver full of them: they shall not be ashamed, but they shall speak with the enemies in the gate.

3. Children are sources of great joy and grief to parents and grandparents.

Proverbs 10:1

... A wise son maketh a glad father: but a foolish son is the heaviness of his mother. Also 15:20.

Proverbs 17:6, 21, 25

6 Children's children are the crown of old men; and the glory of children are their fathers. A mutual delight! *21 He that begetteth a fool doeth it to his sorrow: and the father of a fool hath no joy. 25 A foolish son is a grief to his father, and bitterness to her that bare him.*

Proverbs 19:13, 26

13 A foolish son is the calamity of his father .... 26 He that wasteth his father, and chaseth away his mother, is a son that causeth shame, and bringeth reproach.

Proverbs 23:15, 16, 24, 25

15 My son, if thine heart be wise, my heart shall rejoice, even mine. 16 Yea, my reins shall rejoice when thy lips speak right things. Also 27:11.

Examples of grief:

Genesis 27

Jacob deceives his father, Isaac; Isaac is heart-broken and angry; Esau plans to kill his brother; Jacob has to flee and the family is separated for many years.

2 Samuel 15:14-18

Absalom is a source of grief to his father, David. Finally David and his followers have to flee from Jerusalem because of Absalom's takeover.

4. Children are important to God.

Exodus 1:16-21

Pharaoh orders the killing of Hebrew baby boys; the midwives fear God and refuse to obey the king. God honors their actions. Infanticide is sin in God's eyes!

Exodus 2:2-10

Moses' parents refuse to follow Pharaoh's orders and instead save Moses. God preserves Moses and uses him greatly.

Leviticus 18:21; 20:1-5; Deuteronomy 18:9, 10

No Israelite child was to be given to the heathen god, Molech.

Matthew 18:1-10

Jesus says several things here about the importance of a child: his humble attitude is a pattern for adults who would enter God's kingdom; one who receives a child in His name receives Him; one who offends a believing child is worthy of death by drowning; children are not to be despised.

Luke 18:15-17

Jesus makes it clear that children are important enough for Him to be involved with them. He wants them to come to Him.

5. It is possible to rear children for God, even in a sinful day.

Genesis 6:9-12, 18; 7:1; 8:16-18

Noah's parents did it. So did Noah. His teaching and his life must have taught well for those three sons to remain true to God and enter the Ark, when all the world was wicked around them.

Daniel 1:3-6, 8-21

Daniel and his friends had parents, whom we do not

know, who brought them up to be godly men, even as captive in a strange land.

2 Timothy 1:3-6

Timothy's mother and grandmother so conveyed their faith to him that Paul was proud to associate with him.

V. Parental responsibility for children

1. God holds parents responsible for their children -- to teach them, to provide for them, to control them, to correct them.

a. Parents must teach their children.

Exodus 10:1, 2

Part of God's reason for the plagues was *2 That thou mayest tell in the ears of thy son, and of thy son's son, what things I have wrought in Egypt, and my signs which I have done among them; that ye may know how that I am the Lord.* See also 12:24-27; 13:8-16, concerning the Passover and redemption money. See also Joshua 4:6, 7.

Deuteronomy 4:9, 10

Moses reminds Israel of his earlier exhortation to teach their children and grandchildren what He had done for them, and to tell them again about God's calling them together on Mount Horeb, when He gave the Commandments.

Deuteronomy 6:6-9, 20-23; 11:18-21

In Israel, God commanded that there should be daily, casual and constant teaching: *7 Thou shalt teach them diligently unto thy children, and shalt talk of them when thou sittest in thy house, and when thou walkest by the way, and when thou liest down, and when thou riseth up.*

Psalm 78:5-8

God explains how he established a testimony and a law in Israel and commanded that parents should make them known to their children, and they in turn to their children. The purpose is given: *6 That the generation to come might know them . . . 7 That they might set their hope in God, and not forget the works of God, but keep his commandments; 8 And might not be as their fathers, a stubborn and rebellious generation; that set not their heart aright, and whose spirit was not stedfast with God.*

Proverbs 4:1-4, 10, 11; 22:6

1 Hear, ye children, the instruction of a father, and attend to know understanding. 2 For I give you good doctrine, forsake ye not my law. 22:6 Train up a child in the way he should go: and when he is old, he will not depart from it.

Ephesians 6:4

And ye fathers, provoke not your children to wrath: but bring them up in the nurture and admonition of the Lord.

b. Parents must provide for their children.

1 Samuel 2:19

An example. Hannah continued to bring coats for Samuel though he was away serving the Lord.

Proverbs 13:22

A good man leaveth an inheritance to his children's children . . . .

Luke 15:20-24

The prodigal's father provided forgiveness and restoration, even after selfishness and wastefulness; and forgiveness included food and clothing and a celebration.

2 Corinthians 12:14

Paul, in speaking of his not wanting to be a burden to the church at Corinth, says: *14 . . . The children ought not to lay up for the parents, but the parents for the children.*

1 Timothy 5:8

Though this passage is dealing with widows in particular, the truth doubtless applies to other family members. *8 But if any provide not for his own, and specially for those of his own house, he hath denied the faith, and is worse than an infidel.*

c. Parents must control their children.

Exodus 20:10; Deuteronomy 5:14

Under the Law, it was the parents' responsibility to see that their children kept the Sabbath day.

Numbers 30:3-5

A father was responsible for the vows his daughter made while she was still under his care. She must submit to him.

Deuteronomy 21:18-21

A mother and father who could not control a rebellious son, undoubtedly an older teen, were required under the Law to take him to the elders of the city for stoning. The initiative was to be theirs!

Deuteronomy 32:46

Moses' last counsel to Israel before his death included these words: *46 . . . Set your hearts unto all the words which I testify among you this day, which ye shall command your children to observe to do, all the words of this law.*

1 Timothy 3:4, 5, 12; Titus 1:6

Only a father whose children are under his control is qualified to be a pastor or deacon.

d. Parents must correct their children.

Proverbs 13:24

He that spareth his rod hateth his son: but he that loveth him chasteneth him betimes.

Proverbs 19:18

Chasten thy son while there is hope, and let not thy soul spare for his crying.

Proverbs 22:15

Foolishness is bound in the heart of a child; but the rod of correction shall drive it far from him. Also 23:13, 14.

Proverbs 29:15, 17

15 The rod and reproof give wisdom: but a child left to himself bringeth his mother to shame. 17 Correct thy son, and he shall give thee rest; yea, he shall give delight unto thy soul.

1 Thessalonians 2:11, 12

Paul treated the Thessalonians as a father would a son: *11 . . . We exhorted and comforted and charged every one of you, as a father doth his children, 12 That ye would walk worthy . . . .*

e. Parents should perform their parental duties out of love for their children, picturing the Lord's love for His own.

Psalm 103:13, 14

13 Like as a father pitieth his children, so the Lord pitieth them that fear him. 14 For he knoweth our frame; he remembereth that we are dust.

Proverbs 3:11, 12

11 My son, despise not the chastening of the Lord; neither be weary of his correction: 12 For whom the Lord loveth he correcteth; even as a father the son in whom he delighteth.

Isaiah 49:15

Can a woman forget her sucking child, that she should not have compassion on the son of her womb? yea, they may forget, yet will I not forget thee. Also 66:13.

Luke 11:11-13

13 If ye then, being evil, know how to give good gifts unto your children: how much more shall your heavenly Father give the Holy Spirit to them that ask him?

Hebrews 12:6-11

7 If ye endure chastening, God dealeth with you as with sons; for what son is he whom the father chasteneth not? 8 But if ye be without chastisement, whereof all are partakers, then are ye bastards, and not sons. 11 Now no chastening for the present seemeth to be joyous, but grievous: nevertheless afterward it yieldeth the peaceable fruit of righteous-ness unto them which are exercised thereby.

PROJECT: Hunt out Bible examples of families in which the members had good and bad relationships with one another, especially in the parent-child relationship. List both positive and negative comments about these families. Here are some starters: Genesis 18:19; 1 Samuel 2:12-29 and 3:13; 1 Samuel 8:3-5; 1 Kings 1:5, 6; 1 Chronicles 22:1-19 and 28:1-21 (note David's preparations for Solomon); Job 1:5.

2. Parents and children must have a mutual respect for one another.

a. Children must give their parents a place of honor and respect.

Exodus 20:12; Deuteronomy 5:16; Matthew 15:4; 19:19; Mark 7:10

12 Honour thy father and thy mother: that thy days may be long upon the land which the Lord thy God giveth thee. 16 . . . and that it may go well with thee . . . .

Exodus 21:15, 17; 20:9; Proverbs 20:20

Under the Law, either striking a parent, or cursing one, was to be punished by death.

Leviticus 18:7; see also Genesis 9:22-25

Children, apparently at any age, were to allow their parents privacy, not intruding on their nakedness.

Leviticus 19:3, 32

In verse 3, the Lord relates respect for parents to the fact that He is holy. *32 Thou shalt rise up before the hoary head, and honour the face of the old man, and fear the Lord your God.* The emphasis here is on respect for age and maturity.

Deuteronomy 27:16

In listing the curses that would come on Israel if they departed from the Lord after entering the land, there is this statement: *16 Cursed be he that setteth light by* [dishonoureth, in *New Scofield Reference Edition*] *his father or his mother . . . .*

1 Kings 2:19

Solomon's example even as the king. When his mother entered to request a favor, he rose to meet her, bowed to her, and set her a place of honor.

1 Kings 8:17-20

At the dedication of the new temple, King Solomon gave credit to his father, David.

Proverbs 19:26; 23:22; 28:24; 30:17

God uses some plain language in emphasizing the many kinds of respect that should be shown to parents. *26 He that wasteth his father, and chaseth away his mother, is a son that causeth shame, and bringeth reproach. 22 Hearken unto thy father that begat thee, and despise not thy mother when she is old. 24 Whoso robbeth his father or his mother, and saith, It is no transgression; the same is the companion of a destroyer. 17 The eye that mocketh at his father, and despiseth to obey his mother, the ravens of the valley shall pick it out, and the young eagles shall eat it.*

Jeremiah 35:18, 19

God promised special blessing to the Rechabites because they obeyed their father's command.

Malachi 1:6

God uses the typical son's honoring his father to illustrate the incongruity of Israel's disobedience in failing to honor Him, the heavenly Father.

Ephesians 6:1-3

1 Children, obey your parents in the Lord: for this is right. 2 Honour thy father and mother; which is the first commandment with promise; 3 That it may be well with thee, and thou mayest live long on the earth.

Colossians 3:20

Children, obey your parents in all things: for this is well pleasing unto the Lord.

1 Timothy 5:1

In instructing Timothy, as a young pastor, Paul urges him to entreat an older man as he would his father, rather than rebuke him.

Hebrews 12:9

God instructs us here concerning His chastening and the results which should come from it. In doing so, He reminds us that human parents chasten for our good and we respect or reverence them. So should we with the Father.

b. Parents must be sensitive to the needs and feelings of their children.

Ruth 1:11-19

A wonderful example of the mother-in-law showing

consideration for the feelings and needs of her daughters-in-law. Naomi was willing to go alone back to Israel, recognizing the fact that the younger women might prefer to marry again among their own people. Her generosity was not lost on Ruth.

Psalm 103:13, 14

God likens His concern for us to that of a father, one who understands his children's limitations. *13 Like as a father pitieth his children, so the Lord pitieth them that fear him. 14 For he knoweth our frame; he remembereth that we are dust.*

Matthew 18:6, 10

Offending a child, or despising a little one, is considered by God a serious sin. Better that a person be drowned than to sin in this manner.

Ephesians 6:4; Colossians 3:21

4 Ye fathers, provoke not your children to wrath.... 21 Fathers, provoke not your children to anger, lest they be discouraged. Here is warning against the danger of expecting the impossible from children, of constantly nagging until they feel they can never please, of teasing or sarcasm which takes advantage of their limitations.

c. **Siblings must show love to one another and not needlessly offend.**

Proverbs 18:19 -- KEY VERSE

A brother offended is harder to be won than a strong city: and their contentions are like the bars of a castle.

Genesis 4:1-8

Cain, in jealousy over his brother's acceptance with God, killed Abel and claimed no responsibility.

Genesis 36:6-8

Even after Jacob and Esau were reconciled following their 20-year parting, they did not trust one another, and Esau kept his distance.

PROJECT: Study the attitudes which showed themselves among David's sons. Make a list of the sons of various wives. Record the instances of jealousies which are recorded among them. See if you can determine any causes that contributed.

1 Samuel 22:3, 4

David's parents and siblings stayed with him in the Cave of Adullam in Moab, when David was fleeing from Saul. Even in adult life, family members can be a significant encouragement when their attitude is right.

Leviticus 18:9-17

God's requirement of modesty, rather than the display of nakedness, was required within the family in all of its relationships.

3. Parents must be fair in their dealings with their children, not showing favoritism.

Genesis 25:28; 27:1-46; 32:3-23; 33:1-17

An example of favoritism and its disastrous results: *28 Isaac loved Esau, because he did eat of his venison: but Rebekah loved Jacob.* There was bickering in the home, deceit which led to Esau's determination to kill his brother, Jacob's escape to Haran, Rebekah's false explanation to her husband (27:42-46), a final meeting of Jacob and Esau after 20 years fraught with great apprehension (32:3-23; 33:1-17).

Genesis 37:3, 4

In spite of Jacob's experience with division in his own parental home brought on by favoritism on the part of his parents, he too repeated the same fault. *3 Now Israel [Jacob] loved Joseph more than all his children, because he was the son of his old age: and he made him a coat of many colours. 4 And when his brethren saw that their father loved him more than all his brethren, they hated him, and could not speak peaceably unto him.* The results: hatred and jealousy, desire to kill Joseph, selling him into slavery, deceiving their father so that he mourned for many years, overwhelming guilt which lasted for years (42:21, 22),

fear when Joseph revealed himself to them (45:3), and again when their father died (50:15-18).

Deuteronomy 21:15-17

Though the situation described here does not fit God's ideal for a family, the principle of fairness in dealing with children is clearly stated. Under the Law, a man with two wives and a son born to each of them could not set aside the firstborn in favor of the second, even if he loved the second mother more.

1 Timothy 5:21

The same principle applies in the church. *21 I charge thee before God, and the Lord Jesus Christ . . . that thou observe these things without preferring one before another, doing nothing by partiality.*

PROJECT: Study the relationship that existed between Moses and Aaron, brothers. Both were used mightily by the Lord. Though the attitudes they showed toward one another were not perfect (Numbers 12), much was exemplary, in spite of the fact that there were many opportunities for jealousy.

4. The lives of parents affect their children and future generations.

a. Righteous living on the part of parents has a positive effect on their children, though outside influences can partially counteract their good example.

Genesis 6:8, 9, 18; 7:1

Because Noah found grace in God's eyes, as he walked with God, his sons and their wives were included in the Ark and in God's covenant.

Genesis 18:18, 19; 22:17, 18

God said of Abraham, *19 For I know him, that he will command his children and his household after them, and they shall keep the way of the Lord, to do justice and judgment; that the Lord may bring upon Abraham that which he hath spoken of him.* When Abraham willingly offered Isaac in obedience to God's command, God renewed His promise of blessing to his seed.

Deuteronomy 4:40; 6:2; 7:12, 13

Repeatedly God promises to bless Israel's future generations as the present generation follows Him.

Joshua 14:8, 9

Caleb said, *8. . . I wholly followed the Lord my God. 9 And Moses sware on that day, saying, Surely the land . . . shall be thine inheritance, and thy children's for ever, because thou hast wholly followed the Lord my God.*

1 Samuel 20:15, 16, 42; 2 Samuel 9:7-10

David and Jonathan convenanted together as friends. Later when David became king, he cared for and honored Mephibosheth.

1 Kings 11:12, 32-36

Many descendants of David were affected for good by his godly life. Here God pronounced judgment on Solomon for his unfaithfulness due to his many foreign wives, but He delayed action for David's sake (v. 12); He also saved one tribe for Solomon's descendants, again for David's sake (32-36).

1 Kings 15:1-5, 11; 2 Kings 8:19; 18:3

Though Abijam *Walked in all the sins of his father. . . and his heart was not perfect with the Lord . . . 4 Nevertheless for David's sake did the Lord his God give him a lamp in Jerusalem, to set up his son after him . . . . 5 Because David did that which was right in the eyes of the Lord . . . .* Also (v. 11), Asa took his example from David. In spite of Jehoram's sins, God remembered Judah for David's sake, and because of His promises to David (8:19). Hezekiah too *did that which was right in the sight of the Lord, according to all that David his father did* (18:3).

PROJECT: Study the kings of Judah, from the books of Kings and Chronicles, specifically looking for the relationships between fathers and sons, in their obedience to the Lord. Which ones followed their fathers? Was it for good or bad? For which ones did God cite particular blessings because of some ancestor's actions or attitudes? How much do parents count in the lives of their children?

Psalm 103:17

But the mercy of the Lord is . . . upon them that fear him, and his righteousness unto children's children

Proverbs 14:26; 20:7

26 In the fear of the Lord is strong confidence: and his children shall have a place of refuge. 7 The just man walketh in his integrity: his children are blessed after him.

b. Sinful living affects future generations.

Genesis 19:14, 31-38

When Lot warned his sons-in-law, he seemed as one that mocked unto his sons-in-law. Apparently his living did not match his words. Lot's immorality taught his daughters that the end justifies the means, and that incest is acceptable if the situation warrants it.

Genesis 34:13-30; 35:22

Jacob's sons were deceitful in their treatment of Shechem and his cohorts, just as their father had been deceitful before them. Jacob's oldest son, Reuben, committed adultery with Bilhah, one of his father's concubines. Jacob had two wives and two concubines, so why should his son be limited to one?

Exodus 20:5, 6; 34:7; Numbers 14:18; Deuteronomy 5:9

In the Commandments, God says, *5 . . . I am a jealous God, visiting the iniquity of the fathers upon the children unto the third and fourth generation of them that hate me; 6 And shewing mercy unto thousands of them that love me and keep my commandments.*

Deuteronomy 23:2-8; 25:17-19; 1 Samuel 15:2, 3

God considered certain sins in Israel so serious that descendants of the guilty persons were not to be admitted into the congregation of the Lord for ten generations. The sins of Amalek were never to be forgotten by Israel.

Joshua 7:24, 25

Though it was Achan who sinned, his sons and daughters were stoned along with him.

2 Chronicles 33:22, 23

Manasseh is known for his sinful practices and idolatrous worship. Though he repented later (33:12-17), his son followed his idolatry, not his repentance.

Jeremiah 9:13-16

God, through Jeremiah, reminds Judah that *they walked after the imagination of their own heart, and after Baalim, which their fathers taught them.* They learned sin from their fathers, yet God holds them responsible.

Jeremiah 32:18; Lamentations 5:7

18 Thou . . . recompensest the iniquity of the fathers into the bosom of their children after them . . . . 7 Our fathers have sinned, and are not; and we have borne their iniquities.

See also many passages in the Kings and Chronicles, including the following: 1 Kgs. 15:26; 21:20-22, 29; 2 Kgs. 3:2, 3; 14:24; 15:9; 17:14, 41; 21:20-22; 2 Chron. 21:1-6; 22:3; 24:7; 33:22, 23; 36:8, 9.

> **"Parents who wish to train up their children in the way they should go, must go in the way in which they would have their children go."**
> --Francis Bacon, 1561-1626

> **"There is no such penalty for error and folly as to see one's children suffer for it . . . . There is no such reward for a well-spent life as to see one's children well started in life, owing to their parents' good health, good principles, fixed character, good breeding, and in general the whole outfit, that enables them to fight the battle of life with success."**
> --William G. Sumner

> **"We never know the love of the parent till we become parents ourselves."**
> --Henry Ward Beecher, 1813-1887

VI. Children's responsibility to parents

1. Children are responsible to God, especially as they come to maturity.

Judges 6:25-27

Gideon, as a young man, was instructed by God to break down the altar to Baal which his father had built and to cut down the grove of trees where it was located, and build an altar to the Lord instead.

1 Kings 15:11-13

Asa followed his ancestor, David, in doing right. He removed the sodomites and the idols which his fathers had made. He even removed his mother from being queen because she made an idol.

2 Chronicles 7:17-22

God reminds Solomon that he cannot depend on his father's obedience for his own blessings. He must walk before the Lord and obey His statutes.

2 Chronicles 28:22-25; 29:2-9

A son can do right in spite of an ungodly father. Ahaz repudiated God and promoted the worship of other gods; Hezekiah, his son, immediately reversed the trend, acknowledged the sin and its results.

2 Chronicles 34:1-8; 2 Kings 22:2, 22-25

Josiah, whose father and grandfather were wicked, began to rule at age eight, and did right; at sixteen, he began to seek the Lord; at twenty, he began to purge Judah and Jerusalem of idol worship and all that went with it. At 26, he began the repair of the house of the Lord and there was revival.

Proverbs 20:11

Even a child is known by his doings, whether his work be pure, and whether it be right.

Ecclesiastes 12:1

Remember now thy Creator in the days of thy youth, while the evil days come not, nor the years draw nigh, when thou shalt say, I have no pleasure in them.

2. Children must obey or submit to their parents.

Exodus 20:12; Deuteronomy 5:16

The fifth commandment: *12 Honour thy father and thy mother: that thy days may be long upon the land which the Lord thy God giveth thee.*

Deuteronomy 21:18-21

Though this command is under the Law, it reveals God's attitude toward rebellion against parents on the part of a young man. *18 If a man have a stubborn and rebellious son, which will not obey the voice of his father, or the voice of his mother, and that when they have chastened him, will not hearken unto them: 19 Then shall his father and his mother lay hold on him, and bring him out unto the elders of his city . . . 21 And all the men of his city shall stone him . . . so shalt thou put evil away from among you; and all Israel shall hear, and fear.*

Judges 11:36-39

An unusual example of godly submission to a father when he had vowed to the Lord.

Proverbs 1:8; 4:1; 6:20; 13:1; 23:22

A series of admonitions to *hear the instruction of thy father*, and *forsake not the law of thy mother*, to pay attention in order to understand, to heed the rebuke of a father, to *hearken unto thy father that begat thee, and despise not thy mother when she is old.*

Jeremiah 35:18, 19

The example of the Rechabites in obedience to their father, and the approval given them. (Read the whole chapter.)

Matthew 15:4

Jesus repeats the Old Testament command to obedience and condemns those who refuse to honor their parents and instead seek to cover their disobedience by gifts to God.

Luke 2:51, 52

Jesus, as a twelve-year-old shown to have remarkable

understanding (v. 46, 47), went back to Nazareth and was subject unto Mary and Joseph. In doing so, He continued to increase in wisdom, stature and in favor with God and man. What an example to us!

Romans 1:30

Listed among the heinous sins that result from refusing to give God His rightful place (v. 28) is *disobedience to parents.* See also 2 Timothy 3:2, where this sin is listed among those characteristic of the last days.

Ephesians 6:1-4; Colossians 3:20

1 Children, obey your parents in the Lord . . . . Four reasons are given: obedience is right; honor to parents is commanded; obedience is rewarded; obedience pleases God.

1 Timothy 3:4, 5, 12; Titus 1:6

Disobedience of children disqualified a father from serving in the church as pastor or deacon.

3. Children must accept responsibility for their parents as they grow older.

Genesis 45:4-15, 21-28; 48:1, 2; 50:7-21

An example. Though Joseph had been mistreated by his brothers, he never lost his concern for them and for his father. He sent substantial gifts, he provided for their needs, he forgave his brothers, he fulfilled his father's requests.

Psalm 127:3-5

In speaking of the blessing that children are to their parents, the Psalmist says: *5 Happy is the man that hath his quiver full of them* [i.e., of children]: *they shall not be ashamed, but they shall speak with the enemies in the gate.* In other words, children will speak in their parents' defense in time of trouble.

Proverbs 23:22

Children are not to despise their parents as they become old.

Matthew 15:4-6; Mark 7:9-13

Jesus severely criticized the Pharisees for urging people to disregard their responsibility to parents by giving to God instead. *9 . . . Full well ye reject the commandment of God, that ye may keep your own tradition. 10 For Moses said, Honour thy father and*

thy mother . . . 11 But ye say, If a man shall say to his father or mother, It is . . . a gift, by whatsoever thou mightest be profited by me; he shall be free. 12 And ye suffer him no more to do ought for his father or his mother; 13 Making the word of God of none effect . . . .

John 19:26, 27

Jesus, in the midst of His suffering on the cross, made provision for His mother. *26 . . . He saith unto his mother, Woman, behold thy son! 27 Then saith he to the disciple, Behold thy mother! And from that hour that disciple took her unto his own home.*

1 Timothy 5:3, 4, 8

3 Honour widows that are widows indeed. 4 But if any widow have children or nephews, let them learn first to shew piety at home, and to requite their parents: for that is good and acceptable before God. 8 But if any provide not for his own, and specially for those of his own house, he hath denied the faith, and is worse than an infidel.

"Let all children remember, if ever they are weary of laboring for their parents, that Christ labored for his; if impatient of their commands, that Christ cheerfully obeyed; if reluctant to provide for their parents, that Christ forgot himself and provided for his mother amid the agonies of the crucifixion. The affectionate language of this divine example to every child is, 'Go thou and do likewise'."
                                                                                --Timothy Dwight, 1752-1817.

8

Social Institutions - Church

BIBLICAL CONCEPTS

I. The CHURCH

1. The CHURCH is the whole body of believers of which Christ is the head.

2. The CHURCH began on the Day of Pentecost, fifty days after the resurrection of Christ.

3. The CHURCH will continue on earth until Christ returns to take believers unto Himself.

4. The CHURCH's union with Christ is pictured by the relationship between the human body and its head, the bride and groom, the temple with its cornerstone and building stones.

5. The CHURCH is the earthly dwelling-place for God in this age, designed to make known God's wisdom.

6. In the CHURCH all distinctions among people disappear: race, sex, nationality, economic condition.

II. Churches, or local bodies

1. A church is a body of believers banded together in one locality to carry out Christ's commands.

2. Churches of the New Testament included in their life and activities: praise and worship, instruction and nurture, counsel and discipline, fellowship and mutual help, observance of the ordinances, evangelism.

3. Churches in the New Testament made their own decisions related to membership, election of officers and messengers, and activities.

4. Decisions in New Testament churches involved the whole church.

5. New Testament believers met together on the first day of the week; much evangelism was done on the Jewish Sabbath.

6. The leaders in local churches of the New Testament are variously called pastors, elders, and bishops, and their qualifications are described.

7. Deacons served in various capacities in the churches, including provision of help to those in need.

8. New Testament churches also recognized apostles, prophets, evangelists and teachers as God's gifts to the CHURCH and to the churches.

III. Church relationships

1. The lives of those united to Christ in the CHURCH should be in marked contrast to those outside of Christ.

2. A church, under the headship of Christ, is independent of any outside human authority.

3. Bible-based churches have much in common, and therefore have often joined in projects of a cooperative nature.

4. Churches should have a positive moral influence on the communities in which they operate.

"The English word *Church* is the translation of the Greek word *ecclesia* which means *called out*. It was used of an assembly or congregation that might be called out for various purposes. The significance of this term as used in the New Testament is twofold. It refers to those who are called out from among the nations as a people for his name who constitute the Church, the Body of Christ. In this sense it is an organism. It also refers to those who are called out of any given community to carry out the principles and precepts of Christ found in the New Testament, as a body of Christians. In this sense it is an organization."

--Emery H. Bancroft, *Elemental Theology* (Binghamton, NY: Conservative Book and Bible Publishing Co., 1932), p. 225.

BIBLICAL BACKGROUND

I. The CHURCH

1. The CHURCH is the whole body of believers of which Christ is the head.

Matthew 16:17, 18

Jesus speaking, after Peter's confession of Christ as Lord: *17 . . . Blessed art thou, Simon Bar-jona: for flesh and blood hath not revealed it unto thee, but my Father which is in heaven. 18 And I say also unto thee, That thou art Peter, and upon this rock I will build my church; and the gates of hell shall not prevail against it.*

1 Corinthians 12:12, 13, 27, 28

12 For as the body is one, and hath many members, and all the members of that one body, being many, are one body: so also is Christ. 13 For by one Spirit are we all baptized into one body, whether we be Jews or Gentiles, whether we be bond or free; and have been all made to drink into one Spirit. 27 Now ye are the body of Christ, and members in particular. 28 And God hath set some in the church, first apostles . . . (a list of gifted persons, given to the CHURCH as a whole follows).

Ephesians 1:22, 23

Paul, speaking of the exaltation of Christ: *22 . . . Gave him to be the head over all things to the church, 23 Which is his body, the fulness of him that filleth all in all.*

Ephesians 5:24-26

25 . . . Christ also loved the church, and gave himself for it; 26 That he might sanctify and cleanse it with the washing of water by the word, 27 That he might present it to himself a glorious church . . . .

2. The CHURCH began on the Day of Pentecost, fifty days after the resurrection of Christ.

Matthew 16:18 (quoted above)

Here Christ indicates that He will build His CHURCH. The time is yet future when He speaks to Peter.

Acts 1:4, 5

At the time of His ascension, Jesus tells His disciples to wait for the promise of the Father, for, He said, *5 . . . Ye shall be baptized with the Holy Ghost not many days hence.* Still future.

Acts 2:1-4, 41-47

1 And when the day of Pentecost was fully come,

they were all with one accord in one place . . . . 4 And they were all filled with the Holy Ghost, and began to speak in tongues, as the Spirit gave them utterance. Then follows Peter's sermon, ending with *38 . . . Repent, and be baptized every one of you in the name of Jesus Christ . . . and ye shall receive the gift of the Holy Ghost. 41 Then they that gladly received the word were baptized and the same day there were* *added unto them about three thousand souls.* Verses 41-47 describe what followed -- a description of the first church in action -- also the CHURCH.

1 Corinthians 12:13 (quoted above)

Here it becomes clear that the baptism of the Holy Spirit is the process by which each individual person becomes part of the body of Christ, the CHURCH.

3. The CHURCH will continue on earth until Christ returns to take believers unto Himself.

John 14:3

A promise before the CHURCH began: *3 . . . I will come again, and receive you unto myself; that where I am, there ye may be also.*

1 Thessalonians 4:15-17

15 . . . We which are alive and remain unto the coming of the Lord shall not prevent [precede] *them* *which are asleep. 16 For the Lord himself shall descend from heaven . . . and the dead in Christ shall rise first: 17 Then we which are alive and remain shall be caught up together with them in the clouds, to meet the Lord in the air: and so shall we ever be with the Lord.* See also 1 Cor. 15:22, 23, 51, 52; also Matt. 16:18.

4. The CHURCH's union with Christ is pictured by the relationship between the human body and its head, the bride and groom, the temple with its cornerstone and building stones.

a. The members of the body and its head

Romans 12:4, 5

4 For as we have many members in one body, and all members have not the same office: 5 So we, being many, are one body in Christ, and every one members one of another.

1 Corinthians 12:12-27

12 For as the body is one, and hath many members, and all the members of that one body, being many, are one body: so also is Christ. Verses 13-27 further discuss this union and the necessity of all the parts. Also Ephesians 1:22, 23, quoted above, and 4:15, 16.

Colossians 1:18; 2:19

18 And he is the head of the body, the church . . . . In verse 19, Paul speaks of the danger of setting up various rules of action rather than holding fast to the Head, *from which all the body . . . increaseth with the increase of God.*

b. The bride and the groom

2 Corinthians 11:2

Paul expressing concern for the Corinthian church: *2 . . . I have espoused you to one husband, that I may present you as a chaste virgin to Christ.*

Ephesians 5:25-32

In presenting the loving relationship between husband and wife, Paul interrelates the relationship of Christ and the CHURCH. *32 This is a great mystery: but I speak concerning Christ and the church.*

Revelation 19:5-9; 21:9

Here is described the marriage supper of the Lamb -- i.e., Christ and the CHURCH, in heaven, after the Rapture.

c. The temple, with its building stones and its cornerstone and foundation

1 Corinthians 3:9-17

Christ is presented as the foundation, and the lives and work of believers as the building on that foundation, with the warning to be sure that they build solidly. There is also the thought that believers are the temple in which God dwells, and that therefore that temple should not be defiled.

Ephesians 2:20-22

Believers *are built upon the foundation of the apostles and prophets, Jesus Christ himself being the chief corner stone; 21 In whom all the building fitly framed together groweth unto an holy temple in the Lord: 22 In whom ye also are builded together for an habitation of God through the Spirit.*

Also 1 Timothy 3:15; 1 Peter 2:4-8

5. The CHURCH is the earthly dwelling-place for God in this age, designed to make known God's wisdom.

Ephesians 2:19-22

19 . . . the household of God . . . 21 . . . an holy temple in the Lord: 22 . . . an habitation of God. Also 3:20.

Ephesians 3:10, 21

In the earlier verse of this chapter Paul shows that the CHURCH was a hidden thing, or mystery, but is now revealed. The intent is stated in 10: *To the intent that now unto the principalities and powers in heavenly places might be known by the church the manifold wisdom of God. 21 Unto him be glory in the church by Christ Jesus throughout all ages, world without end.*

1 Timothy 3:15

15 . . . The house of God, which is the church of the living God, the pillar and ground of the truth.

6. In the CHURCH all distinctions among people disappear: race, sex, nationality, economic condition.

Acts 15:14

Simeon hath declared how God at the first did visit the Gentiles, to take out of them a people for his name.

Galatians 3:27-29

27 For as many of you as have been baptized into Christ have put on Christ. 28 There is neither Jew nor Greek, there is neither bond nor free, there is neither male nor female: for ye are all one in Christ Jesus.

See also Ephesians 2:11-13; 3:6.

II. Churches, or local bodies

1. A church is a body of believers banded together in one locality to carry out Christ's commands.

Acts 2:41-47 and 4:32-37

A description of the first church. Though at the time it was also the CHURCH, it was a body of believers in Jerusalem who were banded together, and who carried out the ministry of a church.

Acts 8:1

1 . . . At that time there was a great persecution against the church which was at Jerusalem; and they were all scattered abroad throughout the regions of Judaea and Samaria . . . . Here is mention of a particular church. This church is also mentioned many times in the Book of Acts.

Acts 11:22, 26; 13:1; 14:27; 15:3, 4, 22

The church at Antioch is mentioned in these verses: the Jerusalem church sent Barnabas to Antioch; Saul and Barnabas assembled with the church and taught there for a year; the name *Christian* was first used there; Paul and Barnabas were commissioned as missionaries in this church; after the missionary journey, Paul and Barnabas reported to the church; dissension arose in the church; this church sent their two missionaries and others to Jerusalem, and provided for their needs enroute. They met with the apostles and elders after being received warmly by the Jerusalem church.

Acts 18:22; 20:17

There was a church at Caesarea, visited by Paul; also at Ephesus.

Romans 16:1, 4, 5; 1 Corinthians 1:2

There was a church at Cenchrea, where Phebe was active and much loved; also several churches of the Gentiles who had appreciated the teaching of Priscilla and Aquila, a church in their home, one in Corinth.

PROJECT: Go through the first verses of each of the Pauline Epistles to find out which are specifically directed to churches in local areas. For locations of other local churches, see Revelation 2, 3.

2. Churches of the New Testament included in their life and activities: praise and worship, instruction and nurture, counsel and discipline, fellowship and mutual help, observance of the ordinances, evangelism.

a. Praise and worship

Acts 2:42-47

Note in these verses describing the church at Jerusalem these words: *breaking of bread...prayers... continuing daily with one accord in the temple, and breaking bread from house to house, did eat their meat with gladness . . . praising God . . . .*

Ephesians 5:19, 20

One of the characteristics Paul says results from being constantly filled with the Holy Spirit is stated here, as instruction to the Ephesian church and to us. *19 Speaking to yourselves in psalms and hymns and spiritual songs, singing and making melody in your heart to the Lord; 20 Giving thanks always for all things unto God and the Father in the name of our Lord Jesus Christ.*

Colossians 3:16

Again, instruction to the Colossian church: *16 Let the word of Christ dwell in you richly in all wisdom; teaching and admonishing one another in psalms and hymns and spiritual songs, singing with grace in your hearts to the Lord.*

1 Thessalonians 5:16

Admonition to the church at Thessalonica: *16 In every thing give thanks: for this is the will of God in Christ Jesus concerning you.*

b. Instruction and nurture

Acts 2:42, 46

42 They continued stedfastly in the apostles' doctrine [teachings] and fellowship . . . . 46 . . . continuing daily with one accord in the temple . . . .

Romans 12:6-8

There were members in the churches who had as their gifts, prophesying, teaching, exhorting. All of these persons were encouraged to use their respective gifts, concentrating in their special areas, all with the purpose of instruction.

1 Corinthians 12:4-31

Again, a diversity of gifts is described. Among them are *8 . . .the word of wisdom . . . the word of knowledge.* A list of gifted persons is given in v. 28; included are apostles, prophets, teachers, all of whom have a teaching ministry. Others are to recognize and appreciate their gifts, as they are to respect the importance of other gifted persons in the CHURCH.

1 Corinthians 14

In all of the instruction about believers speaking in tongues in the assembly, the emphasis is on conducting the meeting in a way that will cause believers to learn and mature. Note such emphases as these: *2 For he that speaketh in an unknown tongue speaketh not unto men . . . for no man understandeth him. . . . 3 But he that prophesieth speaketh unto men to edification, and exhortation, and comfort. 4 . . . He that prophesieth edifieth the church. 5 . . . Greater is he that prophesieth than he that speaketh with tongues, except he interpret, that the church may receive edifying. 12 . . . Seek that ye may excel to the edifying of the church. 15 . . . I will pray with the understanding also . . . and I will sing with the understanding also. 16 Else . . . how shall he that occupieth the room of the unlearned say Amen at thy giving of thanks, seeing he understandeth not what thou sayest? 19 Yet in the church I had rather speak five words with my understanding, that by my voice I might teach others also . . . . Also v. 23-26. 31 For ye may all prophesy one by one, that all may learn. . . .*

Galatians 6:6

Let him that is taught in the word communicate [or share] unto him that teacheth in all good things. There was to be recognition of the contribution of those who teach, and a sharing of materials things.

Ephesians 4:11-16

Again, in verse 11, a list of special leaders given to the churches, several of whom had a teaching ministry. The responsibility of all who are mentioned is to perfect, or equip, the saints so they can do the work of the ministry and edify the body of Christ.

PROJECT: In verses 12-16, pick out all the expressions which have in them the thought of growing up or becoming the mature Christians that we ought to be.

Ephesians 6:4

Fathers are instructed to bring up their children in *the nurture and admonition of the Lord* -- a teaching ministry in the home.

2 Timothy 2:2, 24, 25

Paul's instructions to Timothy, a young pastor, include: *2 The things that thou hast heard of me among many witnesses, the same commit thou to faithful men, who shall be able to teach others also. 24 The servant of the Lord must . . . be gentle unto*

all men, apt to teach, patient, 25 In meekness in-
structing those that oppose themselves; if God
peradventure will give them repentance to the
acknowledging of the truth.

c. Counsel and discipline

Matthew 18:15-17

Before the CHURCH began, Jesus gave instruction
about the settling of differences between believers:
first alone with the other person, then taking one or
two others, then *tell it unto the church: but if he*
neglect to hear the church, let him be unto thee as
an heathen man and a publican - the first mention of
church discipline, with every effort made first to
reconcile the difference and gain the brother.

1 Corinthians 5:1-5, 9-13; 2 Corinthians 2:6-11

Here again is discipline, even excommunication of a
member, in order that he might realize the serious-
ness of his sin. Verse 11 indicates that the same
discipline may be necessary for other offences than
fornication. Paul's second letter indicates that the man
did repent, and was to be restored to church fellowship.

Galatians 6:1

Brethren, if a man be overtaken in a fault, ye which
are spiritual, restore such an one in the spirit of
meekness: considering thyself, lest thou also be
tempted. Here is counseling in the right spirit.

Philippians 4:2, 3

In this letter written to a church, Paul not only urges
Euodias and Syntyche to be of the same mind in the
Lord, but he also urges those with responsibility:
3 . . . Help those women which laboured with me in
the gospel . . . whose names are in the book of life.

d. Fellowship and mutual help

Acts 2:44-46; 4:32-37

Note here the sharing with one another, meeting one
another's needs, eating from house to house, selling
goods in order to give to the church.

Acts 6:1-3

When there were widows in need of assistance, the
church chose seven men to be responsible. See also
1 Tim. 5:3-16.

Acts 11:29, 30

When the church at Antioch heard of need in Judea
29 The disciples, every man according to his ability,
determined to send relief . . . 30 Which also they did,
and sent it to the elders by the hands of Barnabas
and Saul. Also 24:17; Romans 15:25-27; 1 Cor. 16:1-4;
2 Cor. 8, 9. Several churches were involved.

Philippians 4:10-18

In this thank-you letter to the Philippian church, he
expresses appreciation for their many gifts, both now
and previously. Here was not only personal concern
for Paul, but support for worldwide evangelism.

Colossians 3:12-17

Note the emphasis on the fellowship of believers:
on kindness, forbearance, forgiveness, love, appreciation, teaching and admonishing, doing everything
with the Lord in mind.

1 Thessalonians 5:14

Here too is the exhortation to help one another:
comfort the feebleminded [or fainthearted], *support*
the weak, be patient toward all men.

2 Timothy 1:16-18

The Apostle commends Onesiphorus for all the help
he had been to him, both in Ephesus and in Rome.

e. Observance of the ordinances

Baptism

Matthew 28:19; Mark 16:15, 16

The command of the Lord: *19 Go ye therefore, and*
teach all nations, baptizing them in the name of the
Father, and of the Son, and of the Holy Ghost.

Acts 2:41

Those who heard Peter's sermon on the Day of Pentecost and trusted Christ were baptized, and then
continued in the fellowship.

Acts 8:12, 13, 36-38

Philip preached in Samaria and baptized those who
believed. Later he baptized the Ethopian eunuch
whom he led to Christ.

Acts 9:18

Saul, after his Damascus road conversion and a three-
day wait, received his sight through the ministry of
Ananias, and was baptized.

Acts 10:48

When a group of Gentiles gathered in the house of
Cornelius believed and received the Holy Spirit, Peter
commanded that they be baptized in the name of the
Lord.

Also Acts 16:14, 15, 32, 33, where Lydia and her household were baptized, and the Philippian jailer and his
family; 18:8, a synagogue ruler in Corinth, along with
his family; 19:5, followers of John the Baptist in
Ephesus; 22:13, where Paul gives his testimony.

Romans 6:3, 4

The significance of baptism: *3 Know ye not that, as*
many of us as were baptized into Jesus Christ were
baptized into his death? 4 Therefore, we are buried

with him by baptism into death, that as Christ was raised up from the dead by the glory of the Father, even so we also should walk in newness of life. Baptism pictures our identification with Christ in death, burial and resurrection. Also Col. 2:12.

1 Corinthians 12:12, 13

13 For by one Spirit are we all baptized into one body . . . . Just as admission into the CHURCH is by the baptism of the Holy Spirit, so admission into a church is usually based upon water baptism after confession of Christ.

The Lord's Supper

Acts 2:42

Immediately after the Holy Spirit came and the Church was formed, believers engaged in the breaking of bread.

1 Corinthians 11:23-34

Christ's command to observe this Supper is revealed by the Apostle Paul in v. 25, 26: *25 . . . This cup is the new testament in my blood: this do ye, as oft as ye drink it, in remembrance of me. 26 For as oft as ye eat this bread, and drink this cup, ye do shew the Lord's death till he come.* The Lord's Supper then is a commemoration of His death for us, and a reminder of His coming again; it is also a time for self-examination and judging of our own sins (28-32). The Corinthians observed this ordinance, but had desecrated it by gluttony and drunkenness, heresy,

and division (17-22); the Apostle writes here to correct the disorder.

f. Evangelism and missions

Acts 5:25

After the angel released Peter and his co-workers from prison: *25 . . . Behold the men whom ye put in prison are standing in the temple, and teaching the people.*

Acts 6:7

And the word of God increased; and the number of the disciples multiplied in Jerusalem greatly; and a great company of the priests were obedient to the faith.

Acts 9:3, 4

Because of the persecution of the Jerusalem church by Saul, *4 Therefore they that were scattered abroad went every where preaching the word. 5 Then Philip went down to the city of Samaria, and preached Christ unto them; 6 And the people with one accord gave heed unto those things which Philip spake . . . . 25 And they, when they had testified and preached the word of the Lord, returned to Jerusalem, and preached the gospel in many villages of the Samaritans.*

PROJECT: In a study of the Book of Acts, find out where the gospel was preached. Make a chart with these headings: Bible Reference, Location, Who Preached, Results.

3. Churches in the New Testament made their own decisions related to membership, election of officers and messengers, and activities.

Examples:

Matthew 18:15-17

A church is authorized to mediate between members in dispute, and even withdraw fellowship from a person, if necessary. Also 1 Cor. 5:1-5, 9-13.

Acts 6:1-6

A church selects from its members certain ones to perform a service; here it is the deacons to serve the widows.

Acts 13:1-4

A church, under the guidance of the Holy Spirit, selects some to serve as missionaries, and rejoices with them as they report back (14:26-28).

Acts 15:2, 3

A church sends messengers to another church for counsel and help in decision-making. They also provide for the trip.

Acts 15:22-27

A church agrees on a course of action to recommend to another church that has asked counsel, and commissions messengers to communicate both orally and by written letter to that church.

1 Corinthians 14

Here is a church that is disorderly in its services. Paul gives them instructions, but leaves to them the elimination of the confusion.

2 Corinthians 9:19, 23

A church joins with other churches in meeting a financial need, and in giving approval of specific messengers who convey their joint gift. Also 1 Cor. 16:3, 4.

Philippians 2:25

A church sends a messenger to minister to one of its missionaries in time of need.

Philippians 4:14-16

A church may support a missionary or not, according to its own decision. Paul thanked the Philippian church for their repeated gifts, but he recognized that others were within their rights when they did not do likewise.

"As every lord giveth a certain livery to his servants, love is the very livery of Christ. Our Saviour, who is the Lord above all lords, would have his servants known by their badge, which is love."

--Bishop Hugh Latimer, 1490-1555.

4. Decisions in New Testament churches involved the whole church.

Acts 1:15-26

The principle is illustrated before there was a church, in the selection of a man to replace Judas among the apostles. There were about 120 persons involved in the decision. Though Matthias was never prominent, he was numbered with the apostles.

Acts 6:1-6

In the selection of those who should minister to the widows in the Jerusalem church, the idea was stated by the Twelve, but *5 The saying pleased the whole multitude: and they chose Stephen ... Philip ... Prochorus, and Nicanor, and Timon, and Parmenas, and Nicolas ... 6 Whom they set before the apostles: and when they had prayed, they laid their hands on them.*

Acts 11:1-18

After Peter had gone to the house of Cornelius and eaten there, some of the Jewish believers criticized him for his action in going to the uncircumcized. Peter explained how God had directed him, finally ending with these words: *17 Forasmuch then as God gave them the like gift as he did unto us, who believed on the Lord Jesus Christ; what was I, that I could withstand God?* The reaction of the apostles and brethren who were gathered together (v. 1):

18 When they heard these things, they held their peace, and glorified God, saying, Then hath God also to the Gentiles granted repentance unto life. Apparently the whole group agreed.

Acts 15:1-31

In Jerusalem when the Antioch church sent representatives to discuss the question of circumcision, certain believing Pharisees further raised the question. *The apostles and elders came together for to consider the matter* (v. 6). The multitude was present however (v. 12), and after various ones spoke, *22 Then pleased it the apostles and elders with the whole church, to send chosen men of their own company to Antioch ... 23 And they wrote letters ....* In the letters they said, *28 For it seemed good to the Holy Ghost, and to us ....* There was unanimity in the group.

Philippians 2:2-5

The principle by which they seem to have functioned: *2 ... Be like minded, having the same love, being of one accord, of one mind. 3 Let nothing be done through strife or vainglory; but in lowliness of mind let each esteem other better than themselves. 5 Let this mind be in you, which was also in Christ Jesus.*

5. New Testament believers met together on the first day of the week; much evangelism was done on the Jewish Sabbath.

a. Believers gathered on Sunday.

Matthew 28:1; Mark 16:1, 9; Luke 24:1; John 20:1

It was on the first day of the week that various disciples came to the sepulchre and learned that Jesus was risen.

Luke 24:13, 33-45; John 20:19, 26

It was on the first day of the week that the ten gathered in Jerusalem, heard the report from the two who had seen the Lord on the way to Emmaus, compared notes on what they had heard of the resurrection, and then saw the risen Lord Himself. Again a week later, they gathered, this time with Thomas

present.

Acts 20:7

At Troas: *7 Upon the first day of the week, when the disciples came together to break bread, Paul preached unto them ....*

1 Corinthians 16:2

Upon the first day of the week let every one of you lay by him in store, as God hath prospered him, that there be no gatherings when I come.

b. Paul and his co-workers did much preaching and teaching on the Jewish Sabbath, making use of the already established assemblies.

Acts 13:14-16

Paul and Barnabas *14 . . . came to Antioch in Pisidia, and went into the synagogue on the sabbath day, and sat down. 15 . . . The rulers of the synagogue sent unto them, saying, Ye men and brethren, if ye have any word of exhortation for the people, say on. 16 Then Paul stood up and . . . said, Men of Israel, and ye that fear God, give audience.* Verses 17-41 give his message -- an evangelistic theme based on Israel's history and God's promises.

Acts 13:42-44

After the Jews left the synagogue, the Gentiles asked for his preaching the next Sabbath. Much personal conversation concerning the Gospel followed the preaching. The next week there *came almost the whole city together to hear the word of God.*

Acts 16:13

In Philippi, Paul and Silas *went out of the city by a river side, where prayer was wont to be made; and we sat down, and spake unto the women which resorted thither.* It was here that Lydia trusted Christ. The meeting was on the Sabbath.

Acts 17:2; 18:4

2 And Paul, as his manner was, went in unto them [i.e., into the synagogue of the Jews], *and three sabbath days reasoned with them out of the scriptures.* This was in Thessalonica. At Corinth, *4 he reasoned in the synagogue every sabbath, and persuaded the Jews and the Greeks.*

6. The leaders in local churches of the New Testament are variously called pastors, elders, and bishops, and their qualifications are described.

a. Their titles

Elders. Acts 11:30; 14:23; 15:2, 4, 6, 22, 23; 20:17-37; 21:18; 1 Timothy 5:17-19; Titus 1:5; James 5:14; 1 Peter 5:1; 2 John 1; 3 John 1

A study of these passages in context shows that elders were ordained; they were to oversee and feed the flock of God; they served with the apostles in giving leadership in decisions in the early church; they were to be honored and cared for, and not carelessly accused; they were to pray for the sick.

Bishops. Acts 20:28; Philippians 1:1; 1 Timothy 3:1, 2; Titus 1:7

Concern is expressed in these passages that the bishops take heed to their own lives, be concerned about those for whom they are responsible, that they feed the flock, and that they possess high qualifications.

Pastors. Ephesians 4:11

Pastors are listed among the gifts given by Christ to the CHURCH, for the maturing and equipping of saints so that they can fulfill God's expectations. Other uses of the same word carry the thought of shepherding and showing personal concern.

b. Their qualifications

1 Timothy 3:2-7; Titus 1:6-9

2 A bishop then must be blameless, the husband of one wife, vigilant, sober, of good behaviour, given to hospitality, apt to teach; 3 Not given to wine, no striker, not greedy of filthy lucre; but patient, not a brawler, not covetous; 4 One that ruleth well his own house, having his children in subjection with all gravity; 6 Not a novice . . . 7 Moreover he must have a good report of them which are without . . . . 9 Holding fast the faithful word as he hath been taught . . . .

7. Deacons served in various capacities in the churches, including provision of help to those in need.

Acts 6:1-6

The church in Jerusalem chose *seven men of honest report, full of the Holy Ghost and wisdom,* to take responsibility for service to the widows in the congregation.

Philippians 1:1

This epistle is addressed to all the saints at Philippi, but with special mention of bishops and deacons.

1 Timothy 3:8-13

The qualifications for this office: *grave, not double-tongued, not given to much wine, not greedy of filthy lucre; holding the mystery of the faith in a pure conscience . . . proved . . . blameless . . . with wives that are grave, not slanderers, sober, faithful; . . . husbands of one wife, ruling their children and their own houses well.*

8. New Testament churches also recognized apostles, prophets, evangelists and teachers as God's gifts to the CHURCH and to the churches.

Ephesians 4:11

Here are the gifted men whom Christ gave to the churches: *apostles . . . prophets . . . evangelists . . . pastors and teachers.*

Acts 1:20-26

After the Ascension, when preparations were being made to select a successor to Judas, Peter stated the qualifications for an apostle: *21 . . . Men which have companied with us all the time that the Lord Jesus went in and out among us, 22 Beginning from the baptism of John, unto that same day that he was taken up from us . . . a witness with us of his resurrection.* This position is therefore no longer possible.

Acts 11:27; 13:1; 15:32; 21:10

Specific men are mentioned as prophets in several of the churches.

1 Corinthians 12:10; 14:3, 29-33

The gift of prophecy is recognized as a desirable one. Prophecy was to have as its purpose: *3 . . . edification, and exhortation, and comfort.* It was the proclamation of truth, but at this stage in the history of the church, it also included the revelation of truth, as is seen in 30: *If any thing be revealed to another that sitteth by, let the first hold his peace. 31 For ye may all prophesy one by one, that all may learn, and all may be comforted. 32 And the spirits of the prophets are subject to the prophets.*

"The New Testament prophet was not merely a preacher, but an inspired preacher, through whom, until the New Testament was written, new revelations suited to the new dispensation were given (1 Cor. 14:29, 30)."
--The *Scofield Reference Bible,* Note to 1 Cor. 14:1.

Acts 21:8

Philip is called an *evangelist.* Note that he was also one of the deacons in Acts 6:5, and one of the apostles in Matthew 10:3.

2 Timothy 4:5

This letter is addressed to Timothy, who was a pastor, but he is urged to *do the work of an evangelist.* It is apparent that in these churches, as today, there was considerable overlapping of gifts and responsibilities.

Romans 12:7

In this presentation of the varied gifts within the body of Christ, one is teaching. The *teacher* is urged to tend to his teaching -- surely giving the impression that there were persons for whom this was their major ministry. So also in 1 Cor. 12:28, 29.

1 Timothy 2:7; 2 Timothy 1:11

Paul recognized himself as *a preacher, and an apostle . . . a teacher of the Gentiles . . . .* Here again is that overlapping of roles.

James 3:1

James recognizes the responsibility of teachers, urging believers not to be aspiring to be teachers without being willing to take the greater responsibility this position entails.

III. Church relationships

1. The lives of those united to Christ in the CHURCH should be in marked contrast to those outside of Christ.

Romans 12:2

Be not conformed to this world: but be ye transformed by the renewing of your mind, that ye may prove what is that good, and acceptable, and perfect, will of God.

Ephesians 4:17-32; 5:1-10

17 This I say therefore, and testify in the Lord, that ye henceforth walk not as other Gentiles walk, in *the vanity of their mind. 22 That ye put off concerning the former conversation* [way of life] *the old man, which is corrupt according to the deceitful lusts; . . . 24 And that ye put on the new man . . . .*

Galatians 5:19-23

Here is the contrast between the works of the flesh and the fruit of the Holy Spirit in us.

PROJECT: Study Revelation 2, 3, noting what each of the churches was commended for, and what the Lord criticized in each one. Summarize to show what God approves and disapproves in the life and work of a church, and what these churches were told to do.

2. A church, under the headship of Christ, is independent of any outside human authority.

See previous references to Christ as the Head of the CHURCH, and therefore of the churches in local areas.

See also earlier concepts concerning the churches' making their own decisions.

Matthew 23:10

Jesus makes clear that for the believer, He alone is Lord of the conscience. He says, *10 Neither be ye called masters: for one is your Master, even Christ.* If this is true of the individual believer, it is true also of the body of believers.

Matthew 22:17-21

In the question of the tribute money, the Lord made it clear that, while there are things to be rendered to Caesar, there are also areas that belong to God alone, and over which the government has no right.

Acts 4:18-20, 29

In the first persecution of the church in Jerusalem, Peter and John were ordered not to speak to any man in the name of Christ. Their answer: *19 . . . Whether it be right in the sight of God to hearken unto you more than unto God, judge ye. 20 For we cannot but speak the things which we have seen and heard.* Likewise, the second time: *29 . . . We ought to obey God rather than men.*

God has established three institutions: the home, civil government, and the church. Each is independent of the others; each has its own functions and is responsible to God for fulfilling those functions. Each has its own rights, and the others may not legitimately intrude. As individual persons, we have specific responsibilities to each one; these are detailed elsewhere.

3. Bible-based churches have much in common, and therefore have often joined in projects of a cooperative nature.

Ephesians 4:4-6 - common doctrine.

4 There is one body, and one Spirit, even as ye are called in one hope of your calling; 5 One Lord, one faith, one baptism, 6 One God and Father of all, who is above all, and through all, and in you all.

Acts 15:1-35

The churches in Antioch and Jerusalem had a mutual concern about the necessity of circumcision for Gentile believers. Therefore representatives from Antioch met with the Jerusalem church to decide.

Romans 15:26

A common welfare project: *26 For it hath pleased*

them *of Macedonia and Achaia to make a certain contribution for the poor saints which are at Jerusalem.* Also 2 Cor. 8:1-7, where Corinth is also involved.

Romans 16:1, 2

Common hospitality: here the Apostle urges the Roman church to receive and assist Phebe, one who has been involved in the Cenchrea church.

Galatians 1:2; Colossians 4:15, 16

Sharing of Paul's letters: *16 When this epistle is read among you, cause that it be read also in the church of the Laodiceans; and that ye likewise read the epistle from Laodicea.*

4. Churches should have a positive moral influence on the communities in which they operate.

Matthew 5:13-16

Jesus speaking in the Sermon on the Mount: *13 Ye are the salt of the earth . . . . 14 Ye are the light of the world . . . . 16 Let your light so shine before men, that they may see your good works, and glorify your Father which is in heaven.* Though this passage does not deal specifically with church truth, it is an expression of God's will for believers, who make up

churches.

Ephesians 5:22-6:9

As believers submit to the Lord and are filled with the Spirit (v. 18), many relationships improve: husband-wife, parent-child, servant-master.

Philippians 2:14-16

Paul exhorts believers in Philippi, as well as in today's

world, *14 Do all things without murmurings and disputings: 15 That ye may be blameless and harmless, the sons of God, without rebuke, in the midst of a crooked and perverse nation, among whom ye shine as lights in the world; 16 Holding forth the word of life . . . .*

Examples from Genesis:

Genesis 26:28

The Philistines recognized that God was with Isaac.

Genesis 30:27

Laban recognized the fact that God had blessed his house because of Jacob's being with him.

Genesis 39:5, 6

Potiphar, an officer in Egypt, saw that God blessed everything Joseph did. *5 And it came to pass from the time that he had made him overseer in his house, and over all that he had, that the Lord blessed the Egyptian's house for Joseph's sake . . . .*

Genesis 39:21-23

Prison conditions improved when the keeper committed all the prisoners to Joseph.

Genesis 41:55-57

The administration of food during the famine in Egypt was placed under Joseph, and as a result, Egypt and surrounding areas survived.

THOUGHTS YOU CAN USE

"The real democratic American idea is not that every man shall be on a level with every other, but that every one shall have liberty, without hindrance, to be what God made him."

--Henry Ward Beecher, 1813-1887.

"If there were a people consisting of gods, they would be governed democratically; so perfect a government is not suitable to men."

--Jean Jacques Rousseau, 1712-1778.

"If I might control the literature of the household, I would guarantee the well-being of the church and state."

--Francis Bacon, 1561-1626.

"When home is ruled according to God's word, angels might be asked to stay with us, and they would not find themselves out of their element."

--Charles Haddon Spurgeon, 1834-1892.

"It is better to build children than to repair men."   --Bob Peterson, March 10, 1983.

"The family is created and kept together, not because being a parent is so much fun, but because of the commitment of two people who dared to make and keep their promises."

--*The Capsule* (Caravans for Christ) Jan./Feb., 1983, p. 18.

"In families well ordered there is always one firm, sweet temper, which controls without seeming to dictate."

--Edward G. Bulwer-Lytton, 1803-1873.

"The words that a father speaks to his children in the privacy of home are not heard by the world, but, as in whispering galleries, they are clearly heard at the end, and by posterity."

--Jean Paul Richter, 1763-1826.

"It is our sacred duty to transmit unimpaired to our posterity the blessings of liberty which were bequeathed to us by the founders of the republic."

--Andrew Johnson, 1808-1875.

9

Social Problems

BIBLICAL CONCEPTS

I. Basic principles

1. Rebellion against authority is characteristic of man, and is sin.

2. Major social problems are the consequence of man's refusal to recognize God's existence and authority, and to give Him His rightful place.

3. Injustice of all kinds is condemned by God, whether among His people or others.

4. People with particular needs are to have special consideration.

5. Both worship and social concern are required of godly people; neither may be substituted for the other.

II. Specific areas of instruction

1. The safety of others is a responsibility of all.

2. Drug abuse, as illustrated by alcoholism, is sin against God, and a detriment to society.

3. Kindness to animals must characterize godly people.

4. Dealing with the occult should have no place in the lives of believers.

5. Crime must be properly handled to insure a safe environment, and fairness to all who are involved.

BIBLICAL BACKGROUND

I. Basic principles

1. Rebellion against authority is characteristic of man, and is sin.

Examples:

Genesis 11:1-4

The people at Babel say, *Let us make brick . . . let us build us a city and a tower, whose top may reach unto heaven; and let us make us a name, lest we be scattered abroad upon the face of the whole earth.* God had said for them to multiply and replenish the earth (9:1, 2).

Exodus 14:11, 12

Israel rebels against Moses, saying, *Because there were no graves in Egypt, hast thou taken us away to die in the wilderness? wherefore hast thou dealt thus with us . . . ?* So also again and again when they had any need. See 16:2, 3; 17:1-3; Num. 21:5, 6.

Numbers 12:1-3

Miriam and Aaron rebel against the leadership of Moses, using the fact that he married outside of Israel.

Numbers 14:1-4

The people side with the ten spies, against Moses, Caleb and Joshua, and refuse to advance into the land from Kadesh-Barnea. Also Deut. 1:26, 27; 9:23, 24.

Numbers 16:1-3

250 princes of Israel, led by Korah, turn against Moses and Aaron.

Deuteronomy 21:18-21

God decrees stoning for a son who is rebellious against his parents.

Deuteronomy 28:1-68

God promises blessings (v. 1-14) and cursings (15-68) according to Israel's submission to Him or rebellion against Him.

Judges 2:16-19

A summary of the many refusals of Israel to follow God and obey Him. They repeatedly refused to obey the judges appointed by God (v. 17), and as soon as each judge died, they went more deeply into sin, according to their own stubborn ways (v. 19).

Proverbs 30:11-14

God describes a generation that is rebellious against everything.

Romans 1:21-32

God describes man's refusal to acknowledge Him. *21 . . . When they knew God, they glorified him not as God, neither were thankful . . . 25 Who changed the truth of God into a lie, and worshipped and served the creature more than the Creator . . . . 28 . . . They did not like to retain God in their knowledge. . . .*

2 Timothy 3:1-8

A New Testament description of the rebelliousness of the last days.

Revelation 9:20, 21

During the Tribulation period, when God pours out unusual judgment, He, looking down the future, says, *20 And the rest of the men . . . repented not of the works of their hands . . . 21 Neither repented they of their murders, nor of their sorceries, nor of their fornication, nor of their thefts.* Rebellious still!

PROJECT: Study the Book of Judges, noting the sequence of actions and attitudes following the deliverance under each judge. Watch for these: sin, servitude, deliverance, as they occur again and again.

PROJECT: Study carefully Romans 1:18-32. Watch especially for the ways in which rebellion against God showed itself, and the ways in which God responded. Note the kinds of sin which resulted.

2. Major social problems are the consequence of man's refusal to recognize God's existence and authority, and to give Him His rightful place.

Isaiah 24:1-12

Read here a description of the chaos that will result from God's judgment just before the Kingdom Age. The reason for such chaos: *3 . . . The Lord hath spoken this word . . . . 5 . . . Because they have transgressed the laws, changed the ordinance, broken the everlasting covenant.* For a colorful paraphrase of this passage, read the *Living Bible.*

Hosea 4:1-4

Note here again the variety of sin and social disruption: swearing, lying, stealing, adultery, depression, lack of food; note also the basic cause of it all: *1 . . . Because there is no truth, nor mercy, nor knowledge of God in the land.*

Micah 6, 7

Micah lists for us the problems of his day: dishonest business dealings, violence, lies and deceit, unsatisfied appetites for food, women not able to deliver their babies, murder of babies, crop failures, few that can be trusted, bribery, family breakdown. The basic problem behind all this: instead of obeying the Lord, as outlined in 6:8, Israel was following ungodly kings, Omri and Ahab (6:16).

Mark 7:20-23

It is the basic attitude within man that brings all the problems. *21 For from within, out of the heart of men, proceed evil thoughts, adulteries, fornications, murders, 22 Thefts, covetousness, wickedness, deceit, lasciviousness, an evil eye, blasphemy, pride, foolishness: 23 All these evil things come from within, and defile the man.*

Romans 1:18-32

Repeatedly, in these verses, we are told that when man refuses to glorify God, to consider His truth authoritative, to worship Him as Creator, then God gives man up to go his own way. The result is lust, refusal to recognize the sacredness of the human body, homosexuality, a reprobate mind which leads to all kinds of sin, as described in verses 29-31.

2 Timothy 3:1-9

God lists again characteristics of the last days, when men's attention is centered on man (*lovers of their own selves,* v. 2), instead of God (*lovers of God* v. 4). The description parallels other lists of sin against God, families and society.

3. Injustice of all kinds is condemned by God, whether among His people or others.

Job 31:13-23, 29-40

Job was well aware of God's attitude toward sins against people, and examines himself, lest he should be guilty of such sins as wrong attitude toward a servant (v. 13), lack of concern for the poor, or the widow or orphan (16-22), gloating over misfortune to an enemy, cursing one who hated him, or wishing to kill him (29-31), failing in hospitality (32).

Isaiah 1:21-23

God condemns a city full of murder, dilution of that which is pure with something cheaper, rebelliousness, dishonesty, bribery, refusing to judge those who could not pay the fee.

Isaiah 5:20-23

Here God condemns those who do not distinguish between good and evil, those who claim to have all the answers, drunkards, those who pervert justice for the sake of rewards.

Isaiah 59:2-8

2 But your iniquities have separated between you and your God, and your sins have hid his face from you, that he will not hear. 3 For your hands are defiled with blood, and your fingers with iniquity; your lips have spoken lies, your tongue hath muttered perverseness. 4 None calleth for justice, nor any pleadeth for truth . . . .

Jeremiah 5:26-29, 31

26 For among my people are found wicked men: they lay wait . . . they set a trap; they catch men . . . 27 . . . houses full of deceit . . . they are become great, and waxen rich . . . 28 . . . they overpass the deeds of the wicked . . . the right of the needy do they not judge. 29 Shall I not visit for these things? saith the Lord . . . . 31 The prophets prophesy falsely, and the priests bear rule by their means; and my people love to have it so . . . .

Jeremiah 7:5-7

Part of the basis for Judah's dwelling in the land was: *5 . . . If ye thoroughly execute judgment between a man and his neighbour; 6 If ye oppress not the stranger, the fatherless, and the widow, and shed not innocent blood . . . .* Also 9:2-11, where God describes a completely dishonest nation and promises His judgment.

Ezekiel 16:49, 50

God condemns Sodom for pride, idleness, failure to help the poor.

Ezekiel 22:6-13, 27, 29

God speaks strongly against oppression of strangers, widows, orphans; bloodshed, adultery, lewdness; bribery, usury and extortion, dishonest gain.

Micah 3:1-4, 9-12; also Habakkuk 2:9; Zechariah 5:3; 7:10, 11; 8:16, 17

God condemns cannibalism, unfair judgments, building up a city by violence, serving as judges, priests and prophets for money, hypocrisy.

Malachi 3:5

God promises judgment against sorcery, adultery, false swearing, oppression of employees, unfair wages, oppression of widows and orphans, taking advantage of aliens.

Revelation 21:8

But the fearful, and unbelieving, and the abominable, and murderers, and whoremongers, and sorcerers, and idolaters, and all liars, shall have their part in the lake which burneth with fire and brimstone: which is the second death.

See also Romans 1:18-32; Galatians 5:19-21, and many other passages.

4. People with particular needs are to have special consideration.

a. The poor

Exodus 23:10, 11

Israel was to put in crops for six years but let the seventh year grow up itself for the poor to harvest--also with the vineyard and olives. They were to rotate crops so there was provision every year.

Leviticus 19:9, 10; 23:22; Deuteronomy 24:19-22

The corners of the fields and the gleanings were to be left for the poor and strangers.

Leviticus 25:35-54

For the brother who became poor, God directed that others help him and sustain him; they were not to charge interest, make money selling him food, treat him as a bondservant. Even if he sold himself to a master outside of Israel, relatives were to have the right of redemption. These provisions were based on God's relationship to Israel.

Deuteronomy 15:1, 2, 7, 8

Debts to fellow Israelites were to be cancelled every seven years. Generosity was expected: *8 Thou shalt open thy hand wide unto him and shalt surely lend*

him sufficient for his need . . . . Also 9-11.

Proverbs 22:16, 22, 23

16 He that oppresseth the poor to increase his riches . . . shall surely come to want. 22 Rob not the poor, because he is poor: neither oppress the afflicted in the gate: 23 For the Lord will plead their cause, and spoil the soul of those that spoiled them.

Proverbs 29:7, 14

7 The righteous considereth the cause of the poor . . . . 14 The king that faithfully judgeth the poor, his throne shall be established for ever.

Isaiah 3:14, 15

God condemns Judah for taking advantage of the poor. *15 What mean ye that ye beat my people to pieces and grind the faces of the poor? saith the Lord God of hosts.* Also Amos 4:1; 5:11; 8:4-7.

Matthew 19:21; Luke 18:22

Jesus said to the rich young ruler, *21 . . . If thou wilt be perfect, go and sell that thou hast, and give*

to the poor, and thou shalt have treasure in heaven:
and come and follow me.

Luke 3:11

John the Baptist speaking: *11 . . . He that hath
two coats, let him impart to him that hath none; and
he that hath meat, let him do likewise.*

Romans 12:10, 12, 20

*10 Be kindly affectioned one to another with brotherly
love . . . 13 Distributing to the necessity of saints . . . .
20 Therefore if thine enemy hunger, feed him; if he
thirst, give him drink . . . .*

Galatians 2:10

[James, Cephas, and John] . . . *would that we should*

b. Widows and orphans

Exodus 22:22-24

*22 Ye shall not afflict any widow or fatherless child.
23 If thou afflict them in any wise and they cry at
all unto me, I will surely hear their cry; 24 And
my wrath shall wax hot, and I will kill you with the
sword; and your wives shall be widows, and your
children fatherless.* A strong condemnation!

Deuteronomy 14:28, 29; 26:12, 13

*28 At the end of three years thou shalt bring forth
all the tithe of thine increase. . . . 29 And the Levite
. . . and the stranger, and the fatherless, and the
widow . . . shall come and shall eat and be satisfied. . . .*

Psalm 146:9

*The Lord preserveth the strangers; he relieveth the
fatherless and widow . . . .* God shows special concern; so should we.

Isaiah 10:1, 2

God condemns those who make decrees that take

c. Slaves, or other servants or employees

Exodus 20:10; 23:12; Deuteronomy 5:14

The Law required rest on the Sabbath for the servant,
as well as for the master.

Exodus 21:2

A Hebrew slave was to be set free after six years;
special provision was made if he had taken a wife
provided by his master. See 21:3-10.

Exodus 21:26, 27

A slave mistreated by his master was to be set free.

Deuteronomy 15:12-15

The Hebrew slave bought by another Hebrew and set
free in the sabbatical year was to be loaded with

remember the poor; the same which I also was forward to do.

James 2:15, 16

*15 If a brother or sister be naked, and destitute of
daily food, 16 And one of you say unto them, Depart
in peace, be ye warmed and filled; notwithstanding ye
give them not those things which are needful to the
body; what doth it profit?*

**PROJECT: Using a topical Bible or a concordance, look
up all the passages referring to the poor. Try to
determine God's attitude, our responsibility, any
blessings promised for our concern.**

away the rights of the poor, the widows and the
fatherless.

Matthew 23:14

One of the denunciations Jesus made of the Pharisees
was their taking advantage of widows, and salving
their consciences with long prayers.

Acts 6:1-11

In the early church, the deacons were especially
chosen to minister to the widows who needed help.
Note the qualifications listed for this ministry in
verse 3.

1 Timothy 5:3-16

Here are fourteen verses devoted to Paul's instruction
to Pastor Timothy concerning the church's responsibility for widows in the congregation. The first responsibility belongs to family members; the second
to the church, but with certain qualifications.
See also James 1:27 and many other references.

provisions for beginning a new life -- in remembrance
of God's deliverance from Egypt.

Deuteronomy 16:11, 14; also 12:12, 18; 29:10, 11

The bondslave was to have the privilege of partici-
pation in the various feasts and religious events under
the Law.

Galatians 3:28;   also 1 Corinthians 7:21, 22;   12:13;
Ephesians 6:8

In the New Testament church, a bondservant was to
have the same status as a free man. *28 There is
neither . . . bond nor free . . . for ye are all one in
Christ Jesus.*

Ephesians 6:9

And, ye masters, do the same things unto them, for-bearing threatening: knowing that your Master also is in heaven; neither is there respect of persons with him.

d. Prisoners, aliens or strangers, the handicapped

Exodus 22:9

Thou shalt not oppress a stranger: for ye know the heart of a stranger, seeing ye were strangers in the land of Egypt. Also 22:21; Lev. 19:33, 34.

Leviticus 19:14

Thou shalt not curse the deaf, nor put a stumbling-block before the blind, but shalt fear thy God . . . .

2 Samuel 9

The account of King David's kindness to Mephibo-sheth, who was lame on both feet.

Ezekiel 47:22, 23

God commanded that when Israel was restored to the land, even those who were not Jews living among them should receive an inheritance among them. *23 . . . in what tribe the stranger sojourneth, there shall ye give him his inheritance, saith the Lord.*

"The Bible has much to say about helping those in need of this world's goods and also about our responsibilities to make an impact upon the world for Christ. But never are we, nor is the church, expected to Christianize society, to sanctify it. That is impossible."
-Robert P. Lightner, The *Baptist Bulletin,* January, 1972.

Amos 1:3, 6, 11; 2:1

God pronounces judgment on heathen nations because of their cruel treatment of captured nations -- prisoners of war.

Matthew 25:35-46

Though the primary reference, we believe, is to the nations and their treatment of His brethren, the Jews, there is also the teaching of concern for the needs of others.

Luke 14:12-14

The parable of the ambitious guest, who was told to prepare his feast for the poor, the maimed, the lame, the blind.

Hebrews 13:3

Remember them that are in bonds, as bound with them . . . .

Consider also the many examples of Jesus' healing, during His earthly ministry.

5. Both worship and social concern are required of godly people; neither may be substituted for the other.

1 Samuel 15:1-31

God said, *3 Now go and smite Amalek, and utterly destroy all . . . and spare them not . . . 9 But Saul and the people spared Agag, and the best of the sheep . . . . 20 And Saul said unto Samuel, Yea, I have obeyed the voice of the Lord . . . 21 But the people took of the spoil . . . to sacrifice unto the Lord thy God in Gilgal. 22 And Samuel said, Hath the Lord as great delight in burnt-offerings and sacrifices, as in obeying the voice of the Lord? Behold, to obey is better than sacrifice, and to hearken than the fat of rams. 23 For rebellion is as the sin of witchcraft, and stubbornness is as iniquity and idolatry.*

Proverbs 21:3

To do justice and judgment is more acceptable to the Lord than sacrifice.

Matthew 26:6-13

Mary of Bethany anointed the Lord with precious ointment. *8 But when his disciples saw it, they had indignation, saying, To what purpose is this waste? 9 For this ointment might have been sold for much, and given to the poor. 10 Jesus . . . said . . . she hath wrought a good work upon me. 11 For ye have the poor always with you . . . .*

Also Jeremiah 7:4-10; 1 John 3:23; 4:20, 21.

Five basic reasons for the fall of the Roman civilization are listed by Cardinal Gibbons: [1] the undermining of the home, which is the basis for human society; [2] higher and higher taxes; the spending of public money for free bread and circuses for the populace; [3] the mad craze for pleasure; sports becoming every year more exciting, more brutal, more immoral; [4] the building of great armaments when the real enemy was within . . . the decay of individual responsibility; [5] the decline of religion; faith fading into mere form, losing touch with life, losing power to guide the people.
--*The Decline and Fall of the Roman Empire.*

II. Specific areas of instruction

1. The safety of others is a responsibility of all.

Exodus 21:29-32

If an ox, previously known to gore people, killed a man, the owner was to be held liable.

Deuteronomy 22:8

A flat-roofed house must have a parapet around the roof to prevent any person's falling.

2. Drug abuse, as illustrated by alcoholism, is sin against God, and a detriment to society.

a. Abstinance from wine and strong drink was to characterize those in places of special responsibility or separation unto God.

Leviticus 10:8-10

God speaking to Aaron the high priest: *9 Do not drink wine nor strong drink, thou, nor thy sons with thee, when ye go into the tabernacle of the congregation, lest ye die . . . 10 That ye may put a difference between holy and unholy, and between unclean and clean; 11 And that ye may teach the children of Israel all the statutes which the Lord hath spoken . . . .*

Numbers 6:2-4

The Nazarites also were forbidden to drink wine or strong drink, or even to eat grapes.

Judges 13:2-5

The wife of Manoah, before she gave birth to Samson, was forbidden to drink wine or strong drink. Samson was to be a Nazarite.

Proverbs 31:4, 5

4 It is not for kings, O Lemuel, it is not for kings to drink wine nor for princes strong drink. 5 Lest they drink and forget the law, and pervert the judgment of any of the afflicted.

Jeremiah 35:6-8

The Rechabites refused to drink, in obedience to their father; their obedience in this and other respects is in contrast to the disobedience of Israel toward God. See 1-9.

Luke 1:13-15

In the angel's announcement to Zacharias, he said that John the Baptist was to drink no wine nor strong drink, and that he would be filled with the Holy Spirit.

b. Drunkenness in general is condemned.

Proverbs 20:7

Wine is a mocker, strong drink is raging: and whosoever is deceived thereby is not wise.

Proverbs 23:20, 21, 29-35

Here is a detailed description of the results of drunkenness.

Isaiah 28:1, 7, 8

God judged Ephraim for drunkenness and its accompaniments.

Habakkuk 2:15

Woe unto him that giveth his neighbor drink . . . and makest him drunken also, that thou mayest look on their nakedness.

Ephesians 5:18

Be not drunk with wine, wherein is excess; but be filled with the Spirit.

See also Volume 4 of this series, *Fine Arts and Health,* page 51.

3. Kindness to animals must characterize godly people.

Exodus 21:33-35

33 And if a man shall open a pit . . . and not cover it, and an ox or an ass fall therein; 34 The owner of the pit shall make good . . . . 35 And if one man's ox hurt another's that he die; then shall they sell the live ox and divide the money . . . . Also v. 36.

Exodus 23:5

If thou see the ass of him that hateth thee lying under his burden, and wouldest forbear to help him, thou shalt surely help with him.

Exodus 23:11, 12

But the seventh year thou shalt let it [the land] rest and lie still; that the poor of thy people may eat: and what they leave the beasts of the field shall eat . . . . 12 Six days thou shalt do thy work, and on the seventh day thou shalt rest: that thine ox and thine ass may rest . . . . Also Ex. 20:10.

Deuteronomy 22:4

Thou shalt not see thy brother's ass or his ox fall down by the way, and hide thyself from them; thou shalt help him to lift them up again.

Deuteronomy 25:4

Thou shalt not muzzle the ox when he treadeth out the corn. Also 1 Tim. 5:18.

Matthew 6:26

Behold the fowls of the air . . . yet your heavenly Father feedeth them. Also Luke 12:24.

Luke 12:6

Are not five sparrows sold for two farthings, and not one of them is forgotten before God?

See also Gen. 49:5, 6 (NASB, Berkeley, or New Scofield).

4. Dealing with the occult should have no place in the lives of believers.

Exodus 22:18

Thou shalt not suffer a witch to live.

Deuteronomy 18:9-14

9 When thou art come into the land which the Lord thy God giveth thee . . . 10 There shall not be found among you any one . . . that useth divination, or an observer of times, or an enchanter, or a witch, 11 Or a charmer, or a consulter with familiar spirits, or a wizard, or a necromancer. 12 For all that do these things are an abomination unto the Lord . . . . 14 For these nations, which thou shalt possess, hearkened unto obervers of times, and unto diviners: but as for thee, the Lord thy God hath not suffered thee so to do.

1 Samuel 28:7-16

Saul goes to the witch of Endor for counsel. He is rebuked by the witch and by Samuel.

Isaiah 8:19, 20

19 And when they shall say unto you, Seek unto them that have familiar spirits, and unto wizards that peep,

and that mutter: should not a people seek unto their God? . . . 20 To the law and to the testimony: if they speak not according to this word, it is because there is no light in them. Also Isa. 47:12-14.

Nahum 1:4

Nineveh was condemned, among other things, because of her witchcraft.

Galatians 5:19-21

19 Now the works of the flesh are manifest, which are these . . . 20 . . . witchcraft . . . 21 . . . They which do such things shall not inherit the kingdom of God.

Revelation 21:8

But the fearful, and unbelieving, and the abominable, and murderers, and whoremongers, and sorcerers, and idolaters, and all liars, shall have their part in the lake which burneth with fire and brimstone: which is the second death.

5. Crime must be properly handled to insure a safe environment, and fairness to all who are involved.

a. Crime must be paid for.

Genesis 9:6

Whoso sheddeth man's blood, by man shall his blood be shed: for in the image of God made he man.

Exodus 21:12-17, 29

God prescribed, under the Law, the death penalty for certain crimes: premeditated murder, striking one's father or mother, kidnapping, cursing a parent, failing to confine a dangerous ox.

Exodus 22:19, 20

Also for a sexual act with an animal, and for sacri-

ficing to gods other than Jehovah.

Numbers 35:31, 32

One who deserves to die for a crime should not be permitted to pay his way out of the execution or other penalty. To permit such action is to pollute the land.

Deuteronomy 19:11-13

One guilty of murder was not to be pitied, since freedom from such crime in Israel was more important than protecting the guilty. So also with rebellion against parents, Deut. 21:18-21.

b. Punishment should fit the crime.

Exodus 21:12--22:20

Many examples are given in this passage.

Numbers 35:9-28

A distinction is to be made between intentional and unintentional killing -- i.e., between murder (16-21) and manslaughter (9-15, 22-28). See also Ex. 21:12-14.

c. God values life so highly that He prescribes capital punishment as the only suitable punishment for murder.

Genesis 9:6

Whoso sheddeth man's blood, by man shall his blood be shed: for in the image of God made he man.

Exodus 21:12

He that smiteth a man so that he die, shall surely be put to death. Also v. 14. See also Deut. 19:11-13.

Note that the principle stated in Genesis 9 precedes the giving of the Law to Israel.

d. One who is convicted of a crime should not be permitted to pay his way out and escape proper punishment.

Numbers 35:31, 32

31 Moreover ye shall take no satisfaction for the life of a murderer, which is guilty of death: but he shall surely be put to death.

e. False accusation is a serious crime, condemned by God.

Exodus 20:16

Thou shalt not bear false witness against thy neighbor. Also 23:1, 2, 7.

Deuteronomy 19:16-21

If a false witness rise up against any man to testify . . . the judges shall make diligent inquisition . . . if the witness hath testified falsely . . . then shall ye do unto him, as he had thought to have done unto his brother . . . and thine eye shall not pity.

Esther 6, 7

An example of the above principle: Haman was hanged instead of Mordecai.

2 Timothy 3:3

In listing the characteristics of those who have a form of godliness but without the power of God in the latter days, making false accusations is included.

f. A suspected criminal must be protected until his guilt is determined.

Numbers 35:11, 12

God commands Moses concerning the setting up of the cities of refuge for those who accidently kill someone.

Joshua 20:1-6

God confirms this command to Joshua at a later date.

g. One witness is not enough to convict.

Deuteronomy 19:15

One witness shall not rise up against a man for any iniquity . . . ; at the mouth of two witnesses, or . . . three witnesses, shall the matter be established.

1 Timothy 5:19

Against an elder, receive not an accusation, but before two or three witnesses. Also Num. 35:30; Deut. 17:2-11; Prov. 11:14; Matt. 18:16.

h. Bribery has no place in judgment.

Exodus 23:8

Thou shalt take no gift; for the gift blindeth the wise, and perverteth the words of the righteous.

Deuteronomy 16:19

Thou shalt not wrest judgment; thou shalt not respect persons, neither take a gift: for a gift doth blind the eyes of the wise, and pervert the words of the righteous.

Proverbs 17:23

A wicked man taketh a gift out of the bosom to pervert the ways of judgment. Also Prov. 28:21; Ecc. 7:7; Isa. 5:23; 33:15, 16.

i. Justice must not depend on whether one is rich or poor.

Leviticus 19:15

Ye shall do no unrighteousness in judgment: thou shalt not respect the person of the poor, nor honour the person of the mighty: but in righteousness shalt thou judge thy neighbor.

Deuteronomy 1:17

Ye shall not respect persons in judgment; but ye shall hear the small as well as the great; ye shall not be afraid of the face of a man . . . .

Proverbs 22:2

The rich and poor meet together: the Lord is the maker of them all. Also Ex. 23:3, 6; Prov. 24:23; 1 Tim. 5:21; James 2:5-9.

"Biblical law has no prison system. A criminal was held in prison only pending a trial, and then either made restitution, or was a bond-servant until he worked out his restitution, or was executed."
--Rousas J. Rushdoony, *Chalcedon Report*, Dec., 1978.

j. Freedom from crime is even more important than pity for the criminal.

Deuteronomy 19:13

Thine eye shall not pity him [i.e., the one who purposely killed another], *but thou shalt put away the guilt of innocent blood from Israel, that it may go well with thee.* Also v. 20, 21; 21:21.

1 Timothy 5:20

Them that sin rebuke before all, that others may also fear.

k. Bloodshed is against the land as well as against people and against God.

Numbers 35:33, 34

33 So ye shall not pollute the land wherein ye are . . . the land cannot be cleansed of the blood that is shed therein, but by the blood of him that shed it.

l. Crime is more serious in God's eyes than in man's

eyes; God's view includes attitudes and thoughts as well as actions.

Exodus 20:17

Thou shalt not covet thy neighbor's house . . . wife . . . manservant . . . maidservant . . . ox . . . ass, nor anything that is thy neighbor's. In other words, desiring what is not ours is sin in God's eyes. Only when one steals property is it a crime before man.

Matthew 5:21-28

21 Ye have heard that it was said by them of old time, Thou shalt not kill; and whosoever shall kill shall be in danger of the judgment: 22 But I say unto you, That whosoever is angry with his brother without a cause shall be in danger of the judgment . . . whosoever shall say, Thou fool, shall be in danger of hell fire. 27 Ye have heard that it was said of them of old time, Thou shalt not commit adultery: 28 But I say unto you, That whosoever looketh on a woman to lust after her hath committed adultery with her already in his heart.

COMMUNIST RULES FOR REVOLUTION

The following list was published in the Bartlesville *Examiner-Enterprise* in 1919, after the Allied Forces obtained a copy in Dusseldorf, Germany.

1. "Corrupt the young; get them away from religion. Get them interested in sex. Make them superficial; destroy their ruggedness.

2. "Get control of all means of publicity, thereby:
   --get people's minds off their government by focusing their attention on athletics, sexy books and plays, and other trivialities.
   --divide the people into hostile groups by constantly harping on controversial matters of no importance.
   --destroy the people's faith in their natural leaders by holding the latter up to contempt, ridicule and disgrace.
   --always preach true democracy, but seize power as fast and ruthlessly as possible.
   --by encouraging government extravagance, destroying its credit, produce fear of inflation with rising prices and general discontent.
   --incite unnecessary strikes in vital industries, encourage civil disorders, and foster a lenient and soft attitude on the part of government toward such disorders.
   --by specious argument, cause the breakdown of the old moral virtues--honesty, sobriety, self-restraint, faith in the pledged work, ruggedness.

3. "Cause the registration of all firearms on some pretext, with a view to confiscating them and leaving the population helpless."

Quoted from the American Citizenship Education Program *Newsletter*.

Resources

STUDY MATERIALS FOR TEACHERS

Though the preceding chapters have been developed directly from the Bible itself, the following books may prove helpful to the teacher desiring to arrive at a Biblical viewpoint, or trying to find Christian, or at least conservative, writings relevant to the social studies.

This list has been compiled from the recommendations of several scholars in the various fields, as well as from the personal contacts of this writer. It reflects variations in viewpoint among those who are believers. Of necessity this listing is selective, since *of making many books there is no end.*

An asterisk indicates that, as far as can be determined, the book is in print. Some publishers do not list their publications in *Books in Print* however, and their availability is difficult to determine. Libraries and used bookstores can be a great help.

GENERAL BOOKS

Since the most basic problem in education today is the shift from a Bible-based viewpoint to one that is centered in man and science, several resources listed provide insights into the Judeo-Christian versus secular humanistic controversy. A few are specifically related to issues in education, others to the broader field of social studies and of life in general.

Blamires, Harry. *The Secularist Heresy: The Erosion of the Gospel in the Twentieth Century.* Servant Books, 1980. Reprint from 1956, then entitled *The Faith and Modern Error.* 155 p. *The relationship between the Church and the world, between the Christian mind and secular society, with a major concern to retain true Christianity. Also *The Christian Mind: How Should a Christian Think?* 1978. 191 p. Reprint from 1963. * Also *Where Do We Stand? The Christian's Position in the Modern World,* 1980. *

Blumenfield, Samuel. *Is Public Education Necessary?* Devin-Adair, 1981. 263 p. Valuable insights into the forces that promoted public education in the 19th century -- not what is commonly given in education textbooks. Not specifically Christian, but extremely helpful in understanding today's problems. *

Chambers, Claire. *The Siecus Circle: A Humanist Revolution.* Western Islands, 1977. 506 p. A study of the vast network of organizations promoting a secular humanistic viewpoint. *

Dobbs, Zygmund. *The Great Deceit.* Veritas Foundation, 1966. 354 p. Shows how the left wing has captured the whole social science field in America and abroad. Extremely valuable for Christian teachers. *

Duncan, Homer. *Secular Humanism: The Most Dangerous Religion in American,* Missionary Crusader, 1979. Identifies Humanism and its basic tenets and goals; relates Humanism to education, the Church, and other aspects of life. Also *Humanism: In the Light of Holy Scripture.* Christian Focus on Government, 1981. 142 p. *

Howard, Donald R. *To Save a Nation.* ACE, 1976. 186 p. Shows Biblical principles as the basis for American culture, Humanism's destruction of that culture, God's promise of judgment.

Kurtz, Paul. *Humanist Manifestos I and II.* Prometheus Books, 1973, 31 p. Two statements of belief, made in 1933 and 1973 and signed by Humanist leaders, whose names are included. Considered the most definitive statements of secular humanism. Also *Secular Humanist Declaration,* 1980. Valuable and authoritative information. *

LaHaye, Tim. *The Battle for the Mind: A Subtle Warfare.* Revell, 1980. 248 p. The conflict between Biblical Christianity and secular humanism in today's society. * Also *The Battle for the Public Schools: Humanism's Threat to Our Children,* 1983. 283 p. Deals with specific areas of educational curriculum and philosophy. *

Lionni, Paolo, and Lance J. Klass. *The Leipzig Connection: The Systematic Destruction of American Education.* Heron Books, 1980. 110 p. Relates many changes in education since World War I to the experimental psychology of Wilhelm Wundt and his followers. Not specifically Christian. *

McGraw, Onalee. *Family Choice in Education: The New Imperative.* Heritage Foundation, 1978. 60 p. Also *Secular Humanism and the Schools: The Issue Whose Time Has Come,* 1976. 29 p. Also *The Family, Feminism and the Therapeutic State,* 1980. 79 p. Well documented studies on current issues. *

Morris, Barbara M. *Change Agents in the Schools.* The Barbara M. Morris Report, 1979. Also *Why Are You Losing Your Children?* 1976. Present the goals of secular humanism and the methods being used in schools to accomplish these goals. *

North, Gary, comp. *Foundations of Christian Scholarship: Essays in the Van Til Perspective.* Ross House

Books, 1976. Each chapter deals with one subject area, presenting a Christian view.

Rushdoony, Rousas J. *The Philosophy of Christian Curriculum.* Ross House Books, 1981. 194 p. Discusses a Christian viewpoint on curriculum, then provides a chapter on each of twelve subject areas. *

Schaeffer, Francis. *How Should We Then Live?* Revell, 1976. 288 p. A study of the rise and decline of Western thought and culture. Study guide. *

Schimmel, David, and Louis Fischer. *The Rights of Parents in the Education of Their Children.* National Committee for Citizens in Education, 1977. 162 p. Though not specifically Christian, this compilation by two lawyers, who are also professors of education, is very helpful in delineating rights that parents have as parents, and as agents of their children, who also have legal rights as students. Thorough documentation. *

Simon, Sidney, and others. *Values Clarification: A Handbook of Practical Strategies for Teachers and Students.* Hart Publishing Co., 1972. 397 p. Very revealing, by a leader in humanistic education.

Steensma, Geraldine J., and Harro W. Van Brummelen, eds. *Shaping School Curriculum: A Biblical View.* Signal Publishing and Consulting, 1977. 178 p. Chapters 8, 9 deal with historical and social studies, and present a rationale for curriculum development.

Textbook Evaluations, America's Future. Evaluations of specific textbooks in the social sciences fields, based on their treatment of American concepts of government and economic organization. Ask for background information, list of reviews, recommended list. No charge.

Webber, Robert E. *Secular Humanism: Threat and Challenge.* Zondervan, 1982. 144 p. A critique of the *Secular Humanist Declaration* of 1980, roots of secular humanism, and the Christian's response. Examines issues of public education, sexual revolution, violence, and moral legislation. * Also *The Secular Saint: The Role of the Christian in the Secular World,* 1979. Presents a Biblical view of man in the culture, then three historical models followed by Christians and a contemporary Christian perspective.*

Wilkerson, David. *The Vision.* Revell, 1974. "A detailed account of the woes . . . now taking place in the world and which will continue . . . in increasing severity unless drastic action is taken." -- George Otis. *

Zwier, Robert. *Born-Again Politics.* Inter-Varsity Press, 1983. 140 p. How can Christians mix faith and politics in a pluralistic society. A warning against political action without redemption as a force in shaping society. *

HISTORY AND GEOGRAPHY

Ahlstrom, Sidney E. *A Religious History of the American People.* 2 vol. Doubleday, 1975. 720 p. Shows the overwhelmingly Christian origins of the American people at the time of the War of Independence. *

Andrews, Samuel J. *Christianity and Anti-Christianity in Their Final Conflict.* Klock and Klock, 1982. Reprint from 1898. 358 p. A classic showing how the events of history fit Bible prophecy. A dispensational approach. *

Backus, Isaac. *History of New England.* Arno Press, 1969. Reprint from 1871. *

Backus, Isaac. *Isaac Backus on Church, State, and Calvinism Pamphlets,* 1754-1789. Harvard University Press. *

Backus, Isaac. *Your Baptist Heritage - 1620-1804.* Challenge Press, 1976. A primary source, by a participant in the struggle for religious freedom in America.

Boice, James Montgomery. *God and History.* Inter-Varsity Press, 1981. 288 p. A survey of the Biblical view of history, eschatology, and the nature of the church. *

Bradford, M.E. *A Worthy Company: The Role of Christian Statesmen in the Beginnings of the Republic.* Plymouth Rock Foundation, 1983. 281 p. Shows the Christian convictions of the framers of the Constitution. *

Bristol, Frank M. *Providential Epochs in the Renaissance, Reformation, Discovery and Settlement of America.* Hunt and Eatch, 1894.

Bulman, James W. *It Is Their Right: The Declaration of Independence and What Has Followed.* Gateway Publications, 1975. A study of the Declaration: what it says, how it relates to the Constitution, its Bible basis.

Burckhardt, Jacob. *Reflections on History.* Liberty Fund, 1978. Earlier title was *Force and Freedom,* 1943. By an outstanding Christian historian.

Campbell, Tim J. *Central Themes of American Life.* Eerdmans, 1959. The hand of God in U. S. history, and other Christian themes central to our culture and life.

Carson, Alexamder, *Confidence in God in Times of Danger.* Reiner Publications, 1975. A study of God's providence in the Book of Esther. *

Carson, Alexander. *The History of Providence, as Explained in the Bible.* Baker, 1977. 356 p.

Cathcart, William. *Baptist Patriots and the American Revolution.* Guardian Publications, 1976. Reprint from 1876.

Chafer, Lewis Sperry. *Satan*. Zondervan, 1977. A Christian philosophy of history, with emphasis on the role of Satan. *

The Christian Teaching of History. BJU, 1981. 14 p. A Christian philosophy for the teaching of history, based on the University's *Christian Philosophy of Education*. *

Clark, Gordon H. *Histeriography: Secular and Religious*. Presbyterian and Reformed. Shows differences between a God-centered approach and those centered in man.

Cole, Franklin P. *They Preached Liberty*. Liberty Press/Liberty Classics, 1976. 176 p. An anthology of quotations from the New England ministers of the American Revolution, with biographical sketches. *

Coleson, Edward. *The Harvest of Twenty Centuries*. Spring Arbor College, 1967.

Cousins, Norman, ed. *In God We Trust*. Harper and Brothers, 1958. Religious beliefs of the American founding fathers.

Custance, Arthur C. *Genesis and Early Man*. 2 vol. Zondervan, 1975, 1981. *

Davidheiser, J. Bolton. *Evolution and the Christian Faith*. Presbyterian and Reformed, 1969. 379 p. A readable history of evolutionary thought, with refutation of evolutionary principles. *

DeHaan, Martin R. *The Jew and Palestine in Prophecy*. Zondervan, 1978. *

Flavel, John. *The Mystery of Providence*. Banner of Truth Trust (London), 1976. Reprint of 1678. God's providence in the life of a Christian. *

Flood, Robert. *America: God Shed His Grace on Thee*. Moody, 1975. 192 p. The spiritual heritage of the American people, showing the superintending hand of God. *

Gaebelein, Arno C. *The Conflict of the Ages*. Pryor N. Russell, 1968. 171 p. Reprint from 1933. Traces origin of socialism and Marxism and on to the final conflict with Anti-Christ.

Gilpin, William. *Mission of the North American People*. Da Capo Press, 1974. Reprint from 1873. Divine Providence in the physical geography of the western states. *

Grunlan, Stephen A., and Marvin K. Mayers. *Cultural Anthropology: A Christian Perspective*. Zondervan, 1979. 309 p. Designed as a Bible college textbook for future missionaries, to help them understand other cultures. *

Hall, Verna M. *The Christian History of the Constitution of the United States*. Foundation for American Christian Education, 1966. 481 p. Also *Self-Government with Union*, 1962; and *The Christian History of the American Revolution: Consider and Ponder*, 1975. 600 p. *

Harvey, Paul. *Our Lives, Our Fortunes, Our Sacred Honor*. Word Books, 1975. Tells of the fate of the 56 signers of the Declaration of Independence. Useful as a patriotic reading.

Hefley, James and Marti. *By Their Blood*. Mott Media, 1978. A new biography of Christian martyrs. *

Herz, Martin F. *How the Cold War Is Taught*. Six American History Textbooks Examined. Ethics and Public Policy Center, Georgetown University, 1978. 76 p. *

Hosmer, William M. *Pilgrims Free Themselves from Communism: Established Free Enterprise*. William M. Hosmer, 1973. 18 p. An essay on Pilgrim history, with a detailed listing of events up to 1623.

Ippel, Henry, and Gordon Oosterman, eds. *The Christian Perspectives on History Series*. Christian Schools International, 1973-1976. A series of booklets including: *The American Revolution; U.S. Involvement in World War I; Ancient Greece; Manifest Destiny: The Mexican War and the Conquest of California; The Reformation*. *

Johnson, William J. *Abraham Lincoln the Christian*. Mott Media, 1976. 228 p. A compilation of Lincoln's statements of a Christian viewpoint. Also *George Washington the Christian*, and *Robert E. Lee the Christian*, 1976. 300 p. each. *

Kershner, Howard E. A *Saga of America*. Northwood Institute, 1976. *

LaHaye, Tim. *The Bible's Influence on American History*. Master Books, 1976. 84 p. Many illustrations of the Bible's impact on America in documents, policies, culture.

Lambert, Lance. *Israel: A Secret Documentary*. Tyndale House, 1975. 128 p. The Yom Kippur War in historical and Biblical perspective. Also *Israel: The Unique Land, the Unique People*, 1981. 256 p. *

Ludwig, Charles. *Their Finest Hour*. David C. Cook, 1975. A personal look at men and women of God who changed history.

Marsden, George, and Frank Roberts, eds. *A Christian View of History?* Eerdmans, 1975. 201 p. Essays presenting principles which guide the work of a Christian historian, along with efforts of several Christian scholars in relating history and Christianity.

Mauro, Philip. *The Number of Man*. Revell, 1909. A Christian philosophy of history.

McIntyre, C.T., ed. *God, History and Historians*. Oxford University Press, 1977. 477 p. An anthology of modern Christian views of history.

Marshall, Peter, and David Manuel. *The Light of Glory*. Revell, 1977. 384 p. A fascinating book, with excerpts from the personal writings of Columbus, Washington and many others from early American history, showing viewpoints never given in school history texts. *

Milburn, Robert L. P. *Early Christian Interpretations of History*. Greenwood, 1980. Reprint of 1954. Valuable for a Christian high school library.

Newman, Paul, ed. *In God We Trust*. C. R. Gibson, 1974. America's heritage of faith.

Newman, Robert C. *Baptists and the American Tradition*. Regular Baptist Press, 1976. A readable account of the development of religious freedom in colonial and early federal days, in a Baptist context. *

Noorbergen, Rene, and Ralph W. Hood, Jr. *The Death Cry of an Eagle: The Rise and Fall of Christian Values in the United States*. Zondervan, 1980. 192 p. *

Owen, G. Frederick. *Abraham Lincoln: His Life and Faith*. Tyndale House, 1981. 232 p. A spiritual biography of Lincoln. *

Plantinga, Theodore. *Reading the Bible as History*. Paedeia Press, 110 p. (Distributed in U.S. by Baker Book House) *

Read, Hollis. *The Hand of God in History*, or *Divine Providence Historically Illustrated in the Extension and Establishment of Christianity*. 2 vol. H. E. Robins, 1851, 1855.

Rushdoony, Rousas J. *A Biblical Philosophy of History*. Presbyterian and Reformed, 1960. *

Ryrie, Charles C. *The Best Is Yet to Come*. Moody, 1981. 128 p. Based on the prophecies of Ezekiel, Daniel, Jesus and John the Baptist; shows what the Bible has to say about the future. Good reading.

Schwantes, Siegfried J. *A Short History of the Ancient Near East*. Baker Book House, 1965. 191 p. *

Schwantes, Siegfried J. *The Biblical Meaning of History*. Pacific Press Publishing Association, 1970. What events mean in the light of the Bible.

Singer, C. Gregg. *Christian Approaches: to Philosophy, to History*. Presbyterian and Reformed, 1978. * Also *A Theological Interpretation of American History*, 1964. Shows the ideologies that have shaped American thinking from Biblical Christianity to New Deal socialism. Revised in 1981. *

Slater, Rosalie. *Teaching and Learning America's Christian History*. Foundation for American Christian Education, 1965. To be used with the works of Verna Hall. *

Swanstrom, Roy. *History in the Making*. InterVarsity Press, 1978. 137 p. Shows importance of history and how some problems in the investigation of past events can be solved from a Biblical viewpoint. *

Tonks, A. Ronald, and Charles W. Deweese. *Faith, Stars, and Stripes*. Broadman, 1976. 124 p. The impact of Christianity on the life history of America.

Van Til, L. J. *Liberty of Conscience: History of a Puritan Idea*. Presbyterian and Reformed.

Vos, Howard F. *Archaeology in Bible Lands*. Moody, 1977.

Webster, Noah. *American Dictionary of the English Language*. Foundation for American Christian Education, 1967. 1000 p. Facsimile edition of the original 1828 edition. Helpful in understanding word meanings as understood when our early documents were written. *

Weiss, Benjamin. *God in American History: A Documentation of America's Religious Heritage*. Zondervan, 1966. 256 p. Shown in documents, presidential speeches, state constitutions, inscriptions, songs.

Whitcomb, John C., Jr. *Darius the Mede*. BMH Books. 84 p. A defense of the historical truth of the book of Daniel, showing that secular history and the Bible complement each other. *

Whitcomb, John C. *The Early Earth*. Baker Book House, 1972. 144 p. The case for Biblical creationism. *

Whitehead, John C. *The Separation Illusion: A Lawyer Examines the First Amendment*. Mott Media, 1977. Our nation's heritage, along with great Americans who have contributed to the establishment of a moral American government. *

Wight, Fred. *Manners and Customs of Bible Lands*. Moody, 1953. *

Wilder-Smith, Beate. *The Day Nazi Germany Died*. CLP, 1982. An eye-witness account from inside a Christian home in World War II Germany, showing tactics used to get support for Hitler's rise to power. *

Wood, Leon. *A Survey of Israel's History*. Zondervan, 1970. 460 p. Israel and her prominence in the course of human events. Uses both Biblical and external sources. *

ECONOMICS (personal, family, and general aspects)

Anderson, Douglas, Jr. *Owe No Man Anything: A Practical Guide for Christian Family Financing*. Light and Salt, 1980. 165 p. *

Brown, Harold O. J. *Before the Crash: A Biblical Basis for Economics*. Christian Studies Center. *

Burkett, Larry. *Christian Financial Concepts Series*. Moody, 1982. Three books: *Your Finances in Changing*

Times; How to Manage Your Money (workbook); *The Financial Planning Workbook.* Deals with the present economy, Biblical principles, practical applications. *

Carson, D. A., ed. *From Sabbath to Lord's Day: A Biblical, Historical, and Theological Investigation.* Zondervan, 1982. 432 p. Seven scholars' writings based on the proposition that Sunday is a new day of worship chosen to commemorate the death and resurrection of Christ. *

Catherwood, Fred. *On the Job: The Christian 9 to 5.* Zondervan, 1983. 192 p. Biblical principles and practical suggestions related to work in today's world. *

Chilton, David. *Productive Christians in an Age of Guilt Manipulators.* Institute for Christian Economics, 1981. 242 p. An expose of evangelical socialists, who seek to make Christians feel guilty for having more than the necessities of life. *

Coleson, Edward, *God, Government and the Good Life.* Spring Arbor College, 1970.

Conn, Charles Paul. *Making It Happen.* Revell, 1982. 128 p. A Christian looks at money, competition and success. *

Dollar, Truman. *How to Carry Out God's Stewardship Plan.* Thomas Nelson, 1974. 191 p.

Engstrom, Ted W., and David J. Juroe. *The Work Trap.* Revell, 1979. 224 p. A Scriptural view of work, together with a study of conditions which produce a workaholic and ways to release the worktrap. *

Fooshee, George, Jr. *You Can Be Financially Free.* Revell, 1976. 127 p. Scriptural principles for handling personal and family finance, with practical applications. * Also *You Can Beat the Money Squeeze.* *

Galloway, Dale E. *There Is a Solution to Your Money Problems.* Regal Books, 1977. Practical Christian viewpoint on money and its problems.

Hardisty, George and Margaret. *Successful Financial Planning.* Revell. 192 p. A financial guide for building for the future, and making the most of one's assets. *

Hess, J. Daniel. *Ethics in Business and Labor.* Herald Press, 1977. *

Hollis, Allen. *The Bible and Money.* Hawthorn Books, 1976. 129 p.

Jeremiah, David. *Stewardship Series.* BMH Books. Four booklets, 42-60 pages each on these topics: Biblical stewardship, growing through giving, discovering the grace of giving, learning to give as part of discipleship. *

Kershner, Howard E. *Dividing the Wealth.* Devin-Adair, 1980. *

Kershner, Howard E. *God, Gold and Government.* Prentice-Hall, 1957. 146 p. Excellent, showing the interrelationship of Christianity, freedom, self-government and economic well-being.

MacGregor, Malcolm, with Stanley Baldwin. *Your Money Matters.* Bethany House, 1977. 176 p. *

Martin, Alfred. *Not My Own.* Moody, 1977. 110 p. A Biblical perspective on the stewardship of life, including money and possessions.

North, Gary. *An Introduction to Christian Economics.* Presbyterian and Reformed. *

Otis, George. *God, Money and You.* Jove Publications, 1975. *

Redekop, John, ed. *Labor Problems in Christian Perspective.* Eerdmans, 1971.

Richardson, John R. *Christian Economics: The Christian Message to the Market Place.* St. Thomas Press, 1966. *

Rose, Tom. *How to Succeed in Business.* Institute for Free Enterprise Education, 1975.

Taylor, E. L. H. *Economics, Money and Banking: Christian Principles.* Christian Studies Center. *

Taylor, Jack R. *God's Miraculous Plan of Economy.* Broadman, 1975. 168 p. Emphasis on total giving. *

Thornton, Larry. *The Christian's Economic World.* Central Press, 1975. 71 p. Detailed New Testament study concerning economics.

Webley, Simon. *How to Give Away Your Money.* Inter-Varsity Press, 1979. 60 p. Biblical answers related to Christian giving. *

White, Jerry and Mary. *Your Job, Survival or Satisfaction?* Zondervan, 1976. 191 p. Biblical work ethics, guidelines for success, God's leading in career decisions. *

White, John. *The Golden Cow: Materialism in the 20th Century Church.* InterVarsity Press, 1979. 180 p. *

Young, Samuel. *Giving and Living: Foundations for Christian Stewardship.* Baker, 1974. 94 p. Giving to God as a true Christian response to the grace and generosity of God. *

GOVERNMENT AND POLITICAL SCIENCE

Bastiat, Frederic. *The Law.* Foundation for Economic Education, 1977. 76 p. Reprint from French, 1850. "A primer on the socialistic philosophy of government, showing how socialism perverts the right use of the law. *

Brooks, Pat. *The Return of the Puritans: Christianity and Socialism in Mortal Combat.* New Puritan

Library, 1981 (3rd edition). *

Brown, Harold O. J. *The Reconstruction of the Republic: A Modern Theory of the State "Under God" and Its Political, Social, and Economic Structure.* Arlington House, 1977.

Campbell, Roger. *Justice through Restitution: Making Criminals Pay.* Mott Media, 1977. A challenge to return to Biblical principles of justice. *

Clouse, Robert G., ed. *War: Four Christian Views.* BMH Books, 1982. 210 p. The presentation of Biblical non-resistance, Christian pacificism, just war, and preventive war, together with responses by top level men holding the other views. *

Culver, Robert D. *Toward a Biblical View of Civil Government.* Moody, 1974. 308 p. A careful study of the place of civil government in the world, based on a Biblical view of man, God and Satan. Very helpful.

DeHaan, Richard W. *God, Law, and Capital Punishment.* Radio Bible Class, 1974. 32 p. Monthly Bible study booklet. Also *You, God, and Country,* Victor Books, 1968. 32p. Four studies on the Christian and civil government.

DeKoster, Lester. *Communism and the Christian Faith.* Eerdmans, 1962. Fundamentals of Communism contrasted with Christianity. A call to action.

Helms, Jesse. *When Free Men Shall Stand.* Zondervan, 1976. 122 p. The roots of freedom in America, current social problems, and a call for concern for the family and for recognition of God. *

Ingram, T. Robert. *The World under God's Law: Criminal Aspects of the Welfare State.* St. Thomas Press, 1970. Social implications of the Ten Commandments, how they are embodied in our laws, how they are being modified. *

James, Edgar C. *Arabs, Oil, and Energy.* Moody, 1982. 128 p. *

Kik, J. Marcellus. *Church and State: The Story of Two Kingdoms.* Thomas Nelson, 1963. The Church's conflict with the State, Biblically and historically.

Lee, Francis Nigel. *Communist Eschatology.* Presbyterian and Reformed, 1973. The definitive work on the goals of the Communistic faith, and how it affects all of life.

Lefever, Ernest W., ed. *Values in an American Government Textbook: Three Appraisals.* Ethics and Public Policy Center, Georgetown University, 1978. Not Christian, but thought-provoking, and generally conservative.

Linder, Robert D., and Richard V. Pierard. *Twilight of the Saints.* InterVarsity Press, 1977. 216 p. Biblical Christianity vs civil religion in the United States. Encourages positive interest in politics on the part of the Christian, with views shaped by the Bible. *

Long, Hamilton Abert. *The American Ideal of 1776.* Your Heritage Books, 1976. 398 p. Reprint of *Your American Yardstick,* 1963. Twelve basic American principles underlying the traditional philosophy of man over government. *

McDonald, Lawrence P. *We Hold These Truths.* '76 Press, 1976. A study of the U. S. Constitution and how it has been undermined by liberalism. *

Minear, Paul S. *I Pledge Allegiance: Patriotism and the Bible.* Geneva Press, 1975. 140 p. Examines various aspects of patriotism in the light of the Bible.

Morris, B. F. *The Christian Character of the Civil Institutions of the United States.* G. W. Childs, 1864. Much original material showing Christian origins.

Nisbit, Robert. *The Twilight of Authority.* Oxford University Press, 1977. *

Norris, David A. *Before You Lose It All.* Heartland Press, 1977. 128 p. The philosophy of the Declaration of Independence and the changes from that viewpoint over the last sixty years.

Rushdoony, Rousas J. *Foundations of Social Order.* Presbyterian and Reformed, 1972. Also *The Nature of the American System,* 1965; *This Independent Republic,* 1964; *The Politics of Guilt and Pity,* 1970.

Rushdoony, Rousas J. *Law and Liberty.* Thoburn Press, 1977. Deals with the "use of law to produce either liberty and life, or slavery and death."

Rutherford, Samuel, *Lex Rex,* or *The Law and the Prince.* Sprinkle Publications, 1980. A facsimile reprint of a work which greatly influenced leaders at the time of the War of Independence. Emphasis on the law's being king.

Schaeffer, Francis A. *A Christian Manifesto.* Good News Publishers, 1981. 192 p. A call for Christians to become involved in turning America back to godly principles. *

Taylor, E. L. H. *A Christian Philosophy of Law, Politics and the State.* Presbyterian and Reformed.

Walton, Rus. *One Nation Under God.* Revell, 1975. 309 p. The Christian idea of government and God's laws of freedom, though with confusion between Israel and the Church.

Whitehead, John W. *The Second American Revolution.* David C. Cook, 1982. 253 p. "The issue of church and state: Christian and religious freedom versus a secularist humanistic elite, . . . the most important book I have read in a long, long time." --Francis A. Schaeffer. *

Woods, Dennis. *Where "in the World" Are God's People: A Biblical Guide to Political Involvement.*

Developmental Publications. A series of Bible studies, along with practical suggestions.

LEADERSHIP AND ADMINISTRATION

Alexander, John W. *Managing Our Work.* InterVarsity Press, 1975. 104 p. The problem of work overload, and what to do about it. *

Bowman, George M. *Clockwise.* Revell. 128 p. Time management tools for the believer. *

Butt, Howard. *The Velvet-Covered Brick: Christian Leadership in an Age of Rebellion.* Harper and Row, 1973. 186 p. Christian leadership principles as shown by the pastor-church relationship. *

Dayton, Edward R., and Ted. W. Engstrom. *Strategy for Leadership.* Revell, 1979. 240 p. Leadership skills for Christian organizations. Workbook available. *

Eims, Leroy. *Be a Motivational Leader.* Victor Books, 1981. 144 p. * Also *Be the Leader You Were Meant to Be* , 1975. 132 p. God's methods of leadership, plus illustrations from the Bible and personal experience. *

Engstrom, Theodore W. *The Making of a Christian Leader.* Zondervan, 1976. 214 p. A Biblical view plus practical helps. * Also *The Pursuit of Excellence,* 1982. 112 p. A challenge to shun mediocrity. *

Engstrom, Ted W., and Edward R. Dayton. *The Art of Management for Christian Leaders.* Word Books, 1976. 285 p. * Also *The Christian Executive,* 1979. 216 p. *

Engstrom, Ted W., and R. Alec Mackenzie. *Managing Your Time.* Zondervan, 1967. 242 p. Dedicated to the Christian in a position of management. Practical and Biblical. *

Gangel, Kenneth O. *Competent to Lead.* Moody Press, 1974. 144 p. A New Testament view of leadership and administration, with emphasis on human relations and a critique of motivation theories and the human relations movement. *

Gangel, Kenneth O. *Lessons in Leadership from the Bible.* BMH Books. 156 p. A study of 23 Bible characters in terms of leadership. *

Gangel, Kenneth O. *So You Want to Be a Leader?* Christian Publications, 1973. 167 p. *

Hendrix, Olan. *Management for the Christian Worker.* Quill Publications (Distributed by Mott Media), 1976. 130 p. New methods in problem-solving and goal-setting, with Scripture backing. *

Johnson, James. *The Nine-to-Five Complex.* Zondervan, 1972. 178 p. The problems and dangers in the operation of Christian organizations.

Le Peau, Andrew T. *Paths of Leadership.* InterVarsity Press, 1983. 132 p. A Biblical view of leadership, variety in patterns, importance of character development. *

Lichtenberger, Ruth. *Letters for Reluctant Leaders (and Eager Ones Too).* InterVarsity Press, 1978. Eleven study guides based on First and Second Timothy. *

Overstreet, Sarah B. *Group Control: Studies from the Lives of Early Leaders of Israel.* Bible in the Schools Press, 1973. Reprint from 1954. 27 p.

Wiwcharuck, Peter G. *Christian Leadership Development: Course Outlines with Notes.* Leadership Development Services, 1970. 36 lesson outlines taught by the author in many parts of the world. Detailed, useful for teaching.

FAMILY AND CHURCH

NOTE: Because of the overwhelming number of books related to the family, those dealing with special problems and relationships are omitted here. An attempt has been made to include books that present a Biblical view of the family as it is meant to be.

Brandt, Henry, with Phil Landrum. *I Want My Marriage to Be Better.* Zondervan, 1976. 159 p. Biblical principles portrayed in real life, and the results of failure to portray them. *

Briscoe, Jill. *Fight for the Family: A Plan for Rebuilding the Family.* Zondervan, 1981. 186 p. Lessons from Nehemiah showing how to build strong families in the face of social forces. *

Chapman, Gary D. *Toward a Growing Marriage: A Christian Perspective.* Moody Press, 1979. Designed as a study for couples, with growth assignments included. *

Christenson, Larry. *The Christian Family.* Bethany House, 1978. 224 p. Shows God's order for the family, and the family's relationship to Jesus Christ. Study guide. *

Crabb, Lawrence J., Jr. *The Marriage Builder: A Blueprint for Couples and Counselors.* Zondervan, 1982. 176 p. Designed for married persons seeking to change their marriage from trial to triumph. Strong Biblical emphasis. *

DeJong, Peter, and Donald R. Wilson. *Husband and Wife: The Sexes in Scripture and Society.* Zondervan, 1979. 224 p. Examines the roles biologically, sociologically and Biblically, and integrates these areas in Christian perspective. *

Drescher, John M. *Now Is the Time to Love.* Herald Press, 1970. 110 p. Discusses the importance of parents taking time to show love to their children. Valuable group study. *

Fitch, William. *Christian Perspectives on Sex and Marriage.* Eerdmans, 1971. 214 p. A question and answer book giving a Biblical viewpoint, by a pastor-counselor.

Foster, Timothy. *Dare to Lead.* G/L Publications, 1977. 128 p. Written for men, teaching Biblical principles of home leadership in the light of current issues. Study guide.

Fremont, Walter and Trudy. *Formula for Family Unity.* BJU Press, 1980. 180 p. Bible Action Truths for the Christian family. *

Gangel, Kenneth O. *The Family First.* BMH Books. 140 p. Symptoms and source of family ills; God's purpose in the roles of individuals and the family. *

Gangel, Kenneth O. and Elizabeth. *Between Christian Parent and Child.* Baker Book House, 1974. 89 p. Designed as a discussion prompter for use by parent groups. Much application of Biblical principles. *

Getz, Gene. *The Christian Home in a Changing World.* Moody Press, 1972. 107 p. An excellent study of Biblical principles arranged as a guide for personal study and group interaction.

Getz, Gene. *The Measure of a Church.* G/L Publications, 1975. 159 p. *

Getz, Gene. *The Measure of a Family.* G/L Publications, 1976. 190 p. * Also *The Measure of a Marriage,* 1980. Workbook. *

Getz, Gene. *Sharpening the Focus of the Church.* Moody Press, 1976. 350 p.

Gundry, Patricia. *Heirs Together: Mutual Submission in Marriage.* Zondervan, 1980. 192 p. *

Herr, Ethel. *Chosen Families of the Bible.* Moody Press, 1976. 96 p. A Bible study book helping readers to discover Biblical principles for family living. *

Hindson, Ed. *The Total Family.* Tyndale House, 1981. 119 p. "The best book I have read on how to develop family togetherness." --Jerry Falwell. Each chapter ends with questions for self-evaluation. *

Johnston, O. R. *Who Need the Family?* InterVarsity Press, 1980. 152 p. By a sociologist. The breakdown of the family, plus an analysis of marriage, motherhood and fatherhood. *

LaHaye, Tim. *How to Be Happy though Married.* Tyndale House, 1975. 160 p. The joys, major potential problems, spiritual solutions. *

LaHaye, Tim and Bev. *Spirit-Controlled Family Living.* Revell, 1978. 192 p. *

McDonald, Cleveland. *Creating a Successful Christian Marriage.* Baker Book House, 1975. 392 p. Written as a textbook on Christian courtship and marriage for couples and counselors. Excellent. *

MacDonald, Gordon. *Magnificent Marriage.* Tyndale House, 1976. 183 p. Biblical, well-written, worth reading. *

McRae, William J. *Preparing for Marriage.* Zondervan, 1980. 211 p. A study guide for engaged couples to understand key Bible passages and their implications. *

Meier, Paul D. *Christian Child-Rearing and Personality Development.* Baker Book House, 1977. 222 p. Integrates Scripture passages, findings from psychiatric research and private medical practice. Based on absolute authority of the Bible. *

Narramore, S. Bruce. *Parenting with Love and Limits.* Zondervan, 1980. 176 p. Builds a Biblical framework for parent-child relations, firmly grounded in sound psychology. * Also *You Can Be a Better Parent,* a workbook for the above. *

Narramore, Bruce. *Why Children Misbehave.* Zondervan, 1980. 150 p. Also *The Power of Positive Parenting,* a workbook for study groups, to help parents work through the principles of the above. *

Phillips, Mike. *A Christian Family in Action.* Bethany House, 1977. 188 p. The personal story of a family who put into practice the principles in Larry Christenson's *The Christian Family.* Looks excellent. *

Roberts, Roy R. *God Has a Better Idea--the Home.* BMH Books. 144 p. A well-organized study of the Christian home. *

Schaeffer, Edith. *What Is a Family?* Revell, 1975. 256 p. Explores the many facets of a home as God meant it to be. Many personal illustrations. *

Schaeffer, Francis A. *The Church at the End of the 20th Century.* InterVarsity Press, 1970. An analysis of what the New Testament teaches, and ways in which those principles may show up in the lives of churches.*

Small, Dwight Hervey. *Design for a Christian Marriage.* Revell, 1959. 221 p. Biblical marriage concepts and the relationship of problems in courtship to them.

Small, Dwight Hervey. *Design for a Christian Marriage.* Revell, 1959. 221 p. Biblical marriage concepts and the relationship of problems in courtship to them. Also *Your Marriage is God's Affair,* 1979. 352 p. A series of studies. *

Timmons, Tim. *God's Plan for Your Marriage.* Baker Book House, 1978. 90 p. For newlyweds: how to make the new marriage work as God designs. *

Timmons, Tim. *Maximum Marriage.* Revell, 1977. 128 p. A Biblical game plan for husband and wife to learn to live in complete Christian togetherness. Recommended by Howard Hendricks. *

SOCIAL PROBLEMS AND RELATIONSHIPS

Anderson, J. Kerby. *Genetic Engineering: The Ethical Issues.* Zondervan, 1982. 128 p. *

Anderson, Norman. *Issues of Life and Death.* InterVarsity Press, 1976. 130 p. A well-researched Biblical approach to legalized abortion, genetic engineering, euthanasia, birth control, artificial insemination, capital punishment. *

Bahnsen, Greg L. *Homosexuality: A Biblical View.* Baker Book House, 1978. *

Baker, William. *Worthy of Death: Capital Punishment-- Unpleasant Necessity or Unnecessary Penalty?* Moody Press, 1973. 158 p.

Buzzard, Lynn, and Laurence Eck. *Tell It to the Church: Reconciling Out of Court.* David C. Cook, 1982. *

Carle, Erica. *The Hate Factory.* Erica Carle Foundation, 1974. 77 p. Shows how high school sociology has been used ot indoctrinate students.

Conn, Charles W. *The Anatomy of Evil.* Revell, 1982. 160 p. A clear-cut pattern to today's epidemic of evil, plus abundant assurance of God's sovereignty. *

Court, John H. *Pornography.* InterVarsity Press, 1980. 96 p. An analysis of the arguments used to support pornography, plus scientific studies of its effects. *

Egner, David C. ed., *Morals for Mortals: Biblical Reflections for Making Right Choices.* Radio Bible Class, 1979. 120 p. Deals with a variety of current issues.

Fowler, Richard A., and H. Wayne House. *The Christian Confronts His Culture.* Moody Press, 1983. An analysis of three issues: equal rights for women, the right to life, and homosexuality; by two professors at LeTourneau College. *

Geisler, Norman L. *The Christian Ethic of Love.* Zondervan, 1973. 127 p. Shows love as the basis of ethical behavior, and love's source in the absolute nature of God. * Also *Ethics: Alternatives and Issues,* 1971. 270 p. *

Getz, Gene A. *Building Up One Another.* Victor Books, 1976. Shows the Biblical emphasis on mutual encouragement and help. *

Gorman, Michael J. *Abortion and the Early Church.* InterVarsity Press, 1982. 108 p. Attitudes toward abortion from Greek, Roman, Jewish and Christian perspectives. *

Grunlan, Stephen A., and Milton Reimer, eds. *Christian Perspectives on Sociology.* Zondervan, 1982. 448 p. A college level book of readings presenting a Christian viewpoint on several sociological topics. *

Hess, J. Daniel. *Integrity: Let Your Yea Be Yea.* Herald Press, 1978. A series of lectures studying what it means to live a life of integrity.

Hilliard, Mozelle. *Please Rise!* Mott Media. 201 p. Insights into America's problem of juvenile delinquency.

Ingram, T. Robert. *What's Wrong with Human Rights?* St. Thomas Press, 1979 *

Keysor, Charles. *What You Should Know about Homosexuality* . Zondervan, 1979. 254 p. Biblical teaching, evaluation of various interpretations, teachings of the church fathers, ministries to homosexuals. *

Lutzer, Erwin W. *The Necessity of Ethical Absolutes.* Zondervan, 1981. 112 p. Weighs four major relativistic views of ethics, showing their inadequacy; shows value and necessity of the Judeo-Christian ethic. With response by Mark M. Hanna. *

McCasland, Dave. *The Culture Trap.* Scripture Press, 1982. Helpful for leaders of teens in coping with the culture in which they live. *

Mains, Karen B. *Open Heart--Open House.* David C. Cook, 1980. 199 p. An enthusiastic presentation of a Biblical view of Christian hospitality, with many practical illustrations from the Bible and everyday life. *

Rushdoony, Rousas J. *The Myth of Over-Population.* Thoburn Press.

Ryrie, Charles C. *What You Should Know about Social Responsibility.* Moody Press, 1982. 117 p. A Biblical view of social ethics, including many specific issues. Closes with a set of goals for the believer. *

Schaeffer, Francis. *Back to Freedom and Dignity.* InterVarsity Press. A Christian reaction to Skinner's *Beyond Freedom and Dignity.*

Schaeffer, Francis A., and C. Everett Koop. *Whatever Happened to the Human Race?* Revell, 1979. A serious study of the life and death issues of abortion, infanticide, and euthanasia. *

Schaeffer, Franky. *A Time for Anger.* Good News Publishers, 1982. 192 p. *

Sider, Ronald J. *Rich Christians in an Age of Hunger.* InterVarsity Press, 1977. 252 p. Also *Cry Justice: The Bible on Hunger and Poverty,* 1980. 192 p.

Sider, Ronald J., ed. *Evangelicals and Development.* Westminster Press, 1982. 123 p. Papers from a 1980 conference in England of the Consultation on the Theology of Development. Deals with issues related to undeveloped countries and their needs from a "Christian socialist" viewpoint. *

Smith, Malcolm E. *The Real Marijuana Danger.* Suffold House. 242 p. Summarizes 758 reports on the implications of the use of marijuana. *

Thornton, Larry. *Hospitality in 2nd and 3rd John.* Central Press. 25 p.

Van Impe, Jack, and Roger F. Campbell. *Alcohol: The Beloved Enemy.* Thomas Nelson, 1980. Examines every verse in the Bible containing the word "wine." *

Webber, Robert E. *The Secular Saint: A Case for Evangelical Social Responsibility.* Zondervan, 1979. 208 p. Presents the concerns of the Judeo-Christian heritage, relationship of the church to its culture in church history, and possibilities for today. *

White, Jerry and Mary. *Friends and Friendship: The Secrets of Drawing Closer.* NavPress, 1982. 196 p. *

Wilkerson, David. *The Cross and the Switchblade.*

Chosen Books Publications, 1981. Reprint from 1963. Drugs, crime and teenagers of the inner city. *

Wilkerson, David. *Beyond the Cross and the Switchblade.* Jove Publications, 1976. *

Wilkerson, David. *Suicide.* Revell * Also *Sipping Saints*, 1978. The Bible and alcohol. *

Wilkerson, Don. *Fast Track to Nowhere.* Revell. 192 p. Teenage alcoholism. * Also *Marijuana*, 1980. 128 p. *

CURRICULUM MATERIALS

Materials listed here include a variety of levels. Some are specifically designed for school use; others are supplementary. A few are meant to be used in church youth groups, but can easily be adapted for the classroom.

BOOKS AND PAMPHLETS

America in Person, by George D. Youstra. BJU Press. 320 p. Accounts of 96 events, each told by a participant or a witness to the event. Secondary.

America: One Nation under God, by James C. Hefley. Victor Books, 1975. 144 p. Leader's Guide available. Traces origins of freedoms, law and justice, religious liberty, etc. Secondary.

The American Adventure, Vol. 1. Allyn and Bacon, 1975. Though not specifically Christian, this book is highly recommended by CSI in their *Curriculum Guide, 1977.* Secondary.

The American Covenant: The Untold Story, by Marshall Foster, and Mary-Elaine Swanson. Foundation for Christian Self-Government, 1981. 117 p. Workbook designed to be used with Verna Hall's and Rosalie Slater's books. See list for teachers.

Animal Character Scripts and *People Character Scripts.* Scripture Press. Several puppet scripts available for teaching Christian character traits, how to get along with others, etc.

Beka Social Studies Series. My America, Grade 1; *Our America,* 2; *Our American Heritage,* 3 (U.S. History through the eyes of great people); *The History of Our U.S.,* 4; *Old World History and Geography,* 5; *New World History and Geography,* 6. *History of the World in Christian Perspective* and *U.S. History: Heritage of Freedom,* each 2 vol., high school. A Beka Books, 1976-1983.

Bible Land History and Geography. Rod and Staff. Based on Baker's *Bible Atlas.* Test book available. Grades 7-10.

Character Builders, by Ron and Rebekah Coriell. Revell. Three series of books for three grade spans, designed to help children develop specific Christian character traits. Supplementary, K-8.

Character Foundation Curriculum. Revell. Teacher and student books for each grade, K-8, studying Christian character traits from the Bible. May be used in social studies or in Bible. Highly recommended.

Character Sketches, Vol. 1, 2. Institute in Basic Youth Conflicts, 1976, 1978. 385 p. each. Two beautiful volumes, with emphasis on character qualities, illustrated through the world of nature, and Scriptural events.

Christian Ethics, by James M. Bramblet. ACSI, 1974. Thirty lessons covering the Scriptural basis, personal ethics and social ethics. Grades 7-10.

Burkett, Larry. *Christian Financial Concepts.* Campus Crusade for Christ, 1977. A Bible study course on principles of handling money; a workbook.

Christian Light Social Studies. Christian Light Publications. Available: *Living Together on God's Earth,* Grade 3; *North America Is the Lord's,* 5 (a Christian view of history of U.S. and Canade); *God's World: His Story,* 6, 7 (ancient history).

CSI Social Studies. Christian Schools International. *Social Studies Curriculum Guide,* K-9; *Social Studies Curriculum Guide,* 4-6; *Social Studies Resource Units for the Primary Grades* (thirty units). Also these resource units: *The People: Three Indian Tribes of the Southwest,* 5, 6; *Nigeria,* 6, 7; *Coming to the New World,* 7, 8; *Geneva to Geelong* (on John Calvin), high school; *Christian Perspectives in History Series* (see listing on Page 133).

Also *Under God,* by William C. Hendricks, Fourth Edition, 1981. 252 p. Junior High textbook on Government. Teacher's guide and tests.

Also *Story of the Old World,* by John DiBie. Teacher's guide and tests. Grade 6. *To Find a Better Life: Aspects of Dutch Immigration to Canada and the United States, 1920-1970.* A resource book for teachers and high school students.

Minority Groups in Anglo-America: Curriculum Paper No. 6, by Gordon Oosterman. Selected incidents in U.S. and Canadian history dealing with minority groups. Graded, K-12.

CSI Canadian Social Studies. Christian Schools International. Several resource units: *Famous Persons of New France,* Grades 5, 6; *New France,* 7, 8; *A difficult Journey* (three Indian tribes), 5, 6; *Makers of British Canada,* 5, 6; *Building British Canada,* 7, 8; *Forging a Nation,* 7, 8; *Native Canadians of the Northwest Coast,* 7; *Man in Society: A Study in Hope* (a study of Canadian issues in the light of Biblical principles).

Also *Foundations of Government,* by William C. Hendricks. A Scripturally oriented introduction to government to be used as a supplement in Canadian history. 7-12.

Christopher Columbus and the Discovery of the New World, by Josephine Pollard. A reprint from the late 19th century, for children. The Pilgrim Institute. 224 p.

The Church in History, by B. K. Kuiper. CSI, 1964. 412 p. A church history textbook for Grades 7-12. Extensive teacher's guide.

Curriculum Materials Guide. CSI, 1977, 1982. Reviews many books in all academic disciplines, suggesting those considered most suitable for Christian schools.

Daddy Isn't Coming Home, by Matilda Nordtvedt. Zondervan, 1981. 96 p. Children's fiction to help children understand and be encouraged where there has been divorce, or where their friends have suffered. Grades 3-7.

Economics: Principles and Policy from a Christian Perspective, by Tom Rose. Mott Media, 1977. Instructor's manual. High school level.

Free Market Economics, by Bettina B. Greaves, ed. Foundation for Economic Education, 1975. A syllabus and basic reader. Grades 11, 12.

Fundamentals for American Christians, by Rus Walton. Plymouth Rock Foundation. Student and teacher editions. Grades 11, 12. Volume 2 expected for Fall, 1983.

God and Government: A Biblical and Historical Study, by Gary DeMar. American Vision Press, 1982. 205 p.

A 10-lesson workbook for individual and group study, dealing with Biblical principles of civil government. Senior high and adult.

Guidelines to the American Way of Life Series. Freedoms Foundation at Valley Forge. Vol. 1: *A Teacher's Aid for Elementary Grades;* Vol. 2: *A Guide for Secondary Level Social Studies* (now out of print); Vol. 3: *The American Credo.* Valuable resource guide for teaching basic American principles.

He Freed Britain's Slaves, by Charles Ludwig. Herald Press, 1977. 208 p. A biography of William Wilberforce: his physical problems, faith in God, and great accomplishments. Senior High.

Heritage Studies for Christian Schools. BJU Press. Grades 1-3 available, both in student texts, and teacher's editions; also U.S. History, Grade 11; Family Living, Grades 11, 12. 1982.

Holy Days: Holidays, by Judith Ritchie and others. Mott Media, 1979. 122 p. A resource book giving the story of familiar American holidays from a Christian viewpoint. Grades 3-7.

How to Succeed with Your Money, by George M. Bowman. Moody Press, 1974. Leader's guide includes 12 masters for overhead transparencies.

Joy in Learning, by Arnold DeGraaff and Jean Olthuis, eds. Curriculum Development Centre, 1973. A Christian curriculum for grades 1-3, with many social studies activities suggested.

Levi Coffin and the Underground Railroad, by Charles Ludwig. Herald Press, 1975. 176 p. The work of Levi and Catherine Coffin in freeing blacks from oppression in the South. Senior High.

Life-Pacs for Social Studies. Alpha Omega Publications. Individualized learning packets for various levels and subject areas. 1-12.

The Light and the Glory, by Peter Marshall and David Manuel. Revell, 1977. 384 p. See description under History. Student guide and chart collection available.

Makers of American History. Wilcox and Follett, 1966. A secular textbook for Grade 5, recommended by Christian Schools for America. Study guide and tests available from CSA.

Noah Webster: Father of the Dictionary, by Isabel Proudfit. The Pilgrim Institute, 1942. 219 p. A juvenile biography.

Of America Reading Series. A Beka Books. A series of four readers for Grades 4-6, with an emphasis on our American heritage.

Our Christian Heritage, by Cherie Noel. Published by Our Christian Heritage, 1972. A Christian approach to the study of geography, history and government. Grades 1-8.

Rod and Staff Social Studies. Rod and Staff Publishers. *Our Father's World,* for Grade 2; *Ancient History,* Book 1, for Grade 7.

Rosanna of the Amish, by Joseph W. Yoder. Herald Press, 1940. 319 p. A fascinating factual story of an Irish Catholic girl reared by an Amish lady. Excellent for giving understanding of the Amish faith and life. Senior High.

Rudiments of America's Christian History, by Rosalie Slater and Verna M. Hall. Foundation for American Christian Education, 1968. A workbook for Senior High.

SonPower Series. Scripture Press. A variety of 6-13 lesson courses for junior and senior high level, several of which deal with problems related to the social studies. Each has leader's guide and student book. Some have transparency masters.

The Sower Series of World Heroes. Mott Media. Biographies for grades 3-7: *George Washington, Christopher Columbus, Robert E. Lee, Abigail Adams, Abraham Lincoln.* Excellent.

Streams of Civilization. CLP and Mott Media. 2 vol., 1977, 1980. Vol. 1, Ancient History up to 1572 A.D., by Albert Hyma and Mary Stanton; Vol. 2, The Reformation to the Nuclear Age. Teacher's guides, Christian supplements, home study guides. Junior-Senior High.

The Trouble with Parents: How to Make Peace with Yours, by Tim Stafford. Zondervan, 1978. 159 p. For teenagers. Emphasis on Biblical principles and understanding.

Thunderstorm in Church, by Louise A. Vernon. Herald Press, 1974. 129 p. The story of Martin Luther, as seen by Hans, his teenage son.

Victor Books. A series of paperbacks dealing with home and family. Each has available a leader's guide with transparency masters. Adult level, though many are adaptable for senior high. Some on other social studies topics. Send for list.

Ways of Life Series, by Arnold DeGraaff and Jean Olthuis, eds. The Book Society of Canada and Mott Media, 1977. *Ways of Life: Japan* and *Ways of Life: Kenya* presently available. Grades 6-9. Teacher's manual and student booklet.

We Choose America. A Beka Books. A 48-page book in color, contrasting life styles in America and Russia. High School.

You and Me and Our New Little Baby, by Marla and Benny Alex. Zondervan, 1982. 48 p. Describes the beauty of birth and answers the questions of young children. K-3.

NOTE: Many more books related to the health and sexual area of family life are included in Volume 4 of this series, Fine Arts and Health.

NON-BOOK RESOURCES

The American Vision: 360 Years Later. A sound cassette overview of the founding and development of America, from a Christian perspective. American Vision. No charge, but a $15 donation brings other materials with the tape.

Bible Study Charts, by John C. Whitcomb and others. BMH Books. Charts of both Old and New Testament times in large or notebook sizes.

California Weekly Explorer. A fourth grade newspaper on current events, from a Christian viewpoint.

Debt to the Past: Law and Government. Moody Institute of Science. 16mm film, 1964. Traces history of American system of government, pointing out the Biblical and historical basis for it.

The Freeman. Foundation for Economic Education. Monthly magazine, free on request. Emphasis on free enterprise, private property, limited government, etc.

God, Government and You. Cornerstone Ministry, 1979. Four filmstrips, each with cassette tape narration. Deals with law, authority, government.

It's God's World. A weekly newspaper for Grades 4, 5. Emphasis on current events at an intermediate grade level and from a Christian viewpoint. Primary grade edition coming soon.

The Mel Gablers Newsletter. Gives information about textbook analysis from a Christian viewpoint. Analyses available for many textbooks commonly used in public schools. Write for information about availability and how to order.

The Miracle of America, a lecture series presented by the Freemen Institute, and showing the U. S. Constitution in the tradition of our Founding Fathers. A one-day series scheduled in various parts of the country. Attendance includes tapes and study books. Also tape series.

My America: Her Faith and Freedom. Heritage Music Distributors, 1978. A two-hour presentation of our nation's heritage, using slides, cassette tapes and a book of pictures. Special price to Christian schools. Excellent program material.

The Pilgrim Institute. An organization dedicated to the Principle Approach to American Christian Education. Publishes a periodical, and some books; conducts institutes for teachers.

The Pilgrims: Stories by Aunt Carolyn. Children's Bible Club. Four tape cassettes presenting early American history for intermediate grade children. Each cassette includes two major incidents.

Plymouth Rock Foundation Pilgrim Seminars. Seminars held at Plymouth, Massachusetts, with emphasis on early American history, especially as it relates to the history at Plymouth.

Politics: A Christian Viewpoint. Christian Education and Research Foundation. Encourages high school clubs in Christian high schools to study political and public policy.

Rushdoony Tapes. Chalcedon A-V Ministry. Cassette tapes of lectures given by Dr. Rousas J. Rushdoony. Particularly relevant to the social studies teacher are: *History vs Social Science; History from a Christian Perspective; A Christian Approach to Economics.* Post-millennial viewpoint.

DIRECTORY OF SOURCES

ACE - Accelerated Christian Education
P. O. Box 2205
Garland, TX 75041

ACSI - Association of Christian Schools
P. O. Box 4097   International
Whittier, CA 90607

Allyn and Bacon
Rockleigh, NJ 07647

Alpha Omega Publications
2316 West Huntington
Tempe, AZ 85281

American Vision Press
P. O. Box 720515
Atlanta, GA 30328

America's Future
542 Main Street
New Rochelle, NY 10801

Arlington House
1 Park Avenue
New York, NY 10016

Arno Press
9 Main Street
Salem, NH 03079

Baker Book House
P. O. Box 6287
Grand Rapids, MI 49506

The Barbara M. Morris Report
P. O. 756
Upland, CA 91786

A Beka Book Publications
Box 18000, Station BBC
Pensacola, FL 32523

Bethany House
6820 Auto Club Road
Minneapolis, MN 55438

BJU - Bob Jones University Press
Greenville, SC 29614

BMH Books
Winona Lake, IN 46590

Broadman Press
127 Ninth Avenue North
Nashville, TN 37234

California Weekly Explorer
631 Paularino Avenue
Costa Mesa, CA 92626

Campus Crusade for Christ
P. O. Box 1576
San Bernardino, CA 92402

Carle, Erica, Foundation
P. O. Box 4357
Milwaukee, WI 53210

Central Press
2105 Fremont Avenue North
Minneapolis, MN 55411

Chalcedon AV Ministry
P. O. Box 188
Vallecito, CA 95251

Children's Bible Club
P. O. Box 643
Milton, FL 32570

Chosen Books Publishing Co.
Lincoln, VA 22078
(Dist. by Spring Arbor
P. O. Box 985
Ann Arbor, MI 48106)

Christian Education and Research
  Foundation
418 C Street, N. E., Suite One
Washington, DC 20002

Christian Focus on Government
P. O. Box 3802
Lubbock, TX 79452

Christian Light Publications
P. O. Box 1126
Harrisonburg, VA 22801

Christian Publications
P. O. Box 3404
Harrisburg, PA 17105

CSI - Christian Schools International
3350 East Paris Avenue S.E.
Grand Rapids, MI 49508

CSI-Canada - Christian Schools
P. O. Box 39   International
Norwich, ON NOJ-1P0

Christian Studies Center
P. O. Box 11110
Memphis, TN 38117

Cook, David C., Publishing Co.
850 North Grove Avenue
Elgin, IL 60120

Cornerstone Ministry
P. O. Box 43189
Birmingham, AL 35243

CLP - Creation-Life Publishers
P. O. Box 15666
San Diego, CA 92115

Curriculum Development Centre
229 College Street
Toronto, Ontario M5T1R4

DaCapo Press
233 Spring Street
New York, NY 10013

Developmental Publications
Box 42425
Portland, OR 97242

Devin-Adair Co., Inc.
143 Sound Beach Avenue
Old Greenwich, CT 06870

Doubleday and Co., Inc.
501 Franklin Avenue
Garden City, NY 11530

Eerdmans, William B., Publishing Co.
225 Jefferson Avenue S.E.
Grand Rapids, MI 49503

Ethics and Public Policy Center
1211 Connecticut Avenue N.W.
Washington, DC 20036

Foundation for American Christian
P. O. Box 27035   Education
San Francisco, CA   94127

Foundation for Christian Self-
P. O. Box 1087   Government
Thousand Oaks, CA   91360

Foundation for Economic Education
30 South Broadway
Irvington-on Hudson
New York, NY   10533

Freedoms Foundation at Valley Forge
Valley Forge, PA   19481

The Freeman Institute
P. O. Box 31776
Salt Lake City, UT   84131

Gateway Publications
P. O. Box 6295
Greensboro, NC   27405

Geneva Press
925 Chestnut Street
Philadelphia, PA   19107

Givson, C. R., Co.
Knight Street
Norwalk, CT   06856

G/L - Gospel Light Publications
2300 Knoll Drive
Ventura, CA   93003

Good News Publishers
9825 West Roosevelt Road
Westchester, IL   60153

Guardian Publications
33 West 17th Street
New York, NY   10011

Harper & Row Publishers
10 East 53rd Street
New York, NY   10022

Hart Publishing Co.
15 West Fourth Street
New York, NY   10012

Harvard University Press
79 Garden Street
Cambridge, MA   02138

Hawthorn Books, Inc.
2 Park Avenue
New York, NY   10016

Heartland Press
Box 305
Ames, IA   50010

Herald Press
616 Walnut Avenue
Scottdale, PA   15683

Heritage Foundation
513 C Street N.E.
Washington, DC   20002

Heritage Music Distributors
Melody Center
P. O. Box 112
Montrose, PA   18801

Heron Books
P. O. Box 563
Portland, OR   97207

Hosmer, William M.
P. O. Box 846
San Carlos, CA   94070

Institute for Basic Youth Conflicts
Box 1
Oak Brook, IL   60521

Institute for Christian Economics
P. O. Box 6116
Tyler, TX   75711

Institute for Free Enterprise Education
13601 Preston Road
400 Carillon Plaza, Suite 413
Dallas, TX   75240

InterVarsity Press
Downer's Grove, IL   60515

It's God's World
Box 3075
Asheville, NC   28802

Jove Publications
200 Madison Avenue
New York, NY   10016

Klock and Klock Christian Publishers
2527 Girard Avenue North
Minneapolis, MN   55411

Leadership Development Services
6110 48A Avenue
Delta, B.C.

Liberty Press (and Liberty Fund)
7440 North Shadeland
Indianapolis, IN   46250

Light and Salt
Route 1, Box 252
Hampshire, TN   38461

Master Books
P. O. Box 15666
San Diego, CA   92115

The Mel Gablers' Newsletter
P. O. Box 7518
Longview, TX   75607

Missionary Crusader
4606 Avenue H

Lubbock, TX   79404

Moody Institute of Science
12000 East Washington Blvd.
Whittier, CA   90606

Moody Press
1777 Shermer Road
Northbrook, IL   60062

Mott Media
1000 East Huron
Milford, MI   48042

National Committee for Citizens in
   Education
Suite 410, Wilde Lake Village Green
Columbia, MD   21044

NavPress
P. O. Box 6000
Colorado Springs, CO   80934

Nelson, Thomas, Inc.
P. O. Box 14100
Nashville, TN   37214

New Puritan Library
Route 1, Lytle Road
Fletcher, NC   28732

Northwood Institute Press
3225 Cook Street
Midland, MI   48640

Our Christian Heritage
587 Suisse Drive
San Jose, CA   95123

Oxford University Press
16-00 Pollitt Drive
Fair Lawn, NJ   07410

Pacific Press Publishing Association
1350 Villa Street
Mountain View, CA   94042

Paideia Press
Books distributed in U.S., by
Baker Book House

Pilgrim Institute
908 Laurelwood Drive
South Bend, IN   46637

Plymouth Rock Foundation
P. O. Box 425
Marlborough, NH   03455

Prentice-Hall, Inc.
Englewood Cliffs, NJ   07632

Presbyterian and Reformed
   Publishing Co.
Box 817
Phillipsburg, NJ   08865

Prometheus Books
700 East Amherst Street
Buffalo, NY 14215

Quill Publications
1260 Coast Village Circle
Santa Barbara, CA 93108

Radio Bible Class
P. O. Box 22
Grand Rapids, MI 49501

Regal Books
2300 Knoll Drive
Ventura, CA 93003

Regular Baptist Press
P. O. Box 95500
Schaumburg, IL 60195

Reiner Publications
Swengel, PA 17880

Revell, Fleming H., Co.
184 Central Avenue
Old Tappan, NJ 07675

Rod and Staff Publishers
Crockett, KY 41413

Ross House Books
P. O. Box 158
Vallecito, CA 95251

St. Thomas Press
P. O. Box 35096
Houston, TX 77035

Scripture Press
P. O. Box 1825
Wheaton, IL 60187

Servant Publications
237 North Michigan
South Bend, IN 46601

Seventy-Six Press
Box 2686
Seal Beach, CA 90740

Signal Publishing & Consulting
    Corporation
6412 North 30th Street
Terre Haute, IN 47805

Spring Arbor College
Spring Arbor, MI 49283

Sprinkle Publications
Harrisonburg, VA 22801

Suffold House
155 East Main Street
Smithtown, NY 11787

Thoburn Press
11121 Pope's Head Road
Fairfax, VA 22030

Tyndale House
336 Gunderson Drive
Wheaton, IL 60187

Veritas Foundation
P. O. Box 111
West Sayville, NY 11796

Victor Books
P. O. Box 1825
Wheaton, IL 60187

Western Islands
395 Concord Avenue
Belmont, MA 02178

Westminster Press
P. O. Box 718
William Penn Annex
Philadelphia, PA 19105

Wilcox and Follett
1000 West Washington Blvd.
Chicago, Il 60607

Word Books
4800 West Waco Drive
Waco, TX 76796

Your Heritage Books, Inc.
928 Public Ledger Building
Philadelphia, PA 19106

Zondervan Publishing Co.
1415 Lake Drive S.E.
Grand Rapids, MI 49506

Communists Often Put Christians To Shame

A number of years ago the following article appeared in French newspapers and magazines:

"The Gospel is a much more powerful weapon for the renewal of society than is our Marxist philosophy. All the same, it is we Communists who will finally beat you Christians. We are only a handful and you Christians number into the millions. However, if you will remember the story of Gideon and his 300, you will understand why I am right. We Communists do not play at our goal. We are realists and seeing that we are determined to achieve our object, we know how to obtain the means. Of our salaries and wages we keep only what is strictly necessary and we give the rest for propaganda purposes. To this propaganda we also consecrate all of our free time and part of our holidays. You Christians give only a little time and hardly any money for the spreading of the Gospel of Christ. How can you say that you really believe in the supreme value of this Gospel when you do not practice it? No, we Communists will win because we believe in our message and we are ready to sacrifice everything, even our lives, in order that social justice shall triumph. You Christians will lose because you are afraid to soil your hands."

Index

About the Author...

Dr. Ruth Haycock is a recognized leader in the Christian school education field. She serves as a workshop leader for numerous Christian school conventions internationally and is a consultant for the Association of Christian Schools International. She is an instructor each summer at the National Institute of Christian School Administration at Grace College, Winona Lake, Indiana, and was a member of an Advisory Committee for Christian School Curriculum, Division of Fleming H. Revell, publishers.

Dr. Haycock is Chairman of the Department of Christian School Education at Piedmont Bible College in Winston-Salem, North Carolina and is Professor Emeritus at Baptist Bible College of Pennsylvania where she taught for thirty-six years. She holds a Bachelor's Degree from the University of Minnesota, is a graduate of Baptist Bible Seminary, and holds both the Master of Science and Doctor of Education from Syracuse University.

A member of Pi Lambda Theta and Phi Beta Kappa, Dr. Haycock is listed in *Outstanding Educators in America, Who's Who in Religion, International Who's Who in Education, Dictionary of International Biography*, and a number of other national and international publications. She was given a Distinguished Service Award by Baptist Bible Seminary, named the Alumnus of the Year, Baptist Bible College of Pennsylvania, along with numerous other honors.

In addition to the four-volume *Bible Truth for School Subjects*, she has contributed to *An Introduction to Evangelical Christian Education, Church Educational Agencies, Adult Education in the Church, and Childhood Education in the Church*. She is a regular contributor to *Daybreak*, a bimonthly publication of Piedmont Bible College.

BIBLE TRUTH
FOR SCHOOL SUBJECTS

Volume II

LANGUAGE ARTS/ENGLISH

READING
WRITING
LITERATURE
SPEECH
LISTENING
FOREIGN LANGUAGES

by

Ruth C. Haycock